# A POETICS OF JESUS

*A Poetics of Jesus* explores the act of writing within and between the boundaries of nineteenth century biblical criticism and fiction. Reflecting on the work of Christian poetics after Augustine to Baur, Feuerbach, Friedrich Strauss and Victorian novelists of the eighteenth and nineteenth century, this book breaks new ground in juxtaposing the evoked image of Christ arising from Victorian biblical criticism against the image of Christ within fiction, letting both these images and the words that figured them interact.

This book offers a highly accessible introduction to nineteenth century literature and theology through comparisons made to contemporary post-modern theorists. Demonstrating how literature can inform theology without itself becoming 'theology', this book constitutes an important contribution to the literature/theology debate and a much needed contribution to contemporary Christology through its introduction to the literature and the writers central to the beginnings of the historical quest for Jesus.

# ASHGATE NEW CRITICAL THINKING IN THEOLOGY & BIBLICAL STUDIES

*Ashgate New Critical Thinking in Theology & Biblical Studies* presents an open-ended series of quality research drawn from an international field of scholarship. The series aims to bring monograph publishing back into focus for authors, the international library market, and student, academic and research readers. Headed by an international editorial advisory board of acclaimed scholars, this series presents cutting-edge research from established as well as exciting new authors in the field. With specialist focus, yet clear contextual presentation, books in the series aim to take theological and biblical research into new directions; opening the field to new critical debate within the traditions, into areas of related study, and into important topics for contemporary society.

# A Poetics of Jesus

## The search for Christ through writing in the nineteenth century

JEFFREY F. KEUSS

Routledge
Taylor & Francis Group
LONDON AND NEW YORK

First published 2002 by Ashgate Publishing

Reissued 2018 by Routledge
2 Park Square, Milton Park, Abingdon, Oxon OX14 4RN
711 Third Avenue, New York, NY 10017, USA

*Routledge is an imprint of the Taylor & Francis Group, an informa business*



A Library of Congress record exists under LC control number: 2002100760

ISBN 13: 978-1-138-73332-9 (hbk)
ISBN 13: 978-1-138-73322-0 (pbk)
ISBN 13: 978-1-315-18774-7 (ebk)

# Table of Contents

# Acknowledgements

While attempting to acknowledge all by name is impossible, I wish to briefly acknowledge the following:

My family in Seattle whose belief in this venture helped set this work in motion and have reminded me of 'first things' throughout these years in Scotland.

The University of Glasgow for their generous financial support of my work through the University Postgraduate Scholarship as well as the Glasgow Cathedral Faculty of Divinity Scholarship. Needless to say, without these sources of financial support this book may not have been possible.

The many voices of individuals such as Michael Neelley, Randy Rowland, Pete Smith, Steven Purcell, Jim and Erika Fox, Dave and Sandy Goudie, Paul Watson, Ian and Joanna Meacock, Brett and Janet Nicholls, Tim MacKenzie, Faith Hobbis, Derrick Coyle and Stephen Mitchell whose words often reminded me of that which lies outside the Cloisters and which dwells at the heart of ultimate concern.

Lastly, I wish to note three people to whom this work is dedicated:

First, and most importantly, to my wife Diana who knew the wonder of George Eliot's prose before I did and whose life and love have continued to be that "deep which calls out to deep." As George Eliot wrote in *Adam Bede*: "What greater thing is there for two human souls, than to feel that they are joined for life – to strengthen each other in all labour, to rest on each other in all sorrow, to minister to each other in all pain, to be one with each other in silent unspeakable memories...?"

Secondly, to my daughter Clara whose life began as this work drew to its close and has proven the "mystery beneath the processes" more real and embodied than words can describe.

Thirdly, my thanks and gratitude to Professor David Jasper, Dean of the Divinity Faculty at University of Glasgow, for seeing this project through from its slight beginnings to the work that is now before you.

# Introduction

# Writing and Jesus: An Elective Affinity

> *Who shall tell what may be the effect of writing?* If it happens to have been cut in stone, though it lie face down-most for ages on a forsaken beach, or "rest quietly under the drums and tramplings of many conquests", it may end by letting us into the secret of usurpations and other scandals gossiped about long empires ago: this world being apparently a huge whispering-gallery. Such conditions are often minutely represented in our petty lifetimes. As the stone which has been kicked by generations of clowns may come by curious little links of effect under the eyes of a scholar, through whose labours it may at last fix the date of invasions and unlock religions, so a bit of ink and paper which has long been an innocent wrapping or stop-gap may at last be laid open under one pair of eyes which have knowledge enough to turn it into the opening of a catastrophe.[1]

From the start, it is important to note that this study is an endeavour to address a central question that, while familiar to literary criticism, is relatively new to theological inquiry: the effect of writing as giving and releasing of form as a poetics.[2] In particular, this study is an extended

---

[1] George Eliot, *Middlemarch: A Study in Provincial Life* – 1871, 1872 (Oxford: Oxford World's Classics, 1998) pp. 406-407.

[2] In "On the Idea of a Theology of Culture", Paul Tillich distinguishes between content, form, and import, to which he links the terms autonomy, heteronomy, and theonomy. "*Substance or import* is something different from content. By content we mean something objective in its simple existence, which by form is raised up to the intellectual-cultural sphere. By substance or import, however, we understand the meaning, the spiritual substantiality, which alone gives form its significance. We can therefore say: *Substance or import is grasped by means of a form and given expression in a content.* Content is accidental, substance [or import] essential, and form is the mediating element. The form must be appropriate to the content; so there is no opposition

reflection on the question of poetics and how poetics acts as "a declaration of principle with regard to the ideas about literature [and writing] that have been embodied in the events of a given text".[3] Martin Heidegger, in the opening sentence of *Being and Time*, states that what drove him to centre his discussion on the question of Being is that it was, for him, *the* question that had "been forgotten" in Western philosophy.[4] In a similar way, I am asserting that the question of poetics in relation to attempts to form the figure of Jesus in writing has "been forgotten" in most theological discussions. This "forgetfulness" has led to critical misjudgements where the *form* of writing that seeks to figure Jesus as representing the ultimate nexus[5] of subject and sacred

---

between the cultivation of form and the cultivation of content; it is rather that these two represent one extreme, and the cultivation of substance [or import] represents the other" pp. 165-166. According to Tillich, a cultural formation in which form predominates over substance is *autonomous*, while one in which import predominates over form is *heteronomous*. Form in synergistic balance with import is *theonomous*. Theonomous cultural forms (e.g. a poetics of Jesus) are in the nature of the case explicitly open to and disclosive of the unconditioned depth of ultimate meaning. The revelation of a predominant import consists in the fact that the form becomes more and more inadequate to the import. The import in its overflowing abundance shatters the form meant to contain it. For Tillich, this overflowing and shattering of form by import is itself the pre-eminent form of religiously charged cultural products. *My use of form, content, and import throughout this book are in keeping with Tillich's definitions and Tillich's understanding of form in synergistic balance with import as theonomous is central to what I term "a poetics of Jesus".* See Paul Tillich, "On the Idea of a Theology of Culture" in *What is Religion?* Trans. James L. Adams (New York: Harper and Row, 1969) pp. 165ff, "The Nature of Religious Language" in *Theology of Culture* (Oxford: Oxford University Press, 1959) pp. 53ff, and "The Spiritual Presence and the Ambiguities of Culture" in *Sytematic Theology 3: Life and the Spirit/History and the Kingdom of God* (London: SCM Press, 1997) pp. 245-262.

[3] Mieke Bal, *Narratology 2nd edition* (Toronto: University of Toronto Press, 1997) p. 59. The use of the term "poetics" throughout this book will be in keeping with this operational definition.

[4] Martin Heidegger, *Being and Time* trans. Joan Stambaugh (New York: SUNY Press, 1996) p. 1.

[5] I am employing the term "nexus" as the demonstrative moment and place of continual organic connection between agents of cause and effect. *Nexus* has traditionally been utilised to describe properties in philosophy and physics whereby causal agents in seeming opposition come into a mutually causal relationship. In this way it is a term that has heritage across disciplines. Recorded use of *nexus* goes back to Roman law where the term was used (both *nexus* and *nexum*) to describe a transaction whereby a man subjects himself to somebody else's power of seizure, usually as a self-pledge by which a debtor enslaves himself to the creditor until he has worked off a debt. This practice continued until the fourth century when it was

"other"[6] often disregards the import in question. Such a declaration of principle as to how literature functions as an incarnation of this coming together of subject and sacred,[7] and what this embodiment within literary space ultimately concerns is what I am terming a *poetics of Jesus*.[8] It is the search for this poetics of Jesus and the manifested results throughout this search in theology and literature that is the central concern of this work.

Given the questions brought forward during the nineteenth century through Anglo-German higher criticism as to the nature of Jesus, I will focus much of this discussion within the Victorian era. In particular, the work of writer George Eliot will serve to exemplify the tensions surrounding poetics in nineteenth century theological and literary circles. Much has been written throughout the history of George Eliot scholarship in relation to her evangelical childhood, the

---

abolished due to class struggles. In the nineteenth century, writers such as Thomas Carlyle used the term to describe the possible relationship of man to man that transcends the material, as he wrote in chapter VI of *Chartism* that the material is not "the universal nexus of man to man" - *Chartism* (London: Fraser, 1840) p. 49. The currect English term *nexus* has a semantic relation to the mid 17th century French term *nectere* which is "to bind". I am using the term to denote not only the demonstrative moment and place of continual organic connection between agents of cause and effect, but that which evokes a sense of a 'continual passing over' oneself as another which Emmanuel Levinas explores in "La Trace de L'Autre" and "God and Philosophy". See also H. F. Jolowicz, *Historical Introduction to the Study of Roman Law* 3rd ed. (London: Cambridge University Press, 1972) 164ff.

6 See Emmanuel Levinas, "La Trace de L'Autre" trans. A Lingis in *Deconstruction in Context: Literature and Philosophy*. ed. Mark C. Taylor (Chicago: University of Chicago Press, 1986) pp. 346ff.

7 This statement is made with the understanding that Jesus is that manifestation of the ultimate nexus of subject and sacred within the Christian tradition. Other religious systems have similar albeit unique manifestations of a nexus of subject and sacred. Writers such as Joseph Campbell in *The Power of Myth* and *The Hero With A Thousand Faces* and Mircea Eliade in *The Sacred and the Divine* have made foundational work in the area. I am seeking to delimit how such a poetics is attempted within the Christian tradition in which George Eliot was deeply immersed.

8 I am employing Jesus as a linguistic embodiment of the ultimate nexus of the subject and sacred. I am doing so in keeping with Ferdinand de Saussure's assertion in *Cours de linguistique générale* (*Course in General Linguistics*) that the sign or "the link" between signifier and sign is arbitrary within a language system – other terms have been utilized to figure this embodiment and use of the sign Jesus within this book is not to the delimiting of other possible signs that may be employed. See Ferdinand de Saussure, *Course in General Linguistics* trans. Roy Harris (La Salle: Open Court Press, 1986) pp. 67ff.

turning from the faith of her father symbolised by a refusal to take the Eucharist, her extensive reading and translation work of formative German thinkers, and her immersion with her partner, G.H. Lewes, in the scientific developments of the Victorian period. Philosophical themes of Comtean positivism and Feuerbachian humanism have been discussed in relation to her work.[9] As a translator, critic, and ultimately, writer of fiction, George Eliot's prodigious output is a detailed account of questions of meaning raised by a life of nineteenth century scholarship and artistry that sought to find 'the mystery beneath the processes'. In this regard, George Eliot embodies the search for a poetics of Jesus in nineteenth century theology and fiction. As she noted in her oft-quoted journal entry of 6th December 1857 entitled "How I Came to Write Fiction," George Eliot saw her fiction as a "shadowy conception [which] varied, from one epoch of my life to another".[10] The veiled and shadowy cast of her early characters – from Milly Barton to Tina Gilfil, Janet Dempster to Dinah Morris, Hetty Sorrel to Maggie Tulliver – differing though they were, embodied similar questions of meaning that showed different expressions of a common 'face' that troubled Eliot from the beginning of her fictional output. This 'face' that had troubled her and, I will argue, gave form to her resulting fiction, was that which is found in what she termed "the beautiful story" of Jesus.

In her 1868 essay entitled "Notes on Form in Art", Eliot addresses the complex issue of form in artistic representation[11] with

---

[9] T. R. Wright states that the role Positivism plays in George Eliot's thought is difficult to assess since the evidence of her engagement with Auguste Comte comes late in her career. "One of the main difficulties in assessing Comte's influence on George Eliot's philosophical development is its relative lateness. Her first recorded reference to him came in a review of January 1851, and revealed an ignorance of the importance of history in his system." See T.R. Wright, "George Eliot and Positivism: A Reassessment", *Modern Language Review*, LXXVI, Spring 1981, pp. 257ff.

[10] George Eliot, "How I Came to Write Fiction" in *Selected Critical Writings* ed. Rosemary Ashton (Oxford: Oxford University Press, 1992) p. 322. In her reading of Eliot's letters alongside her fiction in *The Real Life of Mary Ann Evans: George Eliot Her Letters and Fiction* (Ithaca: Cornell University Press, 1996), Rosemarie Bodenheimer explores the way in which Eliot wrote 'herself' and 'about herself' simultaneously. This study looks at the ways in which the major crises in her life such as her conflicts with her father, her choice of a pseudonym, and her decision to marry John Cross are 'made flesh' in her letters and fiction. In short, Bodenheimer argues convincingly that fiction played as key a role in Eliot's subjectivity as did her non-fictional writing.

[11] This essay provides an excellent lens with which to view George Eliot's philosophy of poetics. A.S. Byatt makes this comment with regard to her essay in *Selected Essays,*

regard to what she terms 'old subjects', which are those culturally bound artefacts such as "abstract words and phrases which have an excellent genealogy". For Eliot, such things as well-turned phrases, over-used terms, and representations of key figures of cultural import such as the person of Christ,

> are apt to live a little too much on their reputation and even to sink into dangerous impostors that should be made to show how they get their living. For this reason it is often good to consider an old subject as if nothing had yet been said about it; to suspend one's attention even to revered authorities and simply ask what in the present state of our knowledge are the facts which can with any congruity be tied and labelled by a given abstraction.[12]

In order to recover "an old subject" from its demise, Eliot raises the central question of how we derive and delimit the form of a given subject – whether it be a word used in poetry or a key figure in cultural and religious history. For George Eliot, the question of 'Form' is

> distinguished from merely massive impression, [Form] must first depend on the discrimination of wholes and then on the discrimination of parts. Fundamentally, *form is unlikeness*, as is seen in the philosophic use of the word 'Form' in distinction from 'Matter'; and in consistency with this fundamental meaning, every difference is Form. Thus, sweetness is a form of sensibility, rage is a form of passion, and green is a form both of light and of sensibility.[13]

In order to perceive the Form of a given subject, it is first a question of discrimination of wholes that allows for the presentation of Form as unlikeness amidst other wholes before a discrimination of parts can be considered. In this way, "the fullest example of such a whole is the highest example of Form: in other words, the relation of multiplex interdependent parts to a whole which is itself in the most varied and therefore the fullest relation to other wholes".[14]

---

*Poems, and Other Writings* (London: Penguin Classics, 1990): "although written in 1868, at the same time of *The Spanish Gypsy*, its formal preoccupations extend beyond poetry" p. 231.

[12] George Eliot, "Notes on Form in Art" in *Selected Essays, Poems, and Other Writings* ed. A.S. Byatt (London: Penguin Classics, 1990) p. 231.

[13] ibid., p. 232.

[14] ibid.

George Eliot exemplifies this theory of Form by describing the human organism. The human organism is made up of various parts, such as fingernails, toothaches, and a nervous system, which can register a toothache "as the nervous stimulus of muscle manifested in a shout".[15] Yet, although all these 'parts' are part of the human organism, one cannot understand them as part of the human organism in isolation nor can a conception of the whole 'form' be derived merely by categorising the discrimination of parts:

> [The human organism in] all its different elements or parts of experience is bound together in a more necessary wholeness or more inseparable group of common conditions than can be found in any other existence known to us. The highest Form, then, is the highest organism, that is to say, the most varied group of relations bound together in a wholeness, which again has the most varied relations with all other phenomena.[16]

What is interesting in George Eliot's discussion of the nature of Form within her work is the assertion that Form is not dependent upon 'context', but arises within and through the subject itself by its own 'parts' calling back to its own assertion of wholeness. This is true of a work of art, the human organism, or even other cultural signifiers such as Jesus. In speaking of the human organism, George Eliot states that

> the outline defining the wholeness of the human body is due to a consensus or constant interchange of effects among its parts. It is wholeness not merely of mass but of strict and manifold dependence. The word 'consensus' expresses that fact in a complex organism by which no part can suffer increase or diminution without a participation of all other parts in the effect produced and a consequent modification of as a whole.[17]

The analogy of this notion given by Eliot to the arising of Form is that of a shell arising from a snail – the shell does not precede the organism anymore than the Form of a work of art (be that poetry, prose, painting, or any other forming action such the writing of theology regarding the life of Jesus) precedes the work itself:

---

[15] ibid.

[16] ibid.

[17] ibid. p. 234.

> Form was not begotten by thinking it out or framing it as a shell which should hold emotional expression, any more than the shell of an animal arises before the living creature; but emotion, by its tendency to repetition, i.e., rhythmic persistence in proportion as diversifying thought is absent, creates a form by the recurrence of its elements in adjustment with certain given conditions of sound, language, action, or environment. Just as the beautiful expanding curves of a bivalve shell are not first made for the reception of the unstable inhabitant, but grow and are limited by the simple rhythmic conditions of its growing life.[18]

Turning from the question of form to that of import in regards to Eliot's early fiction, scholarship that has considered George Eliot's work in relationship to Christian themes has been dismissive as to the role Jesus had in her work. Many have tended to view Christian themes as manifestations of merely philosophical rather than theological questions, or echoes of Eliot herself as steps along a personal intellectual genealogy that she moved beyond after her departure from the Evangelical period of her childhood. The result is seen as a form of 'Christian humanism'. This is particularly true in many of the biographies of George Eliot, a genre which George Eliot herself called "a disease of English Literature".[19] A number of critical works surmise Eliot's efforts as a novelist as merely revisioning Christianity for a Victorian audience in search of the human condition illumined in a divine light – 'the human face divine'.[20] This book challenges this conclusion. In short, I view Eliot's poetics as seeking to accomplish more than reframing an ethical, iconoclastic, or purely aesthetic stance of Christianity in fictional space. As I will discuss throughout this book, Eliot was indeed concerned with the human condition as scholars such as Knoepflmacher, Paris, and others have argued. Yet, by figuring her fiction through a poetics that is deeply christological, we

---

[18] ibid., p. 235

[19] George Eliot, *The George Eliot Letters* ed. George S. Haight (London: Oxford University Press, 1954-1956) vol. 7, p. 230. As Eliot states, "The best history of a writer is *his* writings – these are his chief actions." ibid.

[20] For examples of this argument, see T.R. Wright, *The Religion of Humanity* (Cambridge: Cambridge University Press, 1986), U.C. Knoepflmacher, *Religious Humanism in the Victorian Novel* (Princeton: Princeton University Press, 1965), B.J. Paris, *Experiments in Life: George Eliot's Quest for Values* (Detroit: Wayne State University Press, 1965), and Bernard M.G. Reardon, *Religious Thought in the Victorian Age: A survey from Coleridge to Gore 2nd Ed.* (London: Longman, 1995).

see that she evidences a concern that is beyond writing for merely utilitarian ends. Unlike the works previously mentioned, this work views George Eliot's poetics as a search for the meaning of what it is to be authentic in relation to what is truly sacred.

In exploring the search for a poetics of Jesus in the nineteenth century, this book will look at the questions that situate George Eliot's early fiction amidst the concerns raised in Anglo-German criticism, in particular the key issues raised by Strauss, Feuerbach, and other key thinkers within the nineteenth century. It is my assertion that George Eliot continued to (re)write throughout her fiction the (re)embodied person of Jesus as a poetics that critics such as D.F. Strauss sought through the limited formalism of theological poetics. It was within fiction that George Eliot sought to actualise the merely theoretical query raised by thinkers such as D.F. Strauss in his magnum opus *Das Leben Jesu*, whose form of writing "made her ill" in its hiding of what she saw as "the beautiful story".[21] As the narrator muses in Middlemarch: *Who shall tell what may be the effect of writing?* I believe George Eliot was fully aware of the effects of writing and saw in works such as Strauss' "Concluding Dissertation" of *Das Leben Jesu* an unwillingness to finish that which he had begun – a figuring of the person of Jesus with authenticity[22]. In looking to contemporary writers of Eliot in the Victorian period such as Froude, Ward, and Pater, one also sees the opting for prescriptive conclusions by these writers in poetics that attempt to recover a false Christ – one that had already been exposed as false, thereby stripping this recovered 'Christ' of his own words and power altogether. It is the disturbingly true Christ, such as Strauss sought to discuss and "critically examine", that remains veiled and unseen. Akin to George Eliot's metaphorical stone - this Christ is one "which has been kicked by generations of clowns [that] may come by curious little links of effect under the eyes of a scholar through whose labours it may at last fix the date of invasions and unlock religions". But George Eliot saw such conclusions to be nothing more than "little links of effect". This Christ sought through the *form* of higher criticism is only authentic through the act of

[21] Gordon S. Haight *George Eliot: A Biography*. (Oxford: Oxford University Press, 1968) p. 58

[22] I use this notion of authenticity in the Heideggerian sense of *existenz* (mode of being-in-the-world) found only through *lichtung* or a "clearing/illuminated moment". I will address this more in depth in chapter 6.

(re)writing as an act of true fiction "under... eyes which [have] knowledge enough to turn it into the opening of a catastrophe".[23] Eliot saw that what was being sought, the 'pale Galilean' of the historical quest, was not the Jesus she sought and would not be found through the employment of systems by those whom she termed "German system-mongers". Rather, "the beautiful story" that she saw under erasure by the likes of Strauss and others could only appear, not in the act of disembodied systems of thought, but through a poetic cartography of embodied truth[24] whereby that which had been viewed as inaccessible in traditional philosophical paradigms is imagined as possible and approachable.[25] In this way, George Eliot announces through the act of writing a subversive power in poetics that offers a *via media* between the Scylla of Higher Criticism and the Charybdis of Victorian fiction that sought only to re-tell a 'life of Jesus' as 'the human face divine'. This search for a poetics as form awake with import has a very contemporary feel to questions raised by post-structuralists. As noted by Kathryn Bond Stockton in her book *God Between Their Lips*,

> *Post-structuralist feminists are caught in the horns of a Victorian obsession: how to chart channels between realms commonly considered approachable and those considered finally inaccessible.* If, for Victorians, 'God' seems the realm that is finally inaccessible, for post-structuralist feminists, as we shall see, it has become the body-apart-from-its-constructions that eludes conceptual, linguistic grasps... *Post-structuralists ... are the new Victorians.*[26]

---

[23] George Eliot *Middlemarch: A Study in Provincial Life.* 1871-72 (Oxford: Oxford World Classics, 1998) pp. 406-407.

[24] By this statement I am inverting the usual image of cartography as a mapping on a two-dimensional field of north/east/west/south. In a poetic cartography, the 'mapping' is not merely of space, but space and that which exists within it. In a poetic cartography that is embodied, the 'mapping' that has no boundary or 'edge' that would announce the end of the world , but is fully enclosed and three-dimensional, moving in time and space. See E. Ann Matter "Internal Maps of an Eternal External" in *Maps of Flesh and Light* ed. Ulrike Wiethaus (New York: Syracuse University Press, 1993) pp. 60ff

[25] As I will discuss in my conclusion, this poetics that Eliot employs in her fiction is a way of saying beyond words – where the form of poetics is itself a means of speaking without being limited by sign/signifier restrictions. As a *poetics of Jesus*, this is an *embodied* poetics that does not restrict, but frees meaning beyond the constriction of the sign/signifier.

[26] Kathryn Bond Stockton, *God Between Their Lips: Desire Between Women in Irigaray,*

The nineteenth century represented, in René Wellek's words, the "attempt, apparently doomed to failure and abandoned by our time, to identify subject and object, to reconcile man and nature, consciousness and unconsciousness by poetry which is 'the first and last of all knowledge.'"[27] At the centre of much of this attempt to reconcile 'man and nature, consciousness and unconsciousness by poetry' was Jesus of Nazareth. Friederich Schleiermacher's platonic dialogue about Christ in his lecture *Christmas Eve Celebrations* in 1806[28] and his later work *The Christian Faith* (1821-22) lead to his conception of Jesus as an archetype (*Urbild*) of authentic humanity in relation to God.[29] As Karl Barth noted, "Jesus of Nazareth fits extremely badly into [nineteenth century] theology... The historical in religion, the objective element, the Lord Jesus is a problem child (*Sorgenkind*) to the theologian, a problem child that ought throughout to be accorded respect and that somehow does receive respect, but a problem child nonetheless".[30] One approach to this *Sorgenkind* is that taken up by post-structuralists such as Stephen D. Moore in the act of recovering the oft overlooked elements of writing as an act of incarnation that reflects the essence of Jesus. As Plato noted in *Phaedrus*,

> once a thing is put into writing, the composition drifts all over the place, getting into the hands not only of those who understand it, but equally of those who have no business with it; it doesn't know how to address the right people, and not address the wrong. And when it is ill-treated and unfairly abused it always needs its parent to come to its help.[31]

---

*Brontë, and Eliot* (Stanford: Stanford University Press, 1994) pp. xvi, 3-4. This theme is also dealt with at great length in Helena Mitchie's *The Flesh Made Word.*

[27] René Welleck. "Romanticism Re-examined," in *Concepts of Criticism.* (New Haven: Yale University Press, 1963) p. 221.

[28] Pelikan states that Schleiermacher's lectures marked the first in the modern University to "lecture publicly on the topic of the life of Jesus" and "making this the subject of academic lectures at the University of Berlin five times between 1819 and 1832, although the book to come out of student notes on the lectures did not appear until 1864". See Jaroslav Pelikan, *Jesus Through the Centuries* (New York: Harper and Row, 1985) p. 195.

[29] "The archetype (*Urbild*) must have become completely historical... and each historical moment of this individual must be born within the archetypal". Friedrich Schleiermacher, *The Christian Faith*, trans. H.R. Mackintosh and J.S. Stewart (Edinburgh: T and T Clark, 1928) chap. 90. Cited by Jaroslav Pelikan, *Jesus Through the Centuries*, p. 195.

[30] Karl Barth, *Die protestantische Theologie im 19. Jahrhundert* (Zurich: Evangelischer Verlag, 1947) pp. 385, 412-13.

Throughout the nineteenth century, many would-be parents arose to "come to the help" of the "ill-treated and unfairly abused" central character of much nineteenth century fiction – Jesus. Where concern arose in the face of the early quest for the Historical Jesus in the projects of D.F. Strauss and F.C. Baur, writers of fiction had found that it was in the continuous act of writing and reading that the very figure that Biblical critics were seeking to stabilise was finding new life. As Stephen D. Moore aptly puts it,

> as writing, Jesus must contend with invisible forces other than demons. As writing, he must be delivered up to powers other than the Jewish and Roman authorities. This force, this power, is the reader. Temma F. Berg asks: "Who is the reader?" She replies: "The reader is legion ('for we are many' – Mark 5:9). And to give oneself to readers, to allow strange others the power of breathing life into you, is to deliver yourself into the unknown. It is to take the greatest risk of all, the risk of annihilation, of death". But if to write is to run the risk of death, it is also to seize the chance of life after death (undead, the author lives on in his or her tome)… writing also offers [Jesus] a body to live on in.[32]

It is this task of developing a *poetics of Jesus* which seeks that which is explicitly open to and disclosive of the unconditioned import as 'the shattering of form' found in the Jesus that is central to much biblical criticism and fiction of the nineteenth century. As will be reflected upon throughout this work, many writers who sought such a poetics in the nineteenth century found merely form devoid of import while others, such as George Eliot, recovered a poetics for the figuring of sacred and subject that recalls a depth of meaning that evokes the genre of gospel – writing which bears good news.

---

[31] Plato, *Phaedrus*. In *The Collected Dialogues of Plato*. ed. Edith Hamilton (Princeton: Princeton University Press, 1961) p. 275.

[32] Stephen D. Moore, ibid. pp. 17,18.

# Chapter Summaries

*Chapter two* discusses how the form within which Christianity has chosen to work out its doctrine of the person of Christ is seen in early Christian poetics. Given the literary foundations of the Church from the New Testament onward, a continued search for the essential *form, content, and import* of the person of Christ has been the very foundation of Christianity's self understanding. Often discussions surrounding the person of Christ have centred on ousiological arguments (*homo* -, *hetero* -, or *homoi* -) that arose from the Council of Chalcedon seeking reasonably to render the 'nature' of Jesus as one who is at once sacred and human. This chapter will instead look at early examples of the search for Jesus in poetics. I argue that it is the dominance of form over content and import found in these early creeds that demonstrates the beginning of arguments for the reasonableness of Christianity as a *system* of beliefs that eclipses the content and import of this system – the figure of Jesus.

*Chapter three* discusses the need for poetics after Augustine's conception of the subject in the form of the sacred. I will argue that an understanding of this conception of Augustine – where the subject is primarily known in its *form* rather than its *content* or *import* – is fundamental to any discussion of how one speaks of the iconic signifier Jesus within poetics and is of particular importance for a reading of George Eliot as an inheritor of Augustine's philosophical project. It was Augustine who took the view that since humanity is fashioned in the *Imago Dei (image of God),* the *form* of the subject must be that of the *form* of God – for Augustine this is a multi-valiant and *gestalt* form resembling the Trinity – triune yet singular. For Augustine, by looking to the *form* of being rather than the *nature* or content of being, one is able to see the affinity of the sacred with the subject – form mirrors form. In this way, Augustine provides what seems to be a reasonable account of the possibility of relationship between God and subject. As will be seen, after Augustine this conception of form regarding subjectivity presumes the subject to have limits given its ultimate grounding in God. This idea will be challenged as the notion of primary subject and object reverses after Kant whereby the 'subject'

God becomes the 'object' of an ever-creative subject – humanity.

*Chapter four* begins an assessment of the nineteenth century's sense of the shifting nature of poetics of the subject and the sacred after Kant. I will first assess the questions raised in the work of such writers as Schiller, Hölderlin, and Goethe to show how literary poetics in Germany had announced many of the issues that would arise in George Eliot's poetics. This reflection is important given the well-researched connection between German literature of the period and George Eliot's fiction. Most scholarship that reflects on Eliot's reading of German literature tends to focus primarily upon plot comparisons[33] or purely philosophical issues arising from German idealism.[34] What I will add to this body of scholarship is a reflection on the question of poetics of the subject and the sacred that George Eliot reflects in her writing, in particular the notion of *morphology as subject* in Goethe's work. This chapter concludes with an assessment of Hegel's concern for the embodied *Geist* in relation to subjectivity and how this notion is then carried into questions that give rise to the quest for the historical Jesus. It is Hegel who offers a reversal of Augustine's conception of the subjective form that, ironically, utilises Augustine's conceptional framing of multiple trinities in relation to the Trinity of the Christian tradition, yet shows the subjective form to be *without* limits and thereby destabilising of the distinction between subject and object, Creator and creation. Hegel develops a notion of the subject whose dominant feature is that of an *expressive* object – *creative and always creating*. Similar to George Eliot's notion of wholeness, Hegel's notion of being argues for inherent unity that precedes wholeness as a compilation of isolated parts. Likewise, the subject for Hegel has an overarching, guiding theme whether it is perceived or not. Hegel's project was ultimately a recovery, in some ways, of the unity of Aristotelian form that came

---

[33] Works such as the recent study by Gerlinde Roder-Bolton in the series *Studies in Comparative Literature* entitled *George Eliot and Goethe: An Elective Affinity* is an example of such work that has drawn comparisons of plot between George Eliot's fiction and these writers.

[34] Of particular note is Rosemary Ashton's *The German Idea* which looks at the influence of German idealism upon the writers of the Victorian period of which George Eliot is a central figure. Ashton's work is strong in its reflection on the key philosophical questions raised after Kant and Hegel, but does not engage the question of poetics. That is, Ashton addresses the "what" and the "why" of George Eliot but not the "how".

before the analytic, atomistic view of the Enlightenment and sought to view the subject as unity before parts. The subject therefore is not merely body and thought coexisting but a unity of deep and abiding interpenetration without limit or boundary.

*Chapter five* continues this discussion by showing the effects of a poetics of the self and the sacred as it relates expressly to theological poetics of the nineteenth century which focus on the figuring of Christ in the work of F.C. Baur, Ludwig Feuerbach, and D.F. Strauss. These theological writers had a direct impact on George Eliot's formative poetics through the questions that were raised regarding what should be of primary concern regarding the figuring of Christ. In each theologian, the questions raised suggest the need for what Douglas Templeton has called a 'true fiction' – a means of figuring the Christ in the unbounded realm of fiction (which he argues is the genre of the Gospels) rather than attempting to recover the Christ through an historical quest.

This conclusion, that one needs to employ a religious imagination to truly recover the Christ, is not fulfilled by Baur, Feuerbach, and Strauss. Reaching this conclusion, their respective poetics remain closed and overly systematic. One of the most disappointing aspects of George Eliot scholarship is the seeming disregard and indifference to her work of translating Strauss and Feuerbach and her subsequent poetics.[35] I seek to re-introduce these thinkers into the discussion of George Eliot's poetics with particular attention given to the questioning nature of their projects in relation to the matter of subjectivity and the sacred.

*Chapter six* attends to how Victorian contemporaries of George Eliot sought to address the question of the figuring of Jesus within nineteenth century fictional poetics. I begin my discussion by looking at themes evident within Wordsworth's *Prelude*, arguing that this work serves as a necessary hermeneutical key for unlocking the philosophical undertones found in much of the nineteenth century's attempts in fiction to re-stabilise a poetics that "figures the sacred". It is in *The*

---

[35] Most commentators seem unwilling to engage these texts as writing , either treating them as an "artefact" that merely represents a phase of intellectual development or, given that most focus on these thinkers has been within the disciplines of theology and biblical studies, as something outside the scope of George Eliot scholarship as it pertains to her fictional production.

*Prelude* that the creative act of writing is itself a journey of discovery. *The Prelude* offers a universe that is framed *in* "history brought to its appointed close" and controlled *by* the creating act of the writer which Wordsworth states is the only "work that should endure". *The Prelude* begins by seeking throughout the lived world for meaning and ends with a framing of the never-ending search itself. Eliot continued Wordsworth's project into her own fiction.[36] In this way George Eliot is the extension of Wordsworth – a woman writer of prose who reflects the Wordsworthian project. The Victorian novel provided the ideal space within which to re-create poetics and re-imagine the claims and figuring of Jesus that had been relegated to the space of scripture until (borrowing Ian Watt's title from his now-classic text) "the rise of the Novel". It was in this period that changing assumptions surrounding the nature and status of the church as an institution arose. In addition, doubts regarding theological claims regarding the person of Jesus, and the philosophical challenge arising from scientific thinking, caused a challenge to and a re-imagining of poetics. The novel provided an ideal platform and space for these questions to gain form. I argue that attempts to create a stabilising form within the Victorian novel also attempted to stabilise the nature of subjectivity and provide a stable figuring of the sacred within the space of fiction. I discuss three figurings of Jesus within the Victorian novel in contemporaries of George Eliot: J.A. Froude's *The Nemesis of Faith* (1849), Walter Pater's *Marius the Epicurean* (1885), and Mrs. Humphrey Ward's *Robert Elsmere* (1888).[37] In contrast to these writers, I argue that George Eliot offers a different conception of Jesus that is not formed, fixed, nor exposed but is constantly forming, transient, and strangely veiled within the poetic space.

*Chapter seven* begins with a discussion of George Eliot's first fictional publication, the three short stories that are collected together as *Scenes of Clerical Life*. This chapter argues that George Eliot in *Scenes of Clerical Life* is announcing an incarnational aesthetic that requires "a

---

[36] Notably George Eliot's use of Wordsworth's *The Excursion* as a background for her writing of *Adam Bede*. I will discuss this in more depth in the beginning of chapter seven.

[37] Delimiting texts which represent this period of literary output is extremely difficult. As noted, I will use these as representative, not exhaustive, of various poetic attempts to capture the issues surrounding Victorian "doubt" and the figuring of Jesus within fiction.

phenomenological hermeneutic"[38] in line with the hermeneutic project of Paul Ricoeur. In a phenomenological hermeneutic, interpretation must be focused at the intersection of the two directions of language, that is, neither exclusively with the writer's text nor with the reader, but in the encounter between the two. Secondly, any attempt to reduce or remove the tensional aspect of poetic discourse will impose an arbitrary closure on it. Interpretation must maintain the tensional character of the text. Additionally, the act of interpretation must acknowledge the historicity of the writer's text, and the historicity of the reader, so that the interpretative encounter can engage two spheres of discourse. In this way, the act of interpretation itself must be dialectical and produce on a higher level of conceptual meaning for the reader. At its core, this mode of interpretation is never completed, for the aim cannot be to deplete the text (or life for that matter) of its dynamism. The aim must be to arrive at a *temporary* statement that participates in a tradition of commentary on texts.

In *Scenes of Clerical Life*, Eliot gives rise to a poetics that seeks for a new form of christology that is profoundly a/christological – figuring the Christ as that which is without static form, one that is not dependent upon context and is 'seen' in its absence as much as in its presence. Here, Eliot turns away from the theological methodology of Baur, Feuerbach, and Strauss and asserts in her writing a continued turn toward a telling of "the mystery beneath the processes" that was "clothed in human form", a turn which is always to the particular first and foremost. In this way, her task is a search for an ever-forming and dissolving poetics that is akin to the genre of "Gospel" as opposed to "theology" in its seeking to *tell* the story rather than *form* the story. In *Scenes of Clerical Life*, Eliot addresses the idea of context as form where the façade of context-dependent subjectivity is removed so that "ultimate subjectivity" – subjectivity that is tied to the ultimate concerns of humanity – can be freed.

*Chapter eight* moves to a discussion of George Eliot's second work of published fiction and her first full novel, *Adam Bede*. This chapter discusses how George Eliot continues her developing "poetics of Jesus" through iconographic signs that travel the visual-verbal route. It is in chapter XVII of *Adam Bede* ("Where the story pauses a bit") that

[38] See Mario J. Valdes, *Reflection and Imagination: A Ricoeur Reader* (Toronto: University of Toronto Press, 1991) pp. 15ff.

the reader is provoked not merely to "read" but to "see". Through the act of *visual poetics*, Eliot subverts written language and frees her text by an act of intertexuality in the grafting the *verbal* onto the *visual*. It is in her use of visual poetics that the reader is asked to consider what the true visual counterpart of the written/read word is. In *Adam Bede*, the reader is prompted to view/read the narrative and recognise the "density" of the underlying story that can so easily be overlooked – the role of women, the question of class, the forgotten rural life, the face of God. In this way, George Eliot juxtaposes the evoked with the narrated story (for example, the image of humanity's Fall from Grace with the image of Hetty Sorrel's fall in the garden of Hayslope, the image of Jesus with the image of Dinah Morris), in order to let them interact and to let the tensions between the stories produce new meanings.

*Chapter nine* discusses *The Mill on the Floss* as a culminating point of George Eliot's poetic formation in its thoroughly *autobiographical* quality, which in many ways acts as a hermeneutical key for reading the fiction yet to come. This chapter discusses how the notion of "Jesus as Writing" is reflected in the formation of the novel's central protagonist Maggie Tulliver in relation to the Floss – a symbol for the act of figuring and erasure. Throughout *The Mill on the Floss*, Maggie's development is one of *transfiguration* rather than one of *evolutionary change*. She is one who is "moulded and coloured" and in constant exchanges with her environment, which culminates in a transcending of self whilst descending amidst the flooding of the Floss. Readings of *The Mill on the Floss*, such as in Gillian Beer's *Darwin's Plots*, tend to focus primarily upon the rise in scientific writing of the period as a key influence for the poetics within the novel which George Eliot was fascinated with during the period of her writing of the novel. Unlike Darwin's *On the Origin of Species*, the *Bildung* of Maggie is one of gradual and persistent definition, not of drastic changes, akin to the theories of Jean Lamarck. As if seeking an alternative to the work of Charles Lyell and Charles Darwin, George Eliot is trying to recover writing as a space of transfiguration that is more as an act of clarification of essential and base essence rather than one of explosive and radical changes. Unlike Darwinism, the poetic organicism of St. Oggs on the Floss is one that displays processes of becoming through the gradual transfigurations into what Heidegger would term "Being" after the unnaming of naming – Being that is *what it is* rather than a synthesis of thesis and antithesis that is abstracted and without *spiritus*. This is notably demonstrated by Eliot's use of Thomas à Kempis as the culminating intellectual influence upon Maggie – a recovery of a mode of being that predates the Darwinian theory of the day. I argue that George Eliot is instilling within *The Mill on the Floss* a poetics that seeks to figure the sacred and subject and sees *a poetics of Jesus* as the act of unwriting and writing that recalls an affirmation of God in presence and absence simultaneously.

In conclusion, I posit George Eliot as one whose poetics as a poetics of Jesus offers the reader what I term a "poetic cartography of grace". In this way, George Eliot's poetics acts as a "mapping" not merely of space *within* fiction, but the very fullness of space and time itself – a mapping of meaning. In the poetic cartography of George Eliot, the poetics are embodied both in the poetics and the reader – evoking the sense that "you are in Christ as Christ is in you". This "mapping" has no boundary or "edge" that would announce the end of the world or a limit to the universe that creates a sense of beginning and end, but is fully enclosed and three-dimensional, moving *itself* in the fullest breadth, depth, and height of time and space[39] as a mapping that is not followed, but is one that comes and brings with it good news. In short, it is a poetics that offers "true fiction" as writing that calls forth matter of ultimate concern in an overflowing abundance that shatters the form meant to contain it.

[39] I am seeing this notion of "poetic cartography" as akin to the attempts put forward by women mystics such as Theresa of Avila. See E. Ann Matter "Internal Maps of an Eternal External" and Laurie Finke "Mystical Bodies and the Dialogics of Vision" in *Maps of Flesh and Light* ed. Ulrike Wiethaus (New York: Syracuse University Press, 1993) pp. 28ff.

# Chapter 1

# Christology as Writing into Rupture

> … You think – because it is becoming plain to the modern eye that the ignorant love of his first followers wreathed his life in legend, that therefore you can escape from Jesus of Nazareth, you can put him aside as though he had never been? Folly! Do what you will, you cannot escape him. *His life and death underlie our institutions as the alphabet underlies our literature.*[40]

> Τοῦτο ποῖειτε εἰς την ἐμὴν ἀνάμνησιν[41]

The struggle to "figure the Christ" through various means and media represents a continual search for not only the *content* of the figure in question (what makes up and makes possible this union of human and sacred) but ultimately the *form* within which this figuring is shown and understood. John McIntyre, in his Warfield Lectures delivered at Princeton Theological Seminary, begins his discussion of christology and christocentrism by employing a term not typically used in doctrinal discourse – *shape*. As McIntyre rightly states, "if we were asked to give in a summary form the distinguishing characteristic of Protestant theology in our time, many of us would reply that it is its *christocentric* quality which claims this title. And the evidence would be convincing".[42] As McIntyre goes on to surmise:

> It is by this time clear, then, that christology has come to exercise in theology a range of functions for which it was not originally designed: in this range we find exegetical, expository and hermeneutical as well as normative and critical elements… classical christology has come under severe strain in these new settings in which it has of late found itself and a crisis has begun to develop which can only be resolved by a

---

[40] Mrs. Humphrey Ward, *Robert Elsmere* 9th edition (London: Smith, Elder, and Co., 1888 ) p. 495.

[41] "Do this in remembrance of me" – Luke 22: 19.

[42] John McIntyre, *The Shape Of Christology* (London: SCM Press, 1966) p. 9.

> radical reassessment of the basic *shape* of this central doctrine of the Christian faith as today expressed.[43]

McIntyre rightly notes that there is indeed a continued search for the basic *shape* of this central doctrine of the Christian faith that is the nature of Christ and it goes back to the very foundations of the Church itself.

As one turns to some of the earliest Christian writings, this quest for a *poetics of Jesus* – how the form, content, and import of writing itself makes claims of "ultimate concern"[44] regarding the nature of Christ – is seen particularly in the ecumenical creeds. On the occasion of the Council of Nicaea in CE 325, the dispute within the Church regarding questions brought forward by the Arians as to the very form and definition of Christ's relation to God gave rise to the need for a poetics. As the Arians argued in favour of a radical doctrine of monotheism, they in turn advocated a denial of Christ as being *one* with God, but asserted him to be *created* and therefore *not of the same substance* as God. The Nicene Creed was drafted in response to this assertion. The actual *poetics* of the creed is presented in a manner to assert the orthodox stance of Christ as one who is

> only-begotten Son of God;
> Begotten of his Father before all worlds,
> God of God, Light of Light, Very God of Very God;
> Begotten, not made;
> Being of one substance with the Father;
> By whom all things were made…[45]

Interestingly, it also presents a *condemnation* of those who did not 'fit' Christ into this shape. This is marked in the original form of the Nicene Creed which concludes with a portion originally added as an anathema against the Arians: "But to those who say: 'There is a time

---

[43] ibid., p. 11.

[44] To recollect Paul Tillich's use of the phrase in reference to that which is of highest good and meaning.

[45] Nicene Creed circa CE 325, in *Readings in Christian Thought* 2nd ed. Hugh T. Kerr ed. (Nashville: Abington Press, 1993) p. 76.

when He was not'; and 'He was not before he was made'; and 'He was made out of nothing,' or 'He is of another substance or essence,' or 'The Son of God is created,' or 'changeable or alterable' – they are condemned by the Holy Catholic and Apostolic Church".[46] Where a creed is to be an *assertion* of faith (the term coming from the Latin *credo*, "I believe") this original rendering stands as a statement *against* "I *don't* believe" as much as a statement *for* certain beliefs. The poetics thereby make claims that overturn the very definition of the genre itself (i.e. what constitutes *Credo*) through its construction *as a work* and the claims it makes on how it is to be read. In this way, the *poetics* of the creed (and of much literature as I will argue throughout this book) makes claims that at times are more profound than the actual content or genre the work supposedly represents.

This elevation of poetics is exemplified regarding the further history of the ecumenical creeds in the Council of Chalcedon in CE 451, where the re-writing of the Nicene Creed as a response to such heresies as Arianism as well as Apollinarianism (the denial of the full humanity of Christ), Nestorianism (the denial of the union of the two natures in Christ), and Eutycheanism (which sought to deny the distinction of the two natures) rendered what is commonly known as the *Symbol of Chalcedon*. The very form and limits within which the Church can work out the orthodox doctrine of the person of Christ is given in its poetics. As a *symbol*, it operates as a *frame* within which all subsequent statements made regarding Christ can be seen – that which falls outside the scope of its language and its intent is thereby outside the limits of expression regarding the person of Christ. Due to the density of its very form, the statement forged at Chalcedon is truly more "symbol" than *credo*. Throughout the history of the Church, the Symbol of Chalcedon has "never had a wide liturgical or catechetical use because of the complexity of language and intricacy of definition".[47] This "complexity of language" moves the Symbol of Chalcedon *outside* the orality of language and into a realm of form which seeks to judge subsequent language forms and uses, but does not itself participate in, the common life of language in its fullest capacity.[48]

---

[46] ibid.

[47] Hugh Kerr, *Readings in Christian Thought*- 2nd ed. (Nashville: Abington Press, 1993) p. 75.

[48] Walter Ong makes the distinction in the way in which the very content of information shifts its meaning as it inhabits a different medium since different senses are utilised to make 'sense' of the information received. What Ong terms as a

Figuring a *poetics of Jesus* has continued to challenge subsequent generations in both direct and indirect means with the search to find a poetics that *opens* rather than *closes off* questions of meaning and engagement, allowing for the possibility of the nexus of the sacred and the subject. As mentioned in the Introduction, such a poetics is explicitly open to and disclosive of the unconditioned import of meaning found in Jesus. Finding such a poetics that *flows* in the act of writing as continuous discovery and engagement with ultimate concern, rather than a poetics that *delimits* and ultimately *constricts* the ultimate concerns of the sacred and the subject behind static renderings of dialectical logocentrism was particularly active in the work of writers in Germany and England in the eighteenth and nineteenth centuries. In the writing of those concerned with philosophy and biblical criticism in the eighteenth century, the role of *history* in the discussions regarding the figuring of Jesus of Nazareth became central to christology – attempting to create a figuring of Jesus who *was* rather than the Christ who *is*. As stated by Gregory Dawes in *The Historical Jesus Quest*:

> The question of the historical Jesus is such a familiar one today that it is difficult for us to realise how recent a question it is. For more than 1600 years the idea of asking such a question never arose. More precisely, in the minds of the Christian interpreters of the Bible there was no difference between the Jesus of history and the Jesus of the Church's proclamation. Insofar as the Christian scriptures spoke of the incarnation of God at a particular point in human affairs, the accuracy of their reports was taken for granted.[49]

The challenge to traditional understandings of the person of Jesus during this period is exemplified in the pioneering work of the

---

"sensorium" is the constructed form that communication takes in order to gain access to the subject via given senses. As he notes, the very potency of religion and the message it is trying to convey becomes lost as it moves into a purely literary form since it then becomes delimited by the manifold meanings of language. See Walter Ong, *The Presence of the Word* (New Haven: Yale University Press, 1967) and Robert Detweiler and David Jasper, eds. *Religion and Literature* (Louisville: Westminster John Knox Press, 2000) pp. 36-38.

[49] Gregory W. Dawes, ed. *The Historical Jesus Quest: A Foundational Anthology* (Leiden: Deo Publishing, 1999) p. 1.

late seventeenth century philosopher and ethicist Benedict de Spinoza whose *Ethics* George Eliot translated. In his "Of the Interpretation of Scripture" from Chapter Seven of *Tractatus theologico-politicus*, Spinoza argues that the biblical interpreter is interested in discovering only "the meaning" of the biblical texts and not their "truth":

> But for this task [of interpreting scripture] we need a method and order similar to that which we employ in interpreting Nature from the facts presented before us... we must first seek from our study of Scripture that which is most universal and forms the basis and foundation of all Scripture; in short, that which is commended in Scripture by all the prophets as doctrine eternal and most profitable for all mankind...Scripture does not teach formally, and as eternal doctrine. On the contrary, we have clearly shown that the prophets themselves were not in agreement on these matters, and therefore on topics of this kind we should make no assertion that claims to be the doctrine of the Holy Spirit, even though the natural light of reason may be quite decisive on that point. ... with regard to the meaning of revelation, *it should be observed that this method only teaches us how to discover what the prophets really saw or heard, and not what they intended to signify or represent by the symbols in question. The latter we can only guess at, not infer with certainty from the basis of Scripture.*[50] (emphasis added)

One can hear strains of the eighteenth century writer Hermann Samuel Reimarus, whose writings George Eliot became familiar with through her translation work of D.F. Strauss' *Das Leben Jesu*, in Spinoza's conclusions. In his *Fragments* written in 1777 and first published posthumously by Lessing as fragments of unknown origin found in the Duke of Brunswick's library at Wolfenbüttel (*Fragments of the Wolfenbüttel Unknown*), Reimarus argues for scripture itself as a thoroughly *rewritten* genre – constantly revised and reshaped through the years – thereby overturning both a historical grounding in an "original" text and at the same time supporting, albeit by inference, a view of scripture as a re-imagined space. With regard to Jesus' parables, Reimarus writes:

> But since these secrets [the secrets of the Kingdom of God disclosed in Matthew 13:11; Mark 4:11; Luke 8:10] consist merely of an explanation of figurative concepts and the explanation, insofar as it is stripped of parable, in turn contains nothing more than the common knowledge of

[50] Benedictus Spinoza, *Tractatus Theologico-Politicus*, trans. Samuel Shirley (Leiden: E.J. Brill, 1989) p. 140.

> the promised Kingdom of God under the Messiah, one must confess that no really new or incomprehensible precepts are to be found among these secrets. *Take note from this, to what extent people let themselves be deceived by words!* Today we are accustomed to understanding by the word "faith" or "gospel" the whole body of Christian doctrine that we are to believe, or all the articles of the Christian faith in their interconnection, the entire catechism and the creed, and we particularly call "mysteries" those doctrines that surpass understanding and that are neither to be understood or proved by reason alone.[51]

The notion of Jesus as a person of history whose (to use Spinoza's term) *certainty* as *the* Christ could not be supported by questions put forward by biblical criticism continued in the days following writers such as Spinoza, Reimarus, and Kant. This left a new generation of writers in the eighteenth and nineteenth century suspicious of so-called idle claims regarding the historicity of Jesus, but looking at the effects that such epistemological fractures would have upon the grounding of poetics both in theology and literature after history is rendered non-essential.

One shift in the wake of separating the Jesus of history from the Jesus of the Church's proclamation lay in the notion of *Jesus as the great metaphysical idea* that became an alternative means to support Jesus as the Christ in a new fashion. This opens the opportunity for fiction to be a possible space for the figuring of the nexus of subject and sacred. As Lessing spoke of the "ugly, broad ditch"[52] that existed between the certainty of history and the certainty of reason, he saw the resolution to this proverbial chasm in the advocating for a purely *spiritual* understanding of Christology.[53] This move is further articulated

---

51 Hermann Samuel Reimarus, *Fragments of the Wolfenbüttel Unknown* in *Reimarus: Fragments*, ed. Charles H. Talbert (Minneapolis: Fortress Press, 1970) Part I, section 9, p. 75.

52 Gotthold Ephraim Lessing, "On the Proof of the Spirit and Power" in *Lessing's Theological Writings*, trans. Henry Chadwick (London: Adam & Charles Black, 1956) p. 55.

53 In the early 20th century Karl Barth would later remark that "the Lessing question" regarding this "ugly, broad ditch" was within a much larger context of what Barth termed "the problem of distance" which is the question of the "real" distance that humankind is in relation to God (citing Luke 5:8). For Barth, Christ is the first truly recognisable manifestation of both the problem of this distance and its ultimate

by J.G. Fichte in his statement that "the metaphysical only, and not the historical, can give us blessedness; the latter can only give us understanding".[54] Schelling asserts this notion of the purely metaphysical and idealised rendering of Christ as Idea in his "On the Study of Theology" where he makes the assertion that the "Christ idea" is the "incarnation of eternity" in which "the culmination of this process is Christ assuming visible human form [appearance as the opposite concept to idea], and for this reason it is also its beginning".[55] This "beginning which is also the end" in Schelling's thought prompts the speculative christology of Kant and Hegel. As noted by Otto Weber in his *Dogmatics*, this "speculative Christology" is that which "understood the Christ – idea as the code, disguise, expression, or manifestation of the unity of the absolute, which is realising itself in history, with the relative [the world, man, the human race]".[56] In Kant's *Religion Within the Limits of Reason Alone*, the designation "Son of God" is aligned with the "ideal of a humanity well pleasing to God".[57] This notion is in keeping with Hegel's later conclusions regarding Christ as "a history for the spiritual community because it is absolutely adequate [as] idea".[58] With the notion of the "idea" having the weight of truth that rivalled that of historical fact, the importance of a poetics becomes more apparent. Since it is "the possible" and "the imagined" as well as 'the factual' that can frame the potential of the sacred meeting the subject, the central issue moves beyond *what* is written and read to *how* writing and reading is done.

resolution. In short, Barth takes Lessing's dilemma beyond the philosophical boundaries and places it into what Barth sees as the larger context, that of the salvific. See Karl Barth, *Church Dogmatics*, (Edinburgh: T & T Clark, 1969) part IV, pp. 287ff.

[54] J.G. Fichte, *The Way Toward the Blessed Life, or, The Doctrine of Religion – 1806* trans. W. Smith (London: Chapman, 1849) p. 107.

[55] Schelling, "On the Study of Theology", in *On University Studies*, trans. E.S. Morgan (Athens: Ohio University Press, 1966) p. 94.

[56] Otto Weber, *Foundations of Dogmatics Vol. 2* trans. Darrell Guder (Grand Rapids: Eerdmans Publishing, 1983) p. 3.

[57] Immanuel Kant, *Religion Within the Limits of Reason Alone*, trans. T.M. Greene (New York: Harper & Row, 1960) pp. 54ff. This use of Kant's correlation of the "Son of God" with the "ideal" is manifested in Herder and in a more "emphatic" way in Friedrich Schleiermacher, *The Christian Faith*, trans. H.R. Mackintosh and J.S. Stewart (Edinburgh: T and T Clark, 1928) pp. 377ff.

[58] G.W.F. Hegel, *Lectures on the Philosophy of Religion*, vol. 3, trans. E.S. Haldane (New York: Humanities Press, 1968) pp. 72ff.

As suggested in such works as *Towards a Christian Poetics*[59] by Michael Edwards, the rendering of a poetics that acknowledges the full ramifications of an answer to that question posed to Peter "who do you say that I am?" remains scarce in contemporary poetics, nowhere more so than in the very arena where such a poetics should arise, namely New Testament scholarship. In their recent book entitled *The Meaning of Jesus – Two Visions*, New Testament Scholars N.T. Wright and Marcus Borg come together as representatives of traditionalist and liberal scholarship respectively, in an attempt to dissolve the tensions that surround current academic debates regarding the person of Jesus of Nazareth which have become "acrimonious, with a good deal of name calling and angry polemic in both public and private discourse".[60] The ultimate aim of this "open discussion" is to provide a way through such forms of discussion and hopefully to demonstrate a means by which scholarly discussions surrounding the person of Jesus can take place. As the subtitle of the book denotes, both Wright and Borg attempt to approach the task as "visionaries" of sorts, hoping to guide a new generation toward developing a "new vision" for how one communicates the nature and person of Jesus. What one finds at the end of this attempt is merely a rendering anew of forms and analogies that bring about a closed christology, one that bears little or no resemblance to the Jesus they purport to acknowledge and ultimately seek to locate.[61]

---

[59] Michael Edwards, *Toward a Christian Poetics* (London: Macmilian, 1984). In his address to the conference on Christianity and Literature at Macquarrie University, 5-8 July 1999 in Sydney, Australia entitled "Can We Speak of a Christian Poetics?", David Jasper cited Edward's work as "in Pascal's phrase, *un monstre incompréhensible* – a monster that passes all understanding... because it remains so deeply embedded within the established traditions of Christianity and its theology, his reading of literature exercised only in terms of Christianity, failing to make the radical move which acknowledges the true poet who overturns language which sustains such theology, moving on the boundaries of a silence which, like Augustine, opens our ears and eyes to the profound dichotomy between nature and grace" "Can We Speak of a Christian Poetics?" *Literature and Religion – The Korean Society of Literature and Religion,* (Vol. 5, No. 1 Summer 2000) pp. 139, 140.

[60] N.T. Wright and Marcus Borg, *The Meaning of Jesus – Two Visions* (London: SPCK, 1999) p. x.

[61] Attempts by New Testament scholars to figure the Christ has also seen attempts at fictional accounts with such recent works as Gerard Sloyan's *Jesus in Focus* and Gerd

In his 1990 lecture published in *Granta* entitled "Is Nothing Sacred?" Salman Rushdie discusses the irony whereby traditionally "religious" writing seems to be anything but religious, whilst those who dwell in the space of fiction seem to find openings where the possibility of the sacred is seen. As he compares the genres of "religion" and "literature" he notes that:

> Between religion and literature ... there is a linguistically based dispute. But it is not a dispute of simple opposites. Because whereas religion seeks to privilege one language above all others, one set of values above all others, one text above all others, the novel has always been about the way in which different languages, values and narratives quarrel, and about the shifting relations between them, which are relations of power. The novel does not seek to establish a privileged language, but it insists upon the freedom to portray and analyse the struggle between the different contestants for such privileges.[62]

As Rushdie correctly surmises, the move into the realm of the fictive that is represented by forms such as the novel is a move *away* from the privileging of "one language above all others" and an approach toward a poetics that acknowledges the hope for "the freedom to portray and analyse the struggle" inherent in such a search.

In order to locate such a poetics of Jesus, a poetics that is free to portray and analyse the struggle of figuring the nexus of the subject and sacred, one must place such possibility of a poetics where it is called into judgement before such a poetics can be figured – a disfiguring and figuring at once. This entry into such a poetics is ultimately a *coincidentia oppositorum*. Thomas Altizer asserts that such a space evokes the following:

> a full coming together of total opposites, the opposites of total ending and total beginning, and the totally old world or aeon and a totally new aeon or world ... a *coincidentia oppositorum* is at the very centre of the Christian epic, as is a calling forth and voyage into an apocalyptic totality, and [the Christian] epic totality is an apocalyptic totality if only because it embodies such a radical and total transformation. Here, this

---

Theissen's *The Shadow of the Galilean*. While these seek to project a re-figured Christ, these fall back onto poetics that limits and is primarily dependent upon historical inquiry.

[62] Salman Rushdie, "Is Nothing Sacred?" – Herbert Read Memorial Lecture in *Granta* 31, Spring 1990 pp. 102, 103.

> transformation is deepest in envisioning the depths of the Godhead itself, depths that are apocalyptic depths, and hence depths unveiling a new Godhead only by bringing an old Godhead to an end.[63]

As Altizer maintains, at the centre of the Christian epic, that is, the centre of writing that brings to mind the person of Christ, one must acknowledge that the question of the person of Jesus is the ultimate *coincidentia oppositorum*, that is a disturbing centre-point to all concerns. This acknowledgement is one of, as Altizer argues, "eschatological proclamation and parabolic enactment" that, like the true Jesus, will "reverse every given form of God and the world". To enter this parabolic enactment through the medium of literature is to take on a *poetics of Jesus* which will

> reverse every image of Jesus we have known if we are to be open to his contemporary and apocalyptic presence. Just such a reversal has continually occurred in the Christian imagination, a reversal not only of given images of Jesus, but also, and even thereby, a reversal of all given Christian images of God.[64]

This bears striking similarity to contemporary post-structuralist writers such as Jacques Derrida, who, while resolutely determined not to be considered as a "religious" writer, actually attempts to form such a poetics that Altizer argues is at the very heart of the person of Jesus. Jesus, as that subject of writing where subjectivity is both constructed and destroyed simultaneously, bears marked resemblance to that which Derrida argues for in his essay "Structure, Sign, and Play in the Discourse of the Human Sciences" from *Writing and Difference.*

In this essay, Derrida is seeking to situate ultimate subjectivity as it is to be determined by a given subject in a place beyond language. Seeking not to destroy the subject, his stated wish is to "...situate it.... [This ultimately is] a question of knowing *where* it [the subject] comes from".[65] In this way, the origin of a subject before language is "named"

---

[63] Thomas J.J. Altizer, *The Contemporary Jesus* (New York: State University of New York Press, 1997) pp. xiv, xv, xxiii.

[64] ibid., p. xxv.

[65] Jacques Derrida, "Structure, Sign, and Play in the Discourse of the Human

by it, prior to seeking definition of pre-existent terms. This point of origin is where one draws meaning from the "history of meanings" that form our understanding. This is what Derrida terms "centre". As one follows his argument, this "centre" resembles the "centre" argued by Altizer to be that of Jesus.

Jean Hyppolite, author of *Logic and Existence*,[66] posed the question to Derrida regarding his lecture on "Structure, Sign, and Play" as to "what a *centre* might mean".[67] In Hyppolite's words, is "the centre the knowledge of the general rules which, after a fashion, allow us to understand the interplay of the elements? Or is the centre certain elements which enjoy a particular privilege with the ensemble?"[68] Derrida's answer was as follows: "I don't mean to say that I thought of approaching an idea of the centre that would be an affirmation".[69] The centre of which he speaks is not a certain place as we shall see, not a place to be affirmed and locked into meaning, for this would do to the word "centre" what Derrida says the term centre now *does* – making a "substitution of *linguistic* centre for *true* centre" – so that "the centre receives different forms or names" and we ultimately lose that which we seek. Derrida's definition of "centre" constitutes abstracted definitions of a communally concerned identity: "The centre, which is by definition unique, constitutes that very thing within a structure which while *governing* that structure, *escapes* structurality".[70]

In the fight to define, definition in its truest sense is lost. To say, for example, that theology has the exclusive role and location for the spiritual formation in people's lives overturns the basic claims of Christianity itself. As noted by David Tracy:[71]

---

Sciences" in *Writing and Difference* (London: Routledge Press, 1978) pp. 278ff.

[66] Jean Hyppolite, *Logic & Existence* (New York: State University of New York Press, 1997).

[67] Richard Macksey and Eugenio Donato, eds. *The Structuralist Controversy: The Languages of Criticism and the Sciences of Man.* (Baltimore: Johns Hopkins University Press, 1972) pp. 265ff. Lee Morrissey makes interesting comparisons between the questions raised by Derrida in "Structure, Sign, and Play" and the political undertones of the essay. See Lee Morrissey, "Derrida, Algeria, and 'Structure, Sign, and Play'" *Postmodern Culture* Volume 9, Issue 2.

[68] ibid.

[69] ibid.

[70] Jacques Derrida, ibid., p. 279.

[71] I am using the notion of the Church collective [Church] as comparable to Tracy's use of the individual christian.

> ...the [Church] lives in a strange and healing paradox disclosed... throughout the scriptures: so deeply into one's existence does the unmasking radicality of the Word strike that the radical contingency and ambiguity of all culture, all civilisation, all institutions, even nature itself [in sum, the "world"] are unmasked by the same Word which commands and enables work *for* the world, and more concretely for the neighbour. This Christian insight into the conventionality, the arbitrariness, the radical contingency of all culture, all nature and all institutions has a reverse side: the radical ambiguity of all culture, nature, institutions – all the world – and their constant temptation to self-aggrandisement and self-delusion. Yet this very same insight into the radical contingency and real ambiguity of the world posits itself not only by negating all "worldly" pretensions to divinity, atemporality, eternity, but also by positing the command and the possibility of living in and for this contingent, ambiguous, created and divinely beloved "world".[72]

Tracy goes on to say that "rather than repeating the domesticated slogans that presume to capture this dialectic ('The [Church] is *in* the world, but not *of* it'), it seems more correct to say that the [Church] is released (the violent imagery is exact) *from* the world, *for* the world".[73]

Attempts to figure Jesus in poetics will *always* have to fight the tendency to build walls and choose a fixed centre rather than an organic one – a poetics that is delimited, static and closed rather than one that provokes eschatological proclamation and parabolic enactment that, like the true Jesus, will reverse every given form of God and the world humanity seeks to figure. As Derrida notes, we seek delimited structures such as a closed and static poetics through a fixed unchanging centerpoint which ultimately "neutralise[s]... [and] reduce[s]" the truth of a subject into merely "a point of presence, a fixed origin".[74] It is this false centre then that controls, in the sense of containing, the structurality of the structure, reducing it. Thus the extremes are neutralised by the centre.

In "Structure, Sign, and Play," Derrida emphasises that true

---

[72] David Tracy, *The Analogical Imagination* (London: SCM Press, 1981) p. 48.

[73] David Tracy, ibid.

[74] Jacques Derrida, op. cit., p. 278.

centre is "not a fixed locus but a *function*".[75] In one sense, then, centring as function, or *import* to recall Tillich's category, need not be put in one place; the function can be distributed throughout the structure. This is another way of understanding that the centre is not the centre; the centre as import need not be at the central place. Moreover, if the centre as import is not a place, then it is highly variable; not only can the function or import be fulfilled from different places, but different centres can fulfil the same function. Derrida states that "[i]f this is so, the entire history of the concept of structure, before the rupture of which we are speaking, must be thought of as a series of substitutions of centre for centre".[76] In short, the functionality of what is "centre" is itself just a substitute for a previous centre; the "function" remains the same even if the centre has moved.

As Derrida notes, "the history of metaphysics, like the history of the West, is the history of metaphors and metonymies".[77] Derrida goes on to state that, "we have no language – no syntax and no lexicon – which is foreign to this history" of metaphors and metonymies.[78] For example, attempts to hold Jesus in place through modifiers such as the "historical" Jesus, the "kerygmatic" Jesus, the "apocalyptic" Jesus, the "liberation" Jesus, or what have you, are merely attempts to stabilise form by evoking metaphors and metonymies. Although metaphors claim to state that "this *is* that", or while metonymies, as the root indicates, make possible changes of names ("we will now re-name this *to be called* that"), they are nothing but descriptions and ultimately barriers. This is central to Derrida's project in "Structure, Sign, and Play" in his arguing that we need to look beyond our need in Western metaphysics to fight for

> the determination of Being as *presence* in all senses of this word. It could be shown that all the names related to fundamentals, to principles, or to the centre have always designated an invariable presence – *eidos*, *arche*, *telos*, *energeia*, *ousia* (essence, existence, substance, subject) *aletheia*, transcendentality, consciousness, God, man, and so forth.[79]

---

[75] ibid., p. 280.
[76] ibid., p. 278.
[77] ibid., p. 279.
[78] ibid., p. 280.
[79] ibid.

This power is, on the one hand, rhetorical, yet on the other hand, substantial and real. But words do not necessarily establish what the object is; they instead participate in "a history of meanings".[80] Moreover, to make a claim of identity based on signifiers such as Jesus takes the form of both a metaphor (a=b or "this" is to "that") and a metonymy (a name change, "Christ" is now "Jesus"), so that what the import sought through form and content may still be different from what either the metaphor or the metonymy can suggest. The face we may seek for – Jesus as Jesus – is not to be found. The face we *do* figure "is neither the face of God nor the figure of man: it is their resemblance. A resemblance which, however, we must think before, or without, the assistance of the Same".[81] We who seek this "face" are in the space between

> the difference between the same and the other, which is not a difference or a relation among others, has no meaning in the infinite... this horizon is not the horizon of the infinitely other, but of a reign in which the difference between the same and the other, *differánce*, would no longer be valid, that is, of a reign in which peace itself will no longer have meaning.[82]

"We live in and of difference," according to Derrida. If Derrida's assertion is true, where does import reside?

For Derrida, given this distinction drawn between true identity and metaphor, it is to be concluded that identity ultimately only exists in "difference" between meaning and the label placed upon it. These labels of metaphors and metonymies only have meaning in their ability to assuage and master a certain degree of anxiety, probably the anxiety of difference, which is also the anxiety of similarity. Anxiety as to what lies behind the veil of signifiers such as Jesus in whatever manifestation, forces institutions to double efforts to re-interpret terms as well as look through these signs to what is beyond. This shift, according to

---

[80] ibid., p. 279.

[81] Jacques Derrida, "Violence and Metaphysics" in *Writing and Difference* (London: Routledge Press, 1978) p. 109.

[82] Jacques Derrida, ibid., p. 129.

Derrida, is the point of "rupture".

"Rupture comes about when the structurality of the structure had to begin to be thought".[83] Once we begin to recognise that the structure of any given sign is merely a structure, and nothing else, a rupture *can* occur. Derrida claims that "perhaps something has occurred in the history of the concept of structure that could be called an event" where "its exterior form would be that of a rupture".[84] Prior to this realisation, when people believe that the structure is something *other* than a structure, they have chosen a mere metaphor instead of import, and in short, chosen form rather than meaning.

According to Lee Morrissey, one way of framing Derrida's attempt in "Structure, Sign, and Play" could be understood as part of what Hal Foster in *Return of the Real* describes as "a shift in conception – from reality as an effect of representation to the real as a thing of trauma",[85] that is, the "real" is something that is beyond critique as "the traumatic" is beyond category and escapes language altogether. This "shift in conception" is an attempt to see *with* reality, not merely form *a* reality to be seen. Similarly, for the question of a *poetics of Jesus* to be resolved, a rupture is needed in the false ways that meaning is made and supported. The reality that there is *no* institution whose task it is to preserve separate fixed centring points needs to be affirmed. Rather, *all* are part of a larger enterprise whose "centre" is shared beyond definition. This calls to mind Thomas Altizer's challenge to seek "a Jesus who was the first truly apocalyptic prophet, the one who first enacted a total apocalyptic ending – but an apocalyptic ending that is apocalyptic beginning, a beginning that has been renewed again and again by those who embody him, or those who embody his acts and words".[86]

In an interview, Derrida stated that "what interests me today is not strictly called either literature or philosophy, I'm amused by the idea that my adolescent desire – let's call it that – should have directed me

---

[83] Jacques Derrida, "Sign, Structure, and Play", ibid., p. 280.

[84] Macksey and Donato, ibid., p. 278.

[85] Hal Foster, *The Return of the Real* (Boston: MIT Press, 1996) p. 146. Foster maintains that this idea of *trauma* is central to critical theory after postmodernity: "Across artistic, theoretical, and popular cultures (in Soho, at Yale, on *Oprah*) there is a tendency to redefine experience, individual and historical, in terms of trauma… Here is indeed a traumatic subject, and it has absolute authority, for one cannot challenge the trauma of another: one can only believe it, even identify with it, or not". p. 168.

[86] Thomas J. J. Altizer, op. cit., p. 17.

toward something in writing which is neither the one or the other. What is it? *Autobiography* is perhaps the least adequate name, because it remains for me the most enigmatic, the most open, even today".[87] This is where I suggest the centering character begins - at its most authentic point. This point which is "the most enigmatic, the most open" is where writing becomes an act of self-creating and encountering that brings such open and enigmatic authenticity. This is characteristic of a poetics of Jesus. George Eliot wrote in one of her letters that writing that is truly autobiography is that which shows how a writer's mind "grew, how it was determined by the joys, sorrows and other influences of childhood and youth – that is a precious contribution to knowledge".[88] In this way, the genre of the Gospels is the true fiction as that which figures the self and the sacred at once, whose story is unique and universal in its writing and, to cite Heidegger, strives to "unname naming" by providing an apocalyptic beginning that has been renewed again and again by those who embody it as an act of "remembrance": re-membering the broken through *poiesis*.

Ultimately, what I am arguing for as a poetics of Jesus is never *formed* and is always *on the way* but never *there*, so to begin this dialogue is not an easy one. As Derrida himself notes in "Structure, Sign, and Play", "there is too much, more than one can say".[89] It is a continuous process that must not be static nor fixed if we are to "recast, if not rigorously refound a discourse ... [O]ne has to go through the experience of deconstruction"[90] to find another way, a new way, all the time.

What I propose here is a rhetorical strategy whereby one actually says more than one appears to have said. The interplay found in the "rupture" of the signs that denote Jesus whether in the poetic space or within the space of a kerygmatic community can lead to new space for Jesus to be "authentic" in the full Heideggerian sense. In

---

[87] Jacques Derrida, " 'This Strange Institution Called Literature': An Interview with Jacques Derrida". *Acts of Literature/Jacques Derrida.* ed. Derek Attridge. Trans. Geoffrey Bennington and Rachel Bowlby (New York: Routledge, 1992) p. 34.

[88] George Eliot, *The George Eliot Letters* ed. George S. Haight (London: Oxford University Press, 1954-1956) vol. 7, p. 230.

[89] Jacques Derrida, "Structure, Sign, and Play", ibid., p. 289.

[90] Jacques Derrida, "This Strange Institution Called Literature", ibid., pp. 33ff.

many ways I am arguing for a poetics of Jesus where entering within is not certain nor safe, a place that is "the undiscovered country" of Hamlet's musings and a place that is closest to Derrida's sense of "autobiography" as writing that is most enigmatic and most open. This is a place that returns to forming questions of life writ large, where people gather and *that* gathering becomes the defining character. It is a place that is open always to possible destruction of the pre-conceived, yet (com)passionate for the clearing act of being-in-the-world and being-for-the-world.

As Derrida has said, the space of literature "allows one to say everything. To say everything is no doubt to gather, by translating, all figures into one another, to totalize by formalizing, but to say everything is also to break out of prohibitions".[91] George Eliot's desire to tell "the simple story" is a concern to tell all stories and ultimately to tell them all through a poetics that finds its form in a poetic incarnation of the one whom Schweitzer felt "comes to us as one unknown…"[92] While most of the so-called Quest of the Historical Jesus concerned itself with the content and facts concerning this one who "comes to us as one unknown", it was the form of Jesus and what this person represents that intrigued and gave noticeable shape to the poetics of Eliot's fiction. In the midst of the "New Quest" for the Historical Jesus, New Testament scholar Günther Bornkamm stated in the opening sentence of *Jesus of Nazerath* that "[n]o one is any longer in the position to write a life of Jesus"[93], yet in works of fiction such as those produced by writers such as George Eliot, that which was sought for – the 'one who comes as one unknown' – does indeed arise.

---

[91] ibid. p. 36.

[92] Albert Schweitzer, *The Quest of the Historical Jesus: A Critical Study of its Progress from Reimarus to Wrede* (London: A & C Black, 1954/1906) p. 401.

[93] Günther Bornkamm, *Jesus of Nazareth* trans. I. McLuskey, F. McLuskey, and J.M. Robinson (London: Hodder and Stoughton, 1960) p. 13.

# Chapter 2

# Augustine and the Form of the Subject in/of the *Imago Dei*

> Before experiencing God you thought you could talk about God; when you begin to experience God you realise that what you are experiencing you cannot put into words.[94]

In western poetics concerning the subject, it is with St. Augustine of Hippo that the move to set *form* above *content* as the indicator of nexus between the subject and the sacred begins and it is Augustine's project that continues to shape poetics of the subject into the present. As Mark Taylor rightly argues, it is Augustine "who first recognised and defined the principles of subjectivity".[95] In his *Confessions,* Augustine attempts to resolve his questions of doubt regarding subjectivity (how does one know self-as-self?) and the possibility of nexus with the sacred through a turn *inward*, and takes a reflexive stance upon one's own selfhood – a move in opposition to that of Aristotle's epistemology. As Augustine notes, the interior realm is vastly more complex than the exterior and therefore a more likely space to encounter ultimate concerns.[96] As Mark Taylor notes, "The world within [for Augustine],

---

[94] Augustine, Homily on Psalm 99.6, cited by Marcus Borg, *The God We Never Knew* (San Francisco: Harper Collins, 1997) p. 48.

[95] Mark C. Taylor, *Erring: A Postmodern A/Theology* (Chicago: University of Chicago Press, 1984) pp. 38ff.

[96] In Book X of *Confessions,* Augustine uses the metaphor of the inner life as one of deep "secret caverns". Questions to the great questions of being (P), such as "Does P exist? What is P? What kind of thing is P?" are informed by the senses (sight, hearing, touch, taste, smell) yet the true meaning of this sensory data is only known through retrieval of memory. "The answer [Does P exist? What is P? What kind of thing is P?] must be that which is already in the memory, but so remote and pushed into the background, as if in most secret caverns, that unless they [memories held within the mind] were dug out by someone drawing attention to them, perhaps I could not have

proved to be as perplexing as the puzzling world without. Rather than a simple individual or singular substance, Augustine found the self to be complex and inwardly divided".[97] This "complex division" is seen as well throughout the created order where

> opposition of spirit/matter, higher/lower, eternal/temporal, immutable/changing *is* described by Augustine, not just occasionally and peripherally, but centrally and essentially in terms of inner/outer... And this is not just one way of describing the difference for Augustine. It is in a sense the most important one for our spiritual purposes, because the road from the lower to the higher, the crucial shift in direction, passes through our attending to ourselves as *inner*.[98]

The notable quotation by Augustine in this regard is *Noli foras ire, in teipsum redi; in interiore homine habitat veritas* ("Do not go outward; return within yourself. In the inward man dwells truth").[99] Augustine is in line with Plato before him in his search for a unifying principle under and throughout the oppositions and complex divisions of the world. But Augustine draws a new direction in his avocation of *in interiore homine* as the *habitat veritas*. As noted by Charles Taylor:

> [In] Plato, we find out about this highest principle by looking at the

thought them". Augustine, *Confessions*. trans. Henry Chadwick (Oxford: Oxford University Press, 1998) Book X, section 17, p. 189.

97 ibid.

98 Charles Taylor, *Sources of the Self* (Cambridge: Harvard University Press, 1989) p. 129.

99 Saint Augustine, *De vera Religione[On True Religion]*, XXXIX, 72, in *Augustine: Early Writings*. trans. John H.S. Burleigh (London: SCM Press, 1953) p. 262. "What obstacle then remains to hinder the soul from recalling the primal beauty which it abandoned, when it can make an end of its vices? The Wisdom of God extends from end to end with might. By wisdom the great Artificer knit his works together with one glorious end in view. His goodness has no grudging envy against any beauty from the highest to the lowest, for none can have being except him alone. So that no one is utterly cast away from the truth who has in him the slightest visage of truth. What is it about bodily pleasure that holds fast? You will find that it is agreeableness. Disagreeable things beget grief and agreeable things beget pleasure. Seek therefore the highest agreeableness. *Do not go outward; return within yourself. In the inward man dwells truth.* ...It [agreeableness] has to do no seeking, but you reach it by seeking, not in space, but by a disposition of mind, so that the inward man may agree with the indwelling truth in a pleasure that is not low and carnal but supremely spiritual." ibid.

> domain of objects which it organises, that is, the field of the Ideas. What we saw... in the image of the eye of the soul was the doctrine that the power of seeing doesn't have to be put into it; rather it just has to be turned. Facing the right field is what is decisive. We may have to struggle to rise to this, but the struggle is over the direction of our gaze. For Augustine, too, God can be known more easily through his created order and in a sense can never be known directly... But our principal route to God is not through the object domain but *in* ourselves. This is because God is not just the transcendent object or just the principle of order of the nearest objects, which we strain to see. God is also and for us primarily the basic support and underlying principle of our knowing activity. God is not just what we long to see, but what powers the eye which sees. So the light of God is not just 'out there', illuminating the order of being, as it is for Plato; it is also an 'inner' light.[100]

For Augustine, *Alia est enim lux quae sentitur oculis; alia qua per oculos agitur et sentiatur* ("There is one light which we perceive through the eye, another by which the eye itself is enabled to perceive").[101] This light is a "second light" to the light of God's illumination so that soul is illuminated as bright as the external world: *haec lux qua ista manifesta sunt, utique intus in anima est* . As noted by Gilson, this second light "which watches within is that of the soul itself... so, contrary to all expectations, the analysis of sensation has brought us back from the exterior of things to the interior of the soul... the road which takes the soul to God passes there".[102]

Given the ultimate and seemingly infinite complexity of this notion of *in interiore homine*, Augustine took the stance that humanity, as fashioned in the *Imago Dei (image of God),* sees this *Imago Dei* primarily in searching ever more deeper into the *form* of the self, which is the *form* of God. In this way, by looking to the *form* of being (triune yet singular) rather than the *content or import* of being in order to find possible affinity with God, Augustine provides what seems to be a reasonable account for the possibility of relationship between God and subject – form "fits" form. As Augustine states with regard to this *mimesis* of the Trinitarian God and the Trinitarian self,

---

100 Charles Taylor, ibid.

101 Saint Augustine, cited in Etienne Gilson, *The Christian Philosophy of Saint Augustine* (London: Golancz Press, 1961) p. 65.

102 Gilson, ibid., p. 65.

> We both [the Divine and subject] exist, and know that we exist, and rejoice in this existence and this knowledge. In these three, when the mind knows and loves itself, there may be seen a trinity - mind, love, knowledge; not to be confounded by any intermixture, although each exists in itself, and all mutually in all, or each in the other two, or the other two in each.[103]

Augustine goes on to argue in *De Trinitate, IX* that this notion of *in interiore homine* is constructed of dual trinities – that of the soul and its activity. As noted, the "inner man" resembles the form of God and has this form reflected *to* himself/herself deep within over and over as a mirror held up to a mirror – infinitely repeating the displayed form deeper and deeper without diminishment. This form takes on various dimensions as the Imago Dei is reflected within the most inner man to his ultimate depths of subjectivity. As Augustine notes in *De Trinitate, IX*, the first Trinitarian form of subjectivity is that of mind, knowledge, and love (*mens, notitia, et amor*) which act as idealised concepts. The mind comes to know itself and, in that, love itself. Augustine also speaks of a second trinity, that of memory, intelligence, and will (*memoria, intelligentia, et voluntas*). Where the initial trinity outlines the *qualitative* nature of the subject, the latter trinity evokes the basic *movement* of the trinity in the soul so that both the concept and praxis are in harmony – the initial trinity (*mens, notitia, et amor*) is the known subject, and the secondary trinity (*memoria, intelligentia, et voluntas*) is the knowing subject. "Memory" is the subject's implicit knowledge of itself. The subject holds "memory" within itself, yet this is latent and static. For memory to be brought into awareness, memory must be formulated and awakened. Yet, the latent memory of the subject is overlaid by false images, or "false memory" that distract the self *from* itself. To dissipate distorted memory, the subject is to draw upon the implicit knowledge *within* which also comes from above. This comes about *in verbum* (in a word) that the subject formulates through inwardness upon itself. This is what Augustine terms *intelligentia.* But to understand (*intelligentia*) oneself as subject, the *intelligentia* of awakened

[103] Saint Augustine, cited in Charles N. Cochrane, *Christianity and Classical Culture.* (New York: Oxford University Press, 1957) p. 403.

true memory must be enacted. This enactment of *intelligentia* is *et voluntas* – the will freed to love. In the willing forth of *intelligentia*, the subject ultimately finds self-awareness and, in turn, love, which is the nexus point between the dual trinities. This notion of self-love reminds the subject that this notion of love is not unique to self, but rather from "other than oneself". The subject then reflects back through memory, intelligence, and will, via love, as well as mind and knowledge, which draws the subject into the awareness of the one whose image they share – the *Imago Dei.*

In this way, as the subject looks upon its own *form* which in its dual trinities reflects the *Imago Dei* between them to infinite depths, as one reflects a mirror into another mirror, provoking seemingly infinite reflections, that are never fully plumbed. In this infinite reflexivity, one is led to understand (*intelligentia*) the *form* of God. Augustine introduces here a radical reflexivity that brings to the fore a kind of "presence to oneself which is inseparable from one's being as the agent of experience",[104] something to which access by its very nature is asymmetrical and parenthetical to all other experience. Reflexivity is then a primary requisite for "being". In the act of depth reflexivity, the self also provides a proof for God which

> is a proof from the first-person experience of knowing and reasoning. I am aware of my own sensing and thinking; and in reflecting on this, I am made aware of its dependence on something beyond it, something common... So I recognise that this activity which is mine is grounded on and presupposes something higher than I, something which I should look up to and revere. By going inward, I am drawn upward.[105]

As evidenced in *Confessions*, Augustine took this path out of his concern to show that God is to be found not just *in* the world but also (and more importantly) at the very foundations of subjectivity. For Augustine God is to be found in the intimacy of self-presence that is not organised by the *a priori* but more basically by that "incorporeal light"[106] by which our minds are somehow overturned and renewed, so that we may judge rightly of all these things. In this regard, the subject is so akin to the form of God, and all subjects are made in the *Imago*

---

104 Charles Taylor, ibid. p. 131.

105 ibid., p. 134.

106 "Lucem illam incorpoream". See Augustine, *City of God* (New York: The Modern Library, 1993) XI, 27, p. 372.

*Dei*, that regardless of the seeming differences that may exist between one subject's mind, love, and knowledge and that of another, unity throughout creation is made possible via the "incorporeal light" that illuminated all things. This allows the subject to speak *of itself* in the first person and still live with the possibility of an ethical society amidst other subjects. Ultimately, at the end of its search for selfhood, if the subject goes to the very end of that which is never reached, the subject, becomes aware of the possibility of God.

This experience of radical reflexivity results not in self-illumination, but in *being illuminated* from another source, in receiving the standards of reason from beyond oneself, which the proof of God's existence already brought to light, and which is seen to be very much an experience of inwardness. The more the subject strives to reflect upon itself, the more convinced the subject becomes of the fact that subject and self (knower and known) are one. This unity, coupled with the evidenced multiplicity of selfhood, brings the conviction that God stands alongside and not apart from creation in sharing the *form* of identity and imparting the ability through the "incorporeal light" to judge rightly all things throughout creation and the realm of imagination.

Charles Taylor makes the following observation on the reciprocal nature of form regarding the subject and sacred in Augustine's project:

> ...What is striking here for our purposes is that man shows himself most clearly as the image of God in his inner self-presence and self-love. It is a kind of knowledge where the knower and the known are one, coupled with love, which reflects most fully God in our lives. And indeed, the image of the Trinity in us is the process whereby we strive to complete and perfect this self-presence and self-affirmation. Nothing shows more clearly than these images of the Trinity how Augustinian inwardness is bound up with radical reflexivity, and they also begin to make clear how essentially linked is the doctrine of inwardness to Augustine's whole conception of the relation of man to God.[107]

---

[107] ibid., pp. 136, 137.

One of the issues growing out of this assertion of form over content as to the primary exemplar and ground of subjectivity to the sacred, was the sense that *writing* regarding Christ must also conform to a particular "form" – there was a certain "way" in which the incarnation could be discussed and there were ways that it could not. As mentioned in the Introduction, shortly after Augustine we see that in the forming of the Creeds of the Church, a poetics is employed that makes a statement as to what form literature that seeks to figure the sacred should take. Ultimately, what for Augustine proved to be an answer to the question of God's relation to humanity, and *the priority of form over content*, became the vexation of the eighteenth and nineteenth century as challenges from writers employing a poetics that radically questioned that previously enacted by the Church. While the notion of the *form* of the subject was comforting to Augustine, the question of "*Who* is the subject?" caused intellectual disturbances in different forms from Descartes and Rousseau through Kant and those following. The very question of the form of God and the notion of the Incarnation as the "form of God made flesh" is questioned as to what it (the Incarnation) represents and how is it indeed manifested.

Prior to the Council of Nicaea of 325 CE and the forming of the Symbol of Chalcedon in 451 CE, language used to figure Jesus, as noted by John Hick, "seems generally to have been devotional, or ecstatic, or liturgical (or all three), rather than an exercise in precise theological formulation. *It was analogous to the language of love*, in which all manner of extravagances and exaggerations are entirely appropriate..."[108] As I will assert, it is a recovery of this "language of love" that comes *before* form that writers such as George Eliot have sought and it is this "language" that is at the heart of her poetics.

---

[108] John Hick, *The Metaphor of God Incarnate* (London: SCM Press, 1993) p. 101.

# Chapter 3

# Poetics of the Subject and Sacred into the Nineteenth Century

The Cartesian declaration *assuré que je ne puis avoir aucune connaissance de ce qui est hors de moi, que par l'entremise des idées que j'ai eu en moi* ("certain that I can have no knowledge of what is outside me except by means of the ideas I have within me")[109] had awakened the "resolution and courage" whereby humanity could acknowledge its true capacity for the locus of certainty and truth to be found in its own subjectivity. This was profoundly different from the conclusions reached by Augustine centuries earlier. With the movement from Descartes, through the Enlightenment, to Idealism and Romanticism, attributes traditionally predicated of the divine subject are gradually transferred to the human subject. Through a dialectical reversal, the creator God dies and is resurrected as the creative subject. As Mark C. Taylor states "… In different terms, the modern subject defines itself by its *constructive* activity".[110] As Descartes acknowledges in the *Discours*, the ordering of the *res extensa* by the *res cogitans* is predicated on the possibility of the fictive nature of this ordering: *et supposant mesme de l'orde entre ceux qui ne se precedent point naturellement les uns les autres* ("assuming an order, even if a fictive one, among those which do not follow a natural sequence relatively to one another").[111] Whether fact or fiction, the "world" is ours to form.

Immanuel Kant's summation of the Enlightenment project was that it was the turn toward "man's release from his self-incurred

---

[109] From letter to Gibieuf, 19 January 1642 in René Descartes, *Philosophical Letters*, trans. Anthony Kenny (Oxford: Oxford University Press, 1970) p. 123.
[110] Mark C. Taylor, *Deconstruction in Context: Literature and Philosophy* (Chicago: University of Chicago Press, 1986) p. 3.
[111] René Descartes, *The Philosophical Works of Descartes*, trans. E.S. Haldane and G.R.T. Ross (Cambridge: Dover, 1955) I, p. 92. See also Charles Taylor's commentary on Descartes' Second Rule from *Discours de la méthode* in *Sources of the Self*, pp. 144, 145.

tutelage. Tutelage is man's ability to make use of his understanding without direction from another. Self-incurred is this tutelage when its cause lies not in lack of reason but in lack of resolution and courage to use it without direction from another".[112] In his *Critique of Pure Reason*, Kant furthered the Enlightenment project beyond the mere definitions of *res cogitans* and *res extensa* by categorically critiquing the horizon of reason itself and placing responsibility of the ordering of the world upon the knowing subject. This is what Kant terms as "the synthetic unity of self-consciousness" which stands in conflict to Descartes' notion of "cogito" which is an "analytical unity of self-consciousness". Kant takes the next step beyond Descartes in saying that unity of *form* regarding the subject and the subject's world is merely a synthetic rendering of "spontaneous moments" that come from moments of pure beauty that are not provoked, yet arise and are "gathered" by the forming subject in order that the subject can become self-aware. In this way, subjectivity is not only dependent on the subject himself, as in Descartes' project, but *the very form and unity of the subject is self-created and self-sustained in the context of a first principle* that is articulated as Kant's moral imperative. The split between subject and object in the mediation of an objective God is what Kant's project sought to resolve through the acknowledgement that it is "reason [that] brings unity to the personality by subjecting multiple and conflicting sense inclinations to the directives of the *a priori* moral law. Reason, therefore, in both its theoretical and practical capacities, functions to create unity out of plurality and to reduce manyness to oneness".[113] The form of this oneness is *a priori* and it is for the subject to form and create wholeness within the limits of reason. In this way, we see the ushering in of Idealism into German thought. Idealism "bears its name because ideas are the key to conclusively aligning the metaphysical doctrine put forth by reason with what is evident in self-consciousness".[114] In the Platonic tradition, it is the *Idea* that is purely inhabited within thought yet full of substantial determination. Furthermore, it is the Idea that "cuts through to reveal the actual content of a given thing and... convey the most

---

[112] Immanuel Kant, *On History*, trans. L.W. Beck (New York: Bobbs-Merill, 1965) p. 3.
[113] Mark C. Taylor, op. cit., p. 5.
[114] Rüdiger Bubner, *German Idealist Philosophy* (London: Penguin Books, 1997) p. xv.

basic sediments about reality".[115]

This fundamental point of departure in philosophical thought, introduced by Kant at the end of the eighteenth century, which saw reason turning back onto the subject, was "received as a Copernican revolution".[116] The effects of this Kantian revolution are reflected in German literature by the rejection of concreteness (*Anschaulichkeit*) in favour of abstraction (*Begrifflichkeit*). The "Idea" now had the weight of the "factum" of natural sciences and became a valid currency within the marketplace of thought. This transition is particularly evident in the interpretation of mythology, whose symbols have quite different functions, exemplified in the works of German writers such as Schiller, Hölderlin, and Goethe.

## Friedrich Schiller and the *Mythos* of the Human Spirit

Charles Taylor states that it was "Schiller's aspiration to a condition beyond the forceful imposition of form on matter, and a fusion of the two in beauty" that gave rise to his poetics.[117] Form, for Schiller, is linked to the universal. This aspiration is seen in his attempt to form an anthropologic-aesthetic foundation that is simultaneously dissolved into a symbolic *mythos*, a continuous dissolving of subject and object that defies analytic rationalism. Consequently, Schiller considers his symbolic mythology as a manifestation of human spirit (akin to Hegel's *Absolute Spirit*) in which reason and nature are unified and, in contrast to Kant's practical reason, Schiller sees aesthetics *as* truth, whose realisation takes the form of a mythology which conquers reality. In the *Ninth Letter*, Schiller asserts this claim by stating that the task of the poet is to free the reader through aesthetics: *Wo du sie findest, umgib sie mit edeln, mit geistreichen Formen, schliesse sie ringsum mit den Symbolen des Vortefflichen ein, bis der Schein die Wirklichkeit und die Kunst die Natur öberwindet* ("Surround them wherever you meet them, with the great and noble forms of genius, and encompass them with the symbols of perfection, until Semblance conquer reality and art triumph over nature").[118] In addition to the rejection of concreteness (*Anschaulichkeit*) in favour of abstraction (*Begrifflichkeit*) relative to the subject, the

---

[115] ibid.

[116] ibid., p. xxi.

[117] Charles Taylor, op. cit., p. 421.

[118] Cited by John D. Simons, *Friedrich Schiller* (Boston: G.K. Hall and Co., 1981) p. 41.

development of a distinctive fictional paradigm of identity arises in this literature in the wake of Kant's *Kritik der Urteilskraft* (*Critique of Judgement*). In particular, works written or published in Germany in the last decade of the eighteenth century after the *Kritik der Urteilskraft* include Friedrich Schiller's *Uber die asthetische Erziehung des Menschen in einer Reihe von Briefen*, Friedrich Hölderlin's *Empedokles*, and Johann Wolfgang von Goethe's *Wilhelm Meister's Lehrjahre*. Given the importance of German literature of this period upon the developing poetics of George Eliot, it is important to review some of the key concerns that formed these writers and others of their tradition.

Common to all of these works of Schiller, Hölderlin, and Goethe is a commitment to balancing the claims of the individual with those of the Ideal which had begun to replace the idea of God as the reflexive template where the subject was to gain its assurance of form. Yet while the philosophers of German Idealism (Kant, Schilling, Fichte) create rhetoric to support the agency of the Ideal in relation to the form of the subject, the poetics of writers such as Hölderlin and Goethe showed a loss of form in the subject without God in this Ideal universe. In Kant's *Kritik der Urteilskraft*, he offers Aesthetic judgement, or communal sense, as establishing a base relation between an individual idea and the *apriori* concept; part and the whole:

> In a word, the aesthetic *idea* is a representation of the imagination, annexed to a given *concept*, with which, in the free employment of imagination, such a multiplicity of partial representations are bound up, that no expression indicating a definite concept can be found for it – one which on that account allows a concept to be supplemented in thought by much that is indefinable in words, and the feeling of which quickens the cognitive faculties, and with language, as a mere thing of the letter, binds up the spirit [soul] also.[119]

Yet in turning to key writers, such as Hölderlin in his poem *Empedokles* and Johann Wolfgang von Goethe in *Wilhelm Meister's Lehrjahre,* the idealised subject is not comforted in 'the aesthetic idea [as] the free employment of imagination".

---

[119] Immanuel Kant, *Kritik der Urteilskraft (Critique of Judgement)* in *Deconstruction in Context* ed. Mark C. Taylor (Chicago: University of Chicago Press, 1986) p. 49.

## Friedrich Hölderlin and *Empedokles*

What is argued in Schiller is the assertion that particular sensations and experiences are fundamental and independent but always already bound within some intersubjective structure of the "given concept". *Neither part nor whole serves as an absolute point of origin.* Friedrich Hölderlin exemplifies this in his shorter ode, *Empedokles*:

> *Das Leben suchst du, suchst, und es quillt und glänzt*
> *Ein göttlich Feuer tief aus der Erde dir,*
> *Und du in schauderndem Verlangen*
> *Wirfst dich hinab, in des Aetna Flammen...*
> (You look for life, you look and from deeps of Earth
> A fire, divinely gleaming wells up for you,
> And quick, aquiver with desire, you
> Hurl yourself down into Etna's furnace...)[120]

In *Empedokles*, there is a merging of the subject with concept that departs from a search for form and, ultimately, is the *annihilation of form* altogether in a fire that is not itself divine, but "divinely gleaming". Conversely, the "fire" that Hölderlin speaks of (*das Feuer*) does not emanate from the subject, rather "wells up" *for* the subject. As we see in *Empedokles*, Hölderlin creates a universe in his poetics where, as noted by David Jasper, "Hölderlin's voice, as a poetic one, [suggests] a new mythology which moves from the Bible and beyond syncretism to a new wholeness and coherence as the Bible itself seemed otherwise to disintegrate under the probes of historical criticism".[121] Hölderlin sought to impart through his poetics "... the final realisation of the truly 'mythological' by the poet – not a discovery of the 'key' to all mythologies, but rather a transcending of all systems and historical moments in one great timeless moment of truth, the moment of Being".[122] This mode of being is for Hölderlin the dispersal of the particular into and throughout *the formlessness of concept,* where the seam points of being and non-being, creator and created, cease to be distinguishable. In the emerging role of the writer in later

---

[120] Friedrich Hölderlin, "Empedokles" *Selected Poems and Fragments*, Trans. Michael Hamburger (London: Penguin Books, 1998) pp. 4, 5.

[121] David Jasper *The Sacred and Secular Canon in Romanticism* (London: Macmillian Press, 1999) p. 53.

[122] ibid., p. 50.

Romanticism, Hölderlin took the Promethean task one step beyond the mere stealing of fire. There is an abstraction regarding claims of truth that is evidenced in this arising poetics.[123] In "Empedokles", neither part nor whole could serve as an absolute point of origin, and a "divinely gleaming" fire is all that remained – Prometheus is now both torchbearer and torch. As noted by Michael Hamburger, Hölderlin's "own view of the poet as philosopher, prophet and priest – and as tragic hero – was subject to perpetual crisis and re-examination. The special significance for Hölderlin of Empedokles' mode of death – a physical fusion with the primal elements and return to the very womb of Earth – … [is] intimated in "Empedokles".[124]

Schiller, Hölderlin, and Goethe try to render this ideal of an interdependent relation and irreducible tension between part and whole into, respectively, historical, dramatic, and novelistic accounts. Yet all three, in different measure and with different strategies, simultaneously strive to rebalance this relation, to give greater weight to embodiment and the self than Kant grants.

In his *Aesthetic Letters*, Schiller attempts to hold onto the synthetic and unifying force of beauty while stretching and narrativising Kant's account to lend greater emphasis to sensation which carries certain existentialist leanings. As a result, a space constantly opens up in Schiller's treatise between the empirical and formal dimensions of beauty. The poetics evoked by these writers strive to uphold the tension between universal and particular empirical moments by stressing disjunction and negativity. In both *Empedokles* and *Wilhelm Meister's Lehrjahre*, the gap between an embodied protagonist and the ideal opens up a hermeneutic space which can only be reconciled *by* the reader, yet is destabilising to the very act of reading. As seen earlier in *Empedokles*, a space through which a fire "divinely gleaming" wells up *for* the subject in Hölderlin's universe. Form then dissolves into negativity where that which was embodied is dispersed into the conceptual. Yet this "flame" is not extinguished nor is the fissure through which it came upon the

---

123 As will be discussed in more depth in chapter 4, the destabilising of form regarding the figuring of the subject through poetics has its mimesis in the fall of historicity in biblical criticism.

124 Michael Hamburger, "Introduction" in Friedrich Hölderlin, *Selected Poems and Fragments*. Trans. Michael Hamburger (London: Penguin, 1998) p. xxiv.

subject closed. As the final stanza proclaims:

> *Doch heilig bist du mir, wie der Erde Macht,*
> *Die dich hinwegnahm, kühner Getödteter!*
> *Und folgen möcht' ich in die Tiefe,*
> *Hielte die Liebe mich nicht, dem Helden.*
> (Yet you are holy to me as is the power
> Of Earth that took you from us, the boldly killed!
> And gladly, did not love restrain me,
> Deep as the hero plunged down I'd follow.)[125]

The completion of the work is an open invitation due to the longing ("down I'd follow") of the writer to fulfil the journey. The passive regrets of the writer serve as an offer to the reader to follow "deep as the hero plunged down". This is a hermeneutic invitation to enter fully into the "divinely gleaming" fire that Hölderlin describes in his universe that is without a God yet speaks of divine encounter:

> If biblical criticism in Germany gave rise to Hölderlin's pure "Scripture", it also necessitated, in scholars such as Schleiermacher, the development of the art of hermeneutics which Hölderlin, in a sense, utterly denies. Hermeneutics recognises the gap between the human and the divine realms and the incommensurability finally existing between the word and our interpretation of it. That gap is its very lifeblood.[126]

Turning to Goethe's project in *Wilhem Meister's Lehrjahre* we see that, similar to Schiller and Hölderlin, Goethe creates an abstraction rather than a solidification of the subject in his poetics that results in an unsettled space where poetic form itself is called into question. Ultimately, how one sees "form" in relation to a poetics of the subject and the sacred is shifted.

---

[125] Friedrich Hölderlin, "Empedokles", ibid.
[126] David Jasper, ibid., p. 55.

## Goethe and the Morphological *Bildung* in *Wilhelm Meister's Lehrjahre*

In *The Life and Works of Goethe*, G.H. Lewes made the following observation regarding attempts at critique of Goethe's *Lehrjahre*:

> He [the critic] is not satisfied with what the artist has *given*, he wants to know what he *meant*. He guesses at the meaning; the more remote the meaning lies on the wandering tracks of thought, the better pleased is he with the discovery, and sturdily rejects every simple explanation in favour of this exegetical Idea. Thus the phantom of Philosophy hovers mistily before Art, concealing Art from our eyes. It is true the Idea said to underlie the work was never conceived by anyone before, least of all by the Artist; but that is the glory of the critic: he is proud of having plunged into the depths. Of all horrors to the German of this school there is no horror like that of the *surface* – it is more terrible to him than cold water... The obvious want of unity in the work has given free play to the interpreting imagination. Hillebrand boldly says that the "Idea of *Wilhelm Meister* is precisely this – that it has no Idea", - which does not greatly further our comprehension.[127]

While the assertion that *Wilhelm Meister's Lehrjahre* has no organising Idea may appear at first blush to be a rather extreme assertion, the observations of Lewes do have merit. In his Afterword to *Lehrjahre*, Eric Blackwell raises similar difficulties in approaching the text:

> The main difficulty is the apparent disunity of the book, which seems to begin as one thing – a novel of theatrical life? – and end as something completely different – a novel about social or communal integration? About finding one's way in life?... Add to this that there are elements in the first five books which are hardly encompassable by realistic criteria – the two Strangers, Mignon, and the Harper – characters that seem to be at odds with the generally realistic atmosphere and tone, yet are described realistically. Where does Book Six fit in? Can it be conceived as a transition to the last two; if so, in what sense?... What does it all add up to? What is Philine doing in a

---

[127] G.H. Lewes, *The Life and Works of Goethe* Vol. 2 (London: T. Richards, 37, Great Queen Street, 1855) pp. 201, 202.

> novel of ideas or the Harper in a realistic novel? What is Mignon doing in either?[128]

*Lehrjahre* evidences Goethe creating a space for such questions to be asked that blends his aesthetic and scientific theories. In *Maximen und Reflexionen* he states that "physics must be divorced from mathematics. It must be completely independent, and try to penetrate with all its loving, reverent, pious force into nature and its holy life, quite regardless of what mathematics accomplishes and does".[129] Goethe goes on to note that "mathematics, for its part, must declare itself independent of everything external, go its own distinctive and important way, and cultivate a greater purity than is possible when heretofore it concerns itself with existence and endeavours to win something from it or conform to it".[130]

From his interest in botany, Goethe drew a conception of *morphology*, a word which Goethe himself coined, that was a move beyond the rigidity of classification of type[131] toward a conception of *nature as process.* In this regard, "for Goethe such an enterprise [merely *labelling* natural cause and effect] was not enough. According to him, what we grasp in this way are only the *products*, not the *process* of life. It is into this notion of *life as process* he wanted, not only as a poet, but also as scientist, to win insight; in it he saw what was greatest and highest".[132]

In order to see life as process, Goethe argued that one must look beyond the cataloguing of type in order to gain an appreciation of the whole. In *Naturwiss* he makes the following comment: "... Classes, genera, species and individuals are related as instances to a law; they are contained in it, but they do not *contain* or *reveal* it".[133]

The theme noted previously is continued in Goethe – a desire to look beyond category and type in order to seek after that which is

---

[128] Johann Wolfgang von Goethe, *Wilhelm Meister's Apprenticeship*. Ed. and trans. Eric A. Blackwell (Princeton: Princeton University Press, 1995) pp. 381, 382.

[129] Cited by Ernst Cassirer, *Rousseau, Kant, Goethe* (Princeton: Princeton University Press, 1945) p. 63.

[130] Cassirer, op. cit.

[131] Goethe had read Linnaeus' system of nature whereby understanding of nature is achieved when "we have succeeded in arranging it (nature) in the pigeonholes of our concepts, dividing it into species and genera, into families, classes, and orders". Cassirer, op. cit. p. 69.

[132] ibid.

[133] Cassirer, op. cit., p. 93.

beyond form. For Schiller this is a space that constantly opens between the empirical and formal dimensions of beauty as he strives to uphold the tension between universal and particular through stressing disjunction and negativity. As seen in his poem *Empedokles*, Hölderlin saw the boundary between the subject and the divine dissolve as one thrown into a fire. This space without boundary is seen in Goethe's theory of morphology as well, particularly when seen as an appropriate hermeneutic for reading *Wilhelm Meister's Lehrjahre.* In this regard, *Lehrjahre* is not a quantifiable study where the parts equal the whole, rather

> [Goethe's *Lehrjahre*] narrates the acculturation of a self – the integration of a particular "I" into the general subjectivity of a community, and thus, finally, into the universal subjectivity of humanity… even the knowledge of only a dozen words of German suffices to hear an interplay of representation (*Bild*) and formation (*Bildung*)… [It], in short, *is a trope for the aspirations of aesthetic humanism.*[134]

This "interplay" between representation and formation is key to reading *Lehrjahre,* where the differential between representation (text) and formation (subject) disappear leaving a new hybrid. Before the reader of *Lehrjahre* is neither a solely pedagogic manual nor a purely aesthetic work. *Lehrjahre* does not attempt to be a pre-cursive "novel of manners" in the Victorian vein that offers a manual for self actualisation, nor do the characters chronicled within the text provide an objective means that is necessarily uniform in ethics nor morals. As with Goethe's morphology, this is a new "shape" altogether, that while idealised, is none the less "real".[135] It was Goethe's hope to be the

[134] Marc Redfield, *Phantom Formations: Aesthetic Ideology and the Bildungsroman* (Ithaca: Cornell University Press, 1996) p. 38.

[135] In Goethe's sketch *Gluckliches Ereignis* he reports the following conversation with Schiller regarding his theory of metamorphosis: "We arrived at his house, the conversation began drew me in; there I vigorously expounded the metamorphosis of plants, and with many suggestive strokes of the pen let a symbolic plant arise before his eyes. He listened to and looked at everything with great interest with decided power of comprehension; but when I ended he shook his head and said: 'That is not empirical, that is ideal' (*Das ist keine Erfahrung, das ist eine Idee*). I was taken aback and somewhat vexed; for he had emphatically stated the point that divided us… But I

great liberator of the poetic spirit in his age in his re-imagining of form, as noted by Matthew Arnold: "But to hear Goethe himself: 'If I were to say what I had really been to the Germans in general, and to the young German poets in particular, I should say I had been their *liberator*'".[136] As a liberator, what Goethe was hoping to move beyond is the privileging of *system over essence* as the primary quality of form. As Arnold assesses the beginnings of modernity, he notes the world within which Goethe sought a different path:

> Modern times find themselves with an immense system of institutions, established facts, accredited dogmas, customs, rules, which have come to them from times not modern. In this system their life has to be carried forward; yet they have a sense that this system is not of their own creation, that it by no means corresponds exactly with the wants of actual life... The modern spirit is now awake almost everywhere; the sense of want of correspondence between the forms of modern Europe and its spirit, between the new wine of the eighteenth and nineteenth centuries, and the old bottles of the eleventh and twelfth centuries, or even of the sixteenth century and seventeenth... it is no longer dangerous to affirm that this want of correspondence exists; people are beginning to be shy of denying it... Dissolvents of the old European system of dominant ideas and facts we must all be [after the likes of] Goethe, that grand dissolvent in an age where fewer and fewer are present...[137]

One of the key modes with which Goethe was truly "that grand dissolvent" of traditional form was in his employment of *Bildung* as the poetics of *Lehrjahre*. As noted previously, there is a challenge in deriving a critical reading of *Lehrjahre*, as suggested by Redfield in discussing the *Bildungsroman*:

> The *Bildungsroman* paradox derives from that of aesthetics. The "content" of the *Bildungsroman* instantly becomes a question of form, precisely because the content is the forming-of-content, "*Bildung*" – the formation of the human as the producer of itself as form.[138]

---

collected myself and replied: 'I am very glad that I have ideals without knowing it, and even see them with my eyes'". Cited by Cassirer, op. cit. p. 73.

[136] Matthew Arnold, "from Heinrich Heine" *Poetry and Criticism of Matthew Arnold* ed. A. Dwight Culler (Boston: Houghton Mifflin Company, 1961) p. 289.

[137] Culler, op. cit., p. 290.

[138] Marc Redfield, op. cit., p. 42.

Precisely because Wilhelm's *Bildung* is *shown* more than explained[139], the question of content and form regarding the "how" of his *Bildung* can be troubling, yet a fusion of mind and feeling does progress[140] into the realising of a subject who has completed his apprenticeship and is ready for life.[141] For Goethe, the shift must be made from an empirical reading of the text to a morphological reading in order to see the *Bildung* of Wilhelm take shape. As Goethe notes,

> through me the German poets have become aware that, as man must live from within outwards, so the artist must work from within outwards, seeing that, make what contortions he will, he can only bring to light his own individuality. I can clearly mark where this influence of mine has made itself felt; there arises out of it a kind of *poetry of nature*, and only in this way it is possible to be original.[142]

This notion of a *poetry of nature* is a poetics that knows no systemic limits and is profoundly dialogical rather than dialectical. In the second portion of Kant's *Critique of Judgement* (*Kritik der Urteilskraft*) entitled "Critique of Teleological Judgement", we see Kant's insights into teleology as a heuristic principle for investigation toward understanding. Commenting on the limits of a purely quantified means for understanding of biological nature, Kant writes:

---

139 Book VII of *Lehrjahre* provides an accounting of the "forces" at play in Wilhelm's *Bildung* through the Abbe and the "unveiling" of the Society of the Tower's apprenticeship. Yet pedagogy is not given beyond "forces at work".

140 As noted by Gerlinde Roder-Bolton, "The concept of *Bildung*, as advocated in *Lehrjahre*, is a fusion of mind and feeling in individuals who respond freely to, and are consciously and inseparably part of, the creative forces of nature. Since this creative power is also within them, prompting them to reshape their inner and outer world, they achieve the full development of their potential". Gerlinde Roder-Bolton *Studies in Comparative Literature. Vol. 13: George Eliot and Goethe: An Elective Affinity* (Amsterdam: Rodopi. 1998) p. 164.

141 As noted in the words of the Abbe at the conclusion of Book VII "Hail to thee, young man! Thy apprenticeship is done; Nature has pronounced thee free!" (Goethe, *Wilhelm Meister's Apprenticeship and Travels* Vol. 2 trans. Thomas Carlyle (London: Chapman and Hall, 1858) Book VII, Chapter IX p. 63.

142 Cited by Matthew Arnold, op. cit., p. 290.

> It is quite certain that we can never get a sufficient knowledge of organised beings and their inner possibility, much less get an explanation of them, by looking merely to mechanical principles of nature. Indeed, so certain is it, that we may confidently assert that it is absurd for men even to entertain any thought of so doing, or to hope that maybe another Newton may some day arise, to make intelligible to us even the genesis of but a blade of grass from natural laws that no design has ordered. Such insight we must absolutely deny mankind.[143]

It was here that Goethe made a connection with Kant's philosophy and gained language for his own work. As Kant states, one must never assume that they can capture what he calls the "inner possibilities" of a subject, much less "an explanation" of its truest nature. In his essay entitled "Einwirkung der neuren Philosophie" from *Naturwiss* he describes the impact Kant's "Critique of Teleological Judgement" had upon him:

> But the *Critique of Judgement* fell into my hands, and to this book I owe one of the happiest periods of my life. Here I saw my most diverse interests brought together, artistic and natural production handled the same way; the power of aesthetic and teleological judgement mutually illuminated each other... If my way of thinking was not always able to agree with the author's, if I seemed to miss something here and there, still the main ideas of the work were quite analogous to my previous production, action and thought. The inner life of art as of nature, their mutual working from within outward, were clearly expressed in this book.[144]

In short, for Goethe the process of "becoming" is to be seen through a morphological poetics rather than a mechanistic system - ordering that is organic from the inner realms extending to the outer manifestation of form. Matthew Arnold summarises Goethe's project in this manner:

> Goethe's profound, imperturbable naturalism is absolutely fatal to all routine thinking: he puts the standard, once for all, inside every man instead of outside of him; where he is told, such a thing must be so, there is immense authority and custom in favour of its being so, it has

143 Cited by Cassirer, op. cit., p. 65.

144 ibid., p. 64.

> been held to be so for a thousand years, he answers with Olympian politeness, "But *is* it so? is it so to *me*?"[145]

This "profound, imperturbable naturalism" calls into question the role of writing itself in Goethe's work. The "old Middle-Age machine"[146] that was "still creaking on" in Goethe's time that held the task of writing to be systematic was rendered organic in his work, causing the reader to 'form' with/through the act of reading rather than reading *through* a lens of form. This poetics calls into question large epistemological issues, not the least of which being the nature of destiny and agency in relation to the subject.

Turning to Book I of *Wilhelm Meister's Lehrjahre*, Goethe has the following advice given to his protagonist Wilhelm by a stranger encountered upon the way to an Inn:

> "Do you believe in destiny? No power rules over us, and directs all our ultimate advantage?"
>
> "The question is not now of my belief; nor is this the place to explain how I may have attempted to form for myself some not impossible conception of things which are incomprehensible to all of us: the question is here: What mode of viewing them will profit us the most? The fabric of our life is formed of necessity and chance; the reason of man takes its station between them, and may rule them both: it treats the necessary as the groundwork of its being; the accidental it can direct and guide and employ for its own purposes; and only while this principle of reason stands firm and inexpugnable does man deserve to be named the god of this lower world. But woe to him who, from his youth, has used himself to search in necessity for something of arbitrary will; to ascribe to chance a sort of reason, which it is a matter of religion to obey!"[147]

As Wilhelm unknowingly begins his apprenticeship, a "stranger" offers this advice to him and as well to the reader of the text. In Wilhelm's approach to life, and the reader's approach to the text, one should

---

[145] Matthew Arnold, op. cit., p. 290.
[146] ibid., p. 291.
[147] Johann Wolfgang von Goethe, *Wilhem Meister's Apprenticeship and Travels* trans. Thomas Carlyle (London: Chapman and Hall, 1858) Book 1, Chapter XVII, p. 61.

venture not to find solace in either the seeming security of necessity nor the supposed freedom offered by chance. Instead, there is a middle way where "the reason of man takes its station *between* both".[148] Finding this balance will prove hard to maintain as foreshadowed by Wilhelm in Book II:

> He felt glad as having thus been timefully, though somewhat harshly warned about the proper path of life; while many are constrained to expiate more heavily, and at a later age, the misconceptions into which their youthful inexperience has betrayed them. For, each man commonly defends himself as long as possible from casting out the idols which he worships in his soul, from acknowledging a master error, and admitting any truth brings him despair.[149]

Wilhelm gains a vision for a life that is free from pedagogical prescriptions through his encounter with Shakespeare's *Hamlet.* Relating what is key to an understanding of Hamlet's character, Wilhelm makes the following observation:

> It pleases us, it flatters us to see a hero acting on his own strength; loving and hating as his heart directs him; undertaking and completing; casting every obstacle aside; and at length attaining some great object which he aimed at. Poets and historians would willingly persuade us that so proud a lot may fall to man. In *Hamlet* we are taught another lesson: the hero is without a plan, but the piece is a full and rigidly-accomplished scheme of vengeance: a horrid deed occurs; it rolls itself along with all its consequences, dragging guiltless persons also in its course; the perpetrator seems as if he would evade the abyss which is made ready for him; yet he plunges in, at the very point by which he thinks he shall escape and happily complete his course.[150]

Again, Wilhelm relates both instruction and warning to the reader – "the hero is without a plan". To look for a mechanistic means of connecting events in a logical progression via the protagonist's forethought will be to the reader's dismay. Wilhelm, like the plants that helped Goethe gain a concept of morphology, is himself an organic event rather than a static presence. There is a remarkable freedom that

---

148 ibid.

149 ibid., Book II, Chap. II, p. 67.

150 ibid., Book IV, Chap. XV, p. 207.

is given to Wilhelm upon seeing Hamlet as "a hero without a plan". In the same vein, the poetics that Goethe re-imagines are remarkably free of constraint and morphological in nature – something that George Eliot will exhibit in her writing.

This freedom of poetics to move "without a plan" is carried over into Goethe's re-imagining of scripture in *Faust: Part One* where Goethe employs this free play of form to the subjectivity of words and the Word. As Faust reads the opening verses to the Gospel of John, we see the morphological approach to "word":

> 'Tis writ, "In the beginning was the Word".
> I pause, to wonder what is here inferred.
> The Word I cannot set supremely high:
> A new translation I will try.
> I read, if by the spirit I am taught,
> This sense: "In the beginning was the Thought".
> This opening to need to weigh again,
> Or sense may suffer from a hasty pen.
> Does Thought create, and work, and rule the hour?
> 'Twere best: "In the beginning was the Power'.
> Yet, while the pen is urged with willing fingers,
> A sense of doubt and hesitancy lingers.
> The spirit come to guide me in my need,
> I write, "In the beginning was the Deed."[151]

Faust continues to turn over the possible meanings of the "Word" that is spoken of here and can sense that there is a profound depth to what lies beneath. Each time a rendering is offered (word, thought, power, deed), another possible rendering can be suggested. Goethe demonstrates the manifold meanings that such a "sign" (word) can recall. One must allow the space occupied by the sign continually to open up and offer new renderings as a perpetual discovery of possibilities. In this way, words themselves take on a *morphological* quality.

---

[151] Johann Wolfgang von Goethe, *Faust: Part One* (1808). Trans. Philip Wayne (London: Penguin Classics, 1949) ii, p. 71. Also see David Jasper, *The Sacred and Secular Canon in Romanticism* for further commentary.

In *Lehrjahre*, both the reader and Wilhelm move forward in growth not *through* systematic understanding, but *toward* an end that is the fulfilment of "apprenticeship". In Wilhelm's reflection on the production of *Hamlet*, he makes this observation:

> … In the composition of this play, after the most accurate investigation and the maturest reflection, I distinguish two classes of objects. The first are the grand internal relations of the persons and events, the powerful effects that arise from the characters and proceedings of main figures: these, I hold, are individually excellent; and the order in which they are presented cannot be improved. No kind of interference must be suffered to destroy them, or even essentially to change their form. These are the things which stamp themselves deep into the soul; which all men long to see, which no one dares meddle with. Accordingly, I understand, they have almost wholly been retained in all our German theatres. But our countrymen have erred, in my opinion, with regard to the second class of objects, which may be observed in this tragedy; I allude to the external relations of the persons, whereby they are brought from place to place, or combined in various ways by certain accidental incidents. These they have looked upon as very unimportant; have spoken of them only in passing, or have left them out altogether. Now, indeed, it must be owned, these threads are slack and slender; and yet run through the entire piece, and bind together much that would otherwise fall asunder, and does actually fall asunder, when you cut them off, and imagine you have done enough and more, if you left the ends hanging.[152]

Wilhelm becomes aware that an understanding of one's *Bildung* is found in the space between two poles. The first being "the grand internal relations of the persons and events, the powerful effects which arise from the characters and proceedings of the main figures".[153] This is an acknowledgement of the obvious – that which is seen not only by the self, but also evidenced by others. Yet there is a second class of objects that also play a role in one's *Bildung*, those being "the external relations of the persons, whereby they are brought from place to place, or combined in various ways by certain accidental incidents".[154] One's life cannot be planned. There are "accidental incidents" that arise and give shape to one's identity. These are not to be discounted nor dismissed

[152] ibid., Book V, Chap. IV, 241.
[153] ibid.
[154] ibid.

as Wilhelm's contemporaries "have erred" to do. Throughout *Lehrjahre*, characters continually appear seemingly "by chance" and offer necessary information and direction for Wilhelm as if by mystical means. This comes to its most grandiose epoch with the revealing of Wilhelm's "apprenticeship" in Book VII by the Abbé and the Society of the Tower. As it is revealed to Wilhelm that his life has been guided, he is told:

> "Perhaps," continued his interrogator, "we should now be less at variance in regard to Destiny and Character".
> Wilhelm was about to answer, when the curtain quickly flew together. "Strange!" said Wilhelm to himself: "Can chance occurrences have a connection? Is what we call Destiny but Chance?"[155]

Here Wilhelm echoes the earlier advice of the "stranger" in Book I, quoted earlier, where he is advised that "the fabric of our life is formed of necessity and chance; the reason of man takes its station between them, and may rule them both: it treats the necessary as the groundwork of its being; the accidental it can direct and guide and employ for its own purposes; and only while this principle of reason stands firm and inexpugnable does man deserve to be named the god of this lower world".[156] In order to return to this truth, however, Wilhelm's "apprenticeship" is rendered descriptively rather than prescriptively. He, like the reader, must discover that the "end" is not necessarily easy to discern in an orderly manner. The "threads" of life are indeed "slack and slender; and yet run through the entire piece, and bind together much that would otherwise fall asunder".[157]

As suggested in this chapter, writers in the wake of German Idealism such as Schiller, Hölderlin, and Goethe offer a tension in their work between the subject and the Ideal that is an indeterminate hermeneutic relationship to be determined and reconciled by *and* through the act of writing and being read. Form that was introduced centuries before by Augustine as being the clearest determiner of the necessary relationship of subject to God was challenged through the

---

155 ibid., Book VII, Chap IX, 60.
156 ibid., Book I, Chapter XVII, 61.
157 ibid., Book V, Chap. IV, 241.

assertion of Idealism after Kant, which takes the next step that Descartes began by holding that unity of form regarding the subject and the subject's world is merely a synthetic rendering of "spontaneous moments". These "spontaneous moments" come from moments of pure beauty that are not provoked, but rather the very form and unity of the subject is self-created and self-sustained. The creating God is replaced with the creating subject as primary source of meaning-making. Given the shift of focus toward the subject as the centre of meaning-making, texts as reflections of the subject's creative power now came to take on a new role. This shift is particularly noteworthy as the role of Scripture becomes viewed as a product of human rather than divine formation, designated by Goethe as a part of "Weltliteratur". The role of literature, rather than providing a point of certainty to gather questions of meaning *around*, now becomes a space or gap that is defined by its abstraction rather than traditional modes of certainty. With regard to the nature and person of Jesus, these paradigm shifts in seeing scripture as a product of human creativity as much as a product of divine inspiration is profound. The possibility of new ideas regarding Jesus – who he was and how we are to figure him – becomes a critical question of the eighteenth and nineteenth centuries. Central to much of this discussion is the phenomenological critique of Hegel and his notion of Absolute Spirit (*Geist*) as Subject.

## Hegel and the Unwriting of the Self

The clearest manifestation of the destabilising effect of the poetics announced in writers such as Schiller, Hölderlin, and Goethe is articulated in the philosophical project of Hegel and his notion of Absolute Spirit (*Geist*) as Subject. As noted by Mark C. Taylor, "Hegel's account of reflexive subjectivity forms a significant chapter in the appearance and disappearance of the self".[158] Hegel's project radicalises the notion of reflexivity found in Augustine. According to Hegel, the notions of self-love and self-consciousness combine to form the essence of God or *Geist* (otherwise Absolute Spirit):

> God is self-consciousness. He knows Himself in a consciousness which is distinct from Him, which is potentially [*an sich*] the consciousness of God, but it is also this actuality [*für sich*] in that it

[158] Mark C. Taylor, op. cit.

> knows its identity with God, an identity which is, however, mediated by the negation of finitude. It is this Begriff which constitutes the content of religion. God is this: to distinguish Himself from Himself, to be an object for Himself, but to be in this distinguishing simply indentical with Himself – Spirit.[159]

With this, Hegel points directly to a central tenet of Christian doctrine with regard to the identity of God in this self-love of "Himself for Himself": God *is* love. Hegel notes that

> love implies a differentiation between two who are, however, not merely different from one another. Love is this feeling of being outside of myself, the feeling and consciousness of this identity. I have my self-consciousness not in myself, but in another in whom alone I am satisfied and am at peace with myself – and I am only insofar as I am at peace with myself, for if I do not have this, I am the contradiction that sunders itself.[160]

No longer is there separation of the subject and the sacred (God *gives* love thereby denoting distance and hierarchy). The boundary *between* what is seen as subject and the sacred is removed (God *is* love rather than God *giving* love) leaving categories such as subject and sacred challenged. The space opened by the synthesis of these categories is occupied by the subject alone as both representation and concept. This opening is central to Hegel's philosophy – the spatial differentiation between representation (*Vorstellung*) and concept (*Begriff*). With regard to Hegel's notion of God's love, this love provides "a representation (*Vorstellung*) of God"[161] that points toward the more complete expression of divine subjectivity disclosed in the structure of self-knowledge which is impossible apart from divine self-knowledge. This divine self-consciousness is for Hegel an "act of distinguishing or differentiation which at the same time gives no difference differentiated; and when in His other He is united only with Himself,

---

[159] G.W.F. Hegel, *Lectures on the Philosophy of Religion*, vol. 2, trans. E.S. Haldane (New York: Humanities Press, 1968) p. 327.

[160] G.W.F. Hegel, *Lectures on the Philosophy of Religion*, vol. 3, trans. E.S. Haldane (New York: Humanities Press, 1968) pp. 10-11.

[161] Mark C. Taylor, ibid., p. 39.

He is three with no other but Himself, He is in close union only with Himself, He beholds *Himself* in His other".[162]

In *Science of Logic,* Hegel further interprets divine subjectivity as "self-relating negativity that remains internal to itself".[163] This subjectivity of God is therefore to be understood "in terms of auto-affection and self-consciousness" that is "thoroughly *reflexive*".[164] Mark C. Taylor outlines the Hegelian conceptualisation of reflexivity by delineating and defining the interplay between *cognition, reflection,* and *reflexion.* "Cognition, reflection, and reflexion", states Taylor, "are distinguished by contrasting interpretations of objectivity. In the movement from cognition through reflection to reflexion, subject and object become ever more closely united".[165] This interplay is outlined by Taylor as follows:

> The gaze of the cognitive object is directed outward, toward an object that appears to be other than the knowing object or the knowing self. The aim of cognition is knowledge of the external object. By contrast, the reflective subject turns inward. The object of reflection is, in fact, cognition. In reflection, the subject thinks about itself thinking about an object that seems to be different from itself. Reflexion deepens this inwardness by taking reflection as its object. The reflexive subject thinks about thinking about thinking.[166]

As noted by Robert Scharlemann in *The Being of God*, the reflexive self in Hegel is "an 'absolute' one inasmuch as the experienced phenomenon (reflection) is of the same kind as are the experiencing act (reflecting)

162 G.W.F. Hegel, *Lectures on the Philosophy of Religion*, vol 3. ibid., p. 11.

163 G.W.F. Hegel, *Science of Logic*, trans. A.V. Miller. (New York: Humanities Press, 1969) p. 401.

164 Mark C. Taylor, ibid., p. 39.

165 ibid.

166 Mark C. Taylor, ibid. The notion of "the gaze"(*le regard*) is explored in the twentieth century by Jacques Lacan. Lacan use of *le regard* builds off of his reflections of Jean-Paul Sarte's phenomenological analysis of *le regard*. As noted by Sarte, what is "seen" is not essentially grounded upon the physical act of sight: "Of course what most often manifests a look is the convergence of two ocular globes in my direction. But the look (*le regard*) will be given just as well on occasion when there is a rustling of branches, or the sound of a footstep followed by silence, or the slight opening of a shutter, or a light movement of a curtain". See Jean-Paul Sarte, *Being and Nothingness: An Essay on Phenomenlogical Ontology*, trans. Hazel E. Barnes (London: Methuen, 1958) p. 257.

and the origin of the experience (self-reflection)".[167] This process continues until unity and differentiation is one and the same. It is within what Hegel terms "the sphere of worship" that humanity participates in this unity of Spirit:

> It is this unity, reconciliation, restoration of the subject and of its self-consciousness, the positive feeling of possessing a share in, of partaking in this Absolute, and making unity with it actually one's own – this abolition of the dualism, which constitutes the sphere of worship.[168]

Hegel's project of subjectivity was a reaction against the prevalent view framed through the Enlightenment which asserted both subject and object be thoroughly comprehended via scientific analysis. This philosophical stance was primarily utilitarian in focus and ethically teleological in approach – the ends explained as well as justified the means. At its heart, the Enlightenment project that Hegel reacted against held a view of the subject that was "atomistic in its social philosophy, analytic in its science of man, and which looked to a scientific social engineering to reorganise man and society and bring happiness through perfect mutual adjustment".[169]

In contrast to this Enlightenment notion of the subject, Hegel developed a conception of the subject which held the dominant feature of an expressive object.[170] Human existence for Hegel was seen as having *inherent unity rather than a compilation of isolated parts*, this being analogous to a work of art that only finds meaning in its relation to itself as a whole and completed work. Likewise, the human subject for Hegel has an overarching, guiding theme whether it is seen or not. In

---

[167] Robert Scharlemann, *The Being of God: Theology and the Experience of Truth* (New York: Seabury Press, 1981) p. 26.

[168] G.W.F. Hegel, *Lectures on the Philosophy of Religion*, vol. 1, trans. E.S. Haldane (New York: Humanities Press, 1968) pp. 66-67.

[169] Charles Taylor, *Hegel and Modern Society* (Cambridge: Cambridge University Press, 1979) p. 1.

[170] Charles Taylor cites his utilisation of the term "expressivism" as being in keeping with the definition given by Isaiah Berlin as noted in Earl Wasserman's *Aspects of the Eighteenth Century*. According to Taylor, Berlin uses the term to denote that view of the "self as art" found in Herder and others of the *Sturm und Drang* movement.

this way, Hegel viewed the Enlightenment subject as not only in error, but a "travesty of human self-understanding" and "one of the most grievous modes of self-distortions".[171] Charles Taylor puts it this way:

> To see a human being as in some way compounded of different elements: faculties of reason and sensibility, or soul and body, or reason and feeling, was [for Hegel] to lose sight of the living, expressive unity; and in so far as men tried to live according to those dichotomies, they must suppress, mutilate or severely distort that unified expression which they have it in them to realise.[172]

Hegel's project was ultimately a recovery, in some ways, of the unity of Aristotelian form of self that came before the analytic, atomistic view of the Enlightenment, and sought to view the subject as *unity before parts*. The subject therefore is not merely body and thought coexisting, but a unity of deep and abiding interpenetration without limit or boundary.

Yet how does one derive *form* without limit or boundary? In particular, how does one speak of the form of God in relation to the form of the subject since, as mentioned in regard to Augustine, it is in the form of the subject in relation to the sacred form (rather than nature) where understanding of the sacred by the subject is even possible?

For Hegel this dilemma is resolved by re-assessing how one speaks of the category of form in relation to subjectivity. First of all, subjectivity in Hegel's project is an *embodied* subjectivity:

> It was a basic principle of Hegel's thought that the subject and all his functions, however "spiritual", were inescapably embodied; and this in two related dimensions: as a "rational animal", that is, a living being who thinks; and as an expressive being, that is, a being whose thinking always and necessarily expresses itself in a medium.[173]

Given this essential embodiment, the subject is also organically understood in form rather than atomistically divided. That is, subjectivity is known first in its entirety before it is known in part or portion, as a "functioning unit and not just a concatenation of parts".[174]

---

[171] Charles Taylor, op. cit., p. 2.
[172] ibid.
[173] ibid., p. 18.
[174] ibid., p. 19.

In this way, the subject shows "a sort of proto-purpose, and even a sort of proto-intelligence in adapting to novel circumstances... in other words, [the subject is] not just a functioning unit, but also something in the nature of an agent..."[175]

Like Augustine before him, Hegel transfers his insights with regard to the subject to his concerns regarding that of *Geist*, or the Absolute Spirit, which Augustine would term as God. In Hegel's project, the Absolute is subject and it is this *Geist* which is the foundation and wellspring of all that we call "the Real". Hegel as a product of the *Sturm und Drang* movement saw the Divine flowing through *all* things, not separate from or essentially different from reality both understood and conceived. This is not unlike Spinoza's notion of "substance". As noted previously, Hegel held that the subject is essentially embodied. Therefore, *Geist* (or God) for Hegel "cannot exist separately from the universe which he sustains and in which he manifests himself. On the contrary this universe is his embodiment, without which he would not be, any more than [we] would be without [ours]".[176]

Hegel asserts that *Geist* has both embodiment and form that is paradoxically without limit or boundary. This proves challenging to the key tenet of Christianity – namely the Incarnation. For Hegel, the notion of Christ is the mere example of the unity of the divine and human nature which is the Absolute or Universal Spirit. As noted from *Lectures on the Philosophy of Religion*, Hegel holds that "the history of Christ is a history for the spiritual community because it is absolutely adequate to the idea" of the synthesis of the divine and human, and the previous temporal example of a Christ is "only the effort of Spirit to reach the determination implied in the implicit unity of the divine and human".[177] In the theological context of the period, this becomes a great challenge to christology after Hegel in the attempt to figure Jesus as particular within history. As we will see in the next chapter, with the notion of limit removed from the concept of Christ, theologians such as F.C. Baur, Ludwig Feuerbach, and David Friederich Strauss sought

175 ibid.

176 Charles Taylor, ibid., p. 23.

177 G.W.F. Hegel *Lectures on the Philosophy of Religion*. Vol. 3 Trans. E.B. Speirs and J.B. Sanderson (London: K. Paul, Trench, and Co., 1895) p. 113.

to re-imagine the very form of Jesus as an enactment of the Hegelian project "to reach the determination implied in the implicit unity of the divine and human".[178]

---

[178] ibid.

# Chapter 4

# Theological Poetics of Jesus Amidst Nineteenth Century Higher Criticism

Challenging poetics of the subject by the likes of Schiller, Hölderlin, and Goethe coupled with the limitless possibilities of a Christ without form added to the growing changes in nineteenth century theological poetics surrounding the figuring of Jesus. As this chapter will discuss, the act of writing and reading which had, prior to Higher Criticism, grounded a Christian subject's identity upon the "word of God" as historically and epistemologically indisputable, thereby providing a centre point and focus for answers to build an identity upon, were now called into question. Key to this shift was the questioning of historicity in relation to biblical narratives by Strauss and other Hegelians which destabilised the once essential relationship that was presupposed between "history" and "truth". As noted by Douglas Templeton in *The New Testament as True Fiction*, these shifts affected not only the genre of biblical criticism, but also fiction:

> It was with Strauss that fiction enters the New [era]. A waiting world was struck with a dull thud...In other words, the writers of the Gospels were not following the necessities of *history*, the critical examination of evidence, the sifting, the winnowing, the interrogation, the torture of witnesses. They were following the necessities of the religious *imagination*, as that imagination had been trained by a millennium of poetry to imagine.[179]

179 Douglas A. Templeton, *The New Testament as True Fiction* (Sheffield: Sheffield Academic Press, 1999) p. 37.

While the writers that will be addressed come after Hegel, it will be seen that much of his spirit was certainly evident throughout the nineteenth century, particularly in this area of Higher Criticism.[180]

## F.C. Baur and the "Universal yet Particular" Christ of *Church History*

Ferdinand Christian Baur began his theological training in Tübingen and after serving a time as vicar at Rossag and Mühlhausen near Stuttgart, joined the theological faculty at Blaubeuren in 1817. In 1826, the theological faculty of Tübingen called Baur to the chair of historical disciplines where he taught till his death in 1860. The literary corpus of F.C. Baur can be divided into three periods. His first published work focused on the symbolism and mythology of the ancient world and its relation to Christianity. Published in 1824, the work dealt with the "natural religion" of antiquity and was followed by studies of rationalism, supernaturalism, and Manichaeism in 1827-1829. His second period of scholarly production saw Baur focusing on the history of dogma, with particular attention given to preparing lectures on the chief tenets of Protestantism, Roman Catholicism, Gnosticism, the Trinity, and the history of dogma, which were published after his death in 1865-1868. In his late sixties, Baur began his final literary period which saw the synthesis of the two previous periods into what has been termed his scholarly *opus*, namely the five volume study of Christianity entitled *Geschichte der christlichen Kirche* (*The Church History of the First Three Centuries*). The first two volumes appeared in 1853 and 1859 and were published by Baur himself. The last three volumes were published in succession from 1861 to 1863, the last two volumes published posthumously.

Baur's project in *Church History* is fairly straightforward. His methodology is put forward as seeing:

> ...historical occurrences as the conjunction of the universal and the particular, by which the universal underlies the particular, makes itself

180 "Lower" criticism as research in the texts of the Old and New Testament documents; "Higher" criticism being research pertaining to the historical and theological backgrounds of the documents.

> known through it, and dominates it. Specifically, this task involves inquiry into the essence of Christianity together with that of the period in which it emerged... The requirements for this criticism are threefold: first, to be bound by no dogmatic assumption which might disturb the impartiality of judgement; second, to validate nothing as historical truth which could not be demonstrated from the extant sources; and finally, never to lose sight of the universal.[181]

For Baur, of primary concern was the notion of *essence* and sources for the grounding of Christian faith claims as they pertain to scripture. In *Church History*, Baur directly challenges the presupposition that scripture yields an absolute doctrine of revelation. In his view, "such an assumption... spells the death of all historical observation".[182] In particular, Baur stood against the doctrine of verbal inspiration of scripture stating "what kind of faith must it be that is eternally fearful and anxious that the foundation on which it rests... might be taken and forever removed from it, a faith that encounters... all critical doubts and investigations... with the constant alarm and apprehension that they might finally make a sorry end of it?"[183] In this regard, Baur holds that criticism must be freed from seeing the Gospel writers as "mere reporters", so that the texts may gain "in significance as sources".[184]

Three of the main themes in Baur's project are germane to this discussion and relevant to our consideration of George Eliot's developing poetics. First, the resurrection of Jesus Christ is seen as being beyond historical critique. In *Church History*, as well as his essays on New Testament theology, Baur asserts that reading the Gospel accounts shows Jesus to be more concerned with "inward" faith as opposed to "outward" manifestation, that is, they show a Jesus who disregards *action* in favour of *intention* as conferring moral value. With regard to Jesus' messianic consciousness, Baur asserts that this is evident in Jesus' appearance in Jerusalem, even apart from the triumphal entry, and gives unequivocal proof of this. In reference to the Resurrection accounts, Baur asserts that historical criticism needs to

---

181 F.C. Baur, *Ausgewählte Werke in Einzelausgaben*, ed. Klaus Scholder, 5 volumes (Stuttgart: Friedrich Frommann, 1963-1975) pp. 57ff.

182 Cited by Roy A. Harrisville and Walter Sundberg, *The Bible in Modern Culture: Theology and Historical-Critical Method from Spinoza to Käsemann* (Grand Rapids: Eerdmans, 1995) p. 114.

183 F.C. Baur. ibid. pp. 296ff.

184 Roy A. Harrisville, op. cit., p. 116.

hold only to the fact that *for the disciples* Jesus' resurrection became "the firmest and most irreversible certainty".[185] This is an important statement on Baur's behalf, and will align him (unwittingly) with Strauss as we shall see later. Here, Baur asserts that it is not the fact, but the faith in Jesus' resurrection that should concern us as an object of research. The process by which this faith emerges lies beyond the reach of either psychological analysis or historical verification.

Secondly, Baur implies that Christianity is nothing more than a Hegelian synthesis of Hebraic and Hellenistic ideologies. After Jesus' death, followers of Christ in Jerusalem formed the antitheses of Hebrew and Hellenistic understanding. Baur argues that Jesus' disciples gathered in Jerusalem in two groups, Hebrews and Hellenists, with the latter group sympathetic to Stephen. This latter group of Hellenists would make up the group later to be associated with Paul. Baur then reviews the New Testament corpus through his methodology which he terms *Tendenzkritik*, or "Tendency Criticism".[186] In his words, "I believe I can be certain that no view will succeed… in gaining more universal recognition till mine… will be refuted".[187] Through *Tendenzkritik*, Baur aligns each of the New Testament texts with its "tendency" toward one of three epochs of conflict within early Christianity. In the first epoch, which is the death of Christ, Baur notes that the community in Jerusalem directly following Christ's death became a twin mission between Jewish and Gentile followers in outreach to the poor. This unified mission dissolved with followers of Paul and followers of Peter becoming divided in "tendency". This second epoch extends from the destruction of Jerusalem to the first decades of the second century. The third epoch is seen in the next few decades of the second century where the Christian community is separated into "tendencies" of "Jewish particularism" and "Pauline universalism".[188] It is in this third epoch that Baur notes John the Apostle's move to Ephesus as an act to blend the principles of Jewish Christianity and the 'tendency' of Pauline Christianity. It is in John's Gospel that Baur sees the nexus point of Gospel "tendency" conflict. John's Gospel, states Baur, rests on no

[185] ibid.
[186] F.C. Baur, op. cit., pp. 359, 395, 397-99.
[187] Roy A. Harrisville, op. cit..
[188] ibid., p. 118.

historical grounding, but is a synthesis of the Pauline and Petrine conflict through its announcing of the universal "divine idea" in the notion of the *Logos*. For Baur, it is in the *Logos* that "the relation between Judaism and paganism in Revelation was reversed" and both Pauline and Petrine antitheses are subjected to the "divine idea" of the *Logos* that goes beyond the particularity of Jesus' ministry. This point is key, in that Baur is arguing that an *imagined* space is the point of synthesis which is not an historically rendered "tendency" of either Pauline or Petrine origin. This assertion will be heard by Baur's student, D.F. Strauss, but will not be acted upon fully in his work. It is in Strauss' translator – Marian Evans – that such a spirit is made flesh, in her poetics.

Thirdly, Baur argues that the identity of Christ is both universal and particular or specific. Baur responded in his essays on the New Testament to the claims headed by Heinrich Ewald at the University of Göttingen, and leader of the "Göttingen Seven", that Jesus came to gradual consciousness of his messiahship by restating the assumption behind the assertion; that every individual therefore possessed the possibility of such a consciousness and the "Göttingen Seven" were merely stating that Jesus just "awakened". Yet for Baur the essential question remained unanswered: if this is a universal possibility, where are the other examples? What is not offered up in the underlying assertion, for Baur's satisfaction, is that "the highest in world history is ... never fulfilled"[189] to the position attributed to Jesus. For Baur, the fact that the question remains unanswerable weakens the question itself. Yet, Baur makes this final statement: "But, so long as this is not proved, the other assumption is just as possible [i.e. Universality of messiahship]".[190] In this regard, Baur is also open to the *aufheben* of Jesus (like *dirempt*, a term shared with Hegel, akin to *drawing into* or *absorbing*) whereby the *particular* of Jesus' identity is absorbed into the *universal*, allowing for the expanding identity of Jesus throughout a universal world consciousness.

## Ludwig Feuerbach and *The Essence of Christianity*

Ludwig Feuerbach was born in 1804 and was a student of Hegel at the University of Berlin from 1824 to 1828 and taught Philosophy at

---

[189] ibid., p. 127.
[190] ibid.

Erglangen. Three of his most important works include *The Philosophy of the Future* (*Die Philosophe der Zukunft*, 1843), *The Essence of Religion* (*Des Wesen der Religion*, 1851), and his first and most influential work *The Essence of Christianity* (*Des Wesen des Christentums*, 1841) translated in English by Marian Evans prior to her emergence as George Eliot, the writer of fiction.

In the 1957 edition of *The Essence of Christianity*, an introduction by Karl Barth is included. Barth extracts the kernel of Feuerbach's project from his Heidelberg lectures which became *The Essence of Religion*: "Theology", states Feuerbach, "is anthropology, that is, in the object of religion which we call *Theos* in Greek and *Gott* in German, nothing but the essence of man is expressed".[191] As Barth notes in the introductory essay,

> In Feuerbach's program – the transformation and dissolution of theology into anthropology – one may detect not only the idea that there must be inevitably an end to theology, but also the idea that he always wished to transform theology and make *it* into anthropology. [citing Feuerbach] "While I do reduce theology to anthropology; very much as Christianity while lowering God into man, made man into God".[192]

*In Feuerbach's project God and humanity are not analogous, they are synonymous.* With regard to the nature of Christ, Feuerbach states the following:

> ... Christ was no miracle worker, nor, in general, that which he is represented to be in the Bible. I ...do not inquire what the real, natural Christ was or may have been in distinction from what he has been made or has become in Supernaturalism; on the contrary, I accept the Christ of religion, but I show that this superhuman being is nothing else than a product and reflex of the supernatural mind.[193]

---

[191] Ludwig Feuerbach *The Essence of Christianity*, trans. George Eliot (New York: Harper and Row, 1957) p. xv.

[192] Karl Barth, Introductory essay to Ludwig Feuerbach's *The Essence of Christianity* trans. George Eliot. (New York: Harper and Row, 1957) pp. xiv-xv. Citations of Feuerbach from *The Essence of Christianity* are from Ludwig Feuerbach, *The Essence of Christianity* trans. George Eliot (New York: Prometheus Books, 1989).

[193] Ludwig Feuerbach, *The Essence of Christianity* trans. George Eliot (New York:

This truth has been long evident according to Feuerbach, but remains an open secret:

> It is not I but religion that worships man, although religion, or rather theology, denies this; it is not I, an insignificant individual, but religion itself that says: God is man, man is God; it is not I, but religion itself that denies the God who is *not* man, but it is only an *en rationis* [being for reason], - since it makes God become man, and only then constitues this God, not distinguished from man, having a human form, human feeling and human thoughts, the object of its worship and veneration. I have only found the key to the cipher of the Christian religion, only extricated its true meaning from the web of contradictions and delusions called theology.[194]

Feuerbach's criticism of theism is as much a criticism of his former teacher, Georg Wilhelm Friedrich Hegel, as it was a criticism of Christianity. For Feuerbach, Hegel's notion of *Geist* as the Absolute Spirit that perpetually pours out its life into the finite in the process of becoming its own self-revelation as Absolute Subject was flawed by presupposing an external causal agent that was to have been overcome through the dialectic. Hegel's tendency to conceive of abstract predicates as entities showed him as the *culmination* of Western philosophy since Plato rather than stepping beyond this tradition. Feuerbach notes that Hegel's framing of Absolute Spirit in anthropomorphic visages transfers this predicate into *human* existence and results in the idea rendered a subject. In short, Feuerbach creates a sustained argument throughout *The Essence of Christianity* that the idea of God in Christianity is the idea of humanity unconsciously and involuntarily made into an object of thought and treated as a separate agent. Ultimately, knowledge of God is knowledge of humanity and knowledge of humanity is knowledge of God. In summary, Van Harvey articulates Feuerbach's central argument as follows:

> All of these arguments, as well as others, add up to the conclusion that [for Feuerbach] religion is, so to speak, an acoustical illusion of the consciousness, the means by which the species gradually becomes aware of its own essential nature. Although the religious person is, of

---

Prometheus Books, 1989) p. xxi.

[194] ibid., p. xvi.

> course, not aware of this, every advance in religious consciousness is an advance in self-knowledge, the culmination of which is, paradoxically, athesim.[195]

Feuerbach's dictum that "Man is the beginning, the middle, and the end of religion" is carried into his conception of subjectivity. The subject in Feuerbach's project is a temporal entity delimited by space and through relations with other entities. Knowing the real is forged in the external resistence to our own self-activity in the world and not through accessing some hidden metaphysical realm.[196] Both sense data and internal feelings received by the subject (I) are referenced via relations with other subjects (Thou). In this way, there is no possible awareness of self except as mediated through and with communal encounter. Ultimately, the human subject is a communal subject. It is in the midst of humanity, not in the presense of God as an abstracted and separate entity, that subjectivity is grounded and made manifest. The idea (*idee*) of God for Feuerbach is a distraction and a self-alienating "moment" in the process of humanity becoming authentically human – a moment that humanity is ready to move beyond. Throughout *The Essence of Christianity* Feuerbach shows a strong refusal to attribute predicates to an entity that transcends finite entities. As he states in *The Essence of Christianity*, "as God has renounced himself out of love, so we, out of love, should renounce God; for if we do not sacrifice God to love, we sacrifice love to God, and, in spite of the predicate of love, we have the God – the evil being – of religious fanaticism".[197]

What is at the heart of Feuerbach's first and most notable work is found in its title – *The Essence of Christianity*. While many have used Feuerbach's work as a theory of *religion*, it is merely a critique and attempted theory of *Christianity*. The entire premise of the work rests upon the central argument that *all* religion is merely a projection of the human will. Feuerbach argues this point by constantly interchanging the concepts of "religion" and "Christianity" utilising Christianity as the

---

[195] Van A. Harvey, "Ludwig Feuerbach and Karl Marx" in *Nineteenth Century Religious Thought in the West: Volume I* (Cambridge: Cambridge University Press, 1988) p. 297.

[196] See Ludwig Feuerbach, *Principles of the Philosophy of the Future*, trans. Manfred Vogel (Indianapolis: Bobbs-Merrill, 1966) pp. 51-73.

[197] Ludwig Feuerbach, *The Essence of Christianity*, p. 53.

test case for all religions. As a critique of Christianity as a system that is the manifestation of human will, *The Essence of Christianity* has had strong support. For those who have read Karl Barth, it may seem surprising that Barth goes on to say that Feuerbach's programme is indeed a worthy one. As Barth states in his Introduction to *The Essence of Christianity*:

> ... it is the essence of man that he [Feuerbach] emphatically and enthusiastically affirms, against theology and idealistic theology. When he identifies God with the essence of man, he thereby pays God the highest honour that he can confer; indeed, this is the strange *Magnificat* that Ludwig Feuerbach intones for "the good Lord". Man wants to live. But he is in his existence dependent, limited, threatened. He has needs, wishes, and also something a bit higher – ideals. He loves and fears. He desires and denies and abhors. He knows values and disvalues. He seeks for means to possess the former and to get rid of the latter. Thus his life is a struggle and a tussle.[198]

What Barth assesses in Feuerbach is his desire to free humanity from restrictive modes of belief, be that naïve religion or speculative theology, that can become a religion that proffers salvation but ultimately alienates the very humanity it seeks to save. These thoughts are also seen throughout George Eliot's work and the influence of Feuerbach upon her fiction is certainly evident.[199] Before turning to the resonance of Feuerbach in the poetics of George Eliot, it is important to review her relation to David Friedrich Strauss' *Das Leben Jesu*. It is the comparison of the two works, and the relation between *The Essence of Christianity* and *Das Leben Jesu* have to each other, that assists in such an assessment.

## David Friedrich Strauss and *Mythi* in *Das Leben Jesu*

Like Kant, David Friedrich Strauss spent the majority of his life in and around his birthplace of Stuttgart. In 1831 Strauss went to Berlin to study under Hegel, who died two weeks after his arrival. Strauss made the following remark to his friend Christian Märklin after attending Hegel's funeral:

---

[198] Karl Barth, Introduction to *The Essence of Christianity*, pp. xv-xvi.

[199] This will be explored in chapter nine with regard to George Eliot's sacramental use of water in relation to Feuerbach's conception of the Sacraments in *The Essence of Christianity*.

> We buried him yesterday. At about three o'clock in the hall of the university, Rector Marheineke gave a simple and heartfelt speech, totally pleasing to me. He described [Hegel] not only as a monarch in the realm of thought, but also a true disciple of Christ in his life. Then he said what he would not have said at a church ceremony, that just as Jesus Christ, so he too passed through bodily death to the resurrection of the spirit, a spirit bequeathed to his own. There followed a rather tumultuous procession from the house of mourning to the cemetery.[200]

Strauss stayed on and listened to lectures given by Schleiermacher and noted that he was not radical enough in his conclusions. As Strauss wrote during this time, "Schleiermacher goes only half way... I will write a life of Jesus according to my own idea".[201] Returning to Stuttgart to lecture on the Gospels at University of Tübingen, Strauss published *Das Leben Jesu* in 1835. Writing again to his friend Christian Märklin during the writing of *Das Leben Jesu*, he describes his process as follows: "this way, I would destroy, in part shake the infinite content faith has in [Jesus'] life – indeed, only in order to restore it in a higher order".[202]

The central thesis of Strauss' work is his notion of the *mythi*, which is an attempt to separate out that which is historically derived from that which is nonhistorical in the biblical record though not necessarily untrue religiously or theologically (*mythi*). Strauss begins to create a contextual necessity for this notion of *mythi* in discussing H.E.G. Paulus' *Commentar über das neue Testament* (*Commentary on the New Testament*) published in 1800, arguing for the necessary distinction between *fact* and *opinion*:

---

[200] From a letter to Christian Märklin, 17 November 1831, in Jorg Sandberger, *David Friedrich Strauss als theologischer Hegelianer* (Gottingen: Vandenhoeck und Ruprecht, 1972) p. 192. Cited by Roy A. Harrisville, op. cit., p. 95.

[201] Heinrich Benecke, *William Vatke in seinem Leben und seinen Schriften* (Bonn: E. Strauss, 1883) p. 75. Cited Roy A Harrisville, op. cit.

[202] From a letter to Christian Märklin, 6 February 1832, in Jorg Sandberger, *David Friedrich Strauss als theologischer Hegelianer* (Gottingen: Vandenhoeck und Ruprecht, 1972) p. 193. Cited by Roy A. Harrisville, op. cit., p. 97.

> In the introduction to this [Paulus'] work he states it to be the primary requisite of the biblical critic to be able to distinguish between what is fact, and what is opinion. That which has been actually experienced, internally or externally, by the participants in an event, he calls fact. The interpretation of an event, the supposed causes to which it is referred either by the participants or by the narrators, he calls opinion. But, according to Dr. Paulus, these two elements become so easily blended and confounded in the minds both of the original sharers in an event, and of the subsequent relators and historians, that fact and opinion lose distinction; so that the one and the other are believed and recorded with equal confidence in their historical truth. This intermixture is particularly apparent in the historical books of the New Testament; since at the time Jesus lived, it was still the prevailing disposition to derive every striking occurrence from an invisible and superhuman cause. It is consequently the chief task of the historian who desires to deal with matters of fact, that is to say, in reference to the New Testament, to separate these two constituent elements so closely amalgamated, and yet in themselves so distinct; and to extricate the pure kernel of fact from the shell of opinion. In order to do this, in the absence of any more genuine account which would serve as a correcting parallel, he must transplant himself in imagination upon the theatre of action, and strive to the utmost to contemplate the events by the light of the age in which they occurred.[203]

Paulus represented the "empty form of rationalism" that was supposed to have firmly grounded Higher Criticism in Strauss' day and, in Strauss' estimation, failed to do so. In order to extricate "the pure kernel of fact from the shell of opinion", Strauss called for the task of Higher Criticism to move forward the work done by the Rationalists (Reimarus, Paulus, Lessing, Eichhorn) but with larger strides that fully embrace a wider vista:

> The new point of view... is the mythical. This theory is not brought to bear on the evangelical history for the first time in the present work: it has long been applied to particular parts of that history, and is here only extended to its entire tenor. It is not by any means meant that the whole history of Jesus is to be represented as mythical, but only that every part of it is to be subjected to a critical examination, to ascertain whether it have not some admixture of the mythical. The exegesis of

[203] David Friedrich Strauss, *The Life of Jesus, Critically Examined. 4th Edition.* trans. George Eliot (New York: Swan Sonnenschein and Co., 1848, 1898) p. 49.

> the ancient church set out from the double presupposition: first, that the gospels contained a history, and secondly, that this history was a supernatural one. Rationalism rejected the latter of these presuppositions, but only to cling the more tenaciously to the former, maintaining that these books present unadulterated, though only natural, history. Science cannot rest satisfied with the inquiry must first be made whether in fact, and to what extent, the ground on which we stand in the gospels is historical. This is the natural course of things, and thus far the appearance of a work like the present is not only justifiable, but even necessary.[204]

In this way, Strauss seeks to place scripture under the same scrutiny as other historical documents. In doing so, he intends to dissolve "discrepancies and chronological contradictions" that hold together what is *image or representation* (*Vorstellung*) from the underlying fundamental *concept* (*Begriff*) which for Strauss is what is essential. In this way, the goal of Strauss' project is to separate the husk of *Vorstellung* in order to offer the freed kernel of *Begriff* and, as noted previously, "destroy, in part shake the infinite content faith has in [Jesus'] life – indeed, only in order to restore it in a higher order".[205] As Strauss admits, "as early as in my university years, the most important point of [Hegel's] system appeared to me and my friends to be the distinction between *Vorstellung* and *Begriff* in religion".[206]

Strauss' project in *Das Leben Jesu* is fairly basic in its methodology. The Gospel narratives are organised and discussed in three chronological sections: "History of the Birth and Childhood of Jesus", "History of the Public Life of Jesus", and "History of the Passion, Death, and Resurrection". Each section is then broken into sub-chapters. For example, the section entitled "History of the Birth and Childhood of Jesus" includes five chapters; "Annunciation and Birth of John the Baptist", "Davidical Descent of Jesus according to the Genealogical Tables of Matthew and Luke", "Announcement of the Conception of Jesus and its supernatural character in the visit of Mary

---

204 Strauss, ibid., p. xxix in "Preface to the First German Edition".

205 Letter to Christian Märklin, cited by Harrisville, op. cit.

206 David Friedrich Strauss *Streitschriften zur Vertheidigung meiner Schrift über das Leben Jesu und zur Charakteristik der gegenwärtigen Theologie* (New York: G. Olms, 1930). Cited by Harrisville, op. cit., p. 103.

and Elizabeth", "Birth and Earliest Events of the Life of Jesus", and "The First Visit to the Temple and the Education of Jesus". Within each sub-chapter, Strauss employs a triadic method of critique. First, the account in question is addressed from the orthodox theological view, which Strauss terms the "crude" or "supernaturalist" understanding. Next, the same account is then seen through the critique of the Rationalists which employs a natural and historical rendering (which Strauss terms as "empty" in its results). Finally, Strauss employs his critique of the account as a *mythus*. For example, in chapter ten entitled "The Transfiguration of Jesus and His Last Journey to Jerusalem", Strauss organises the beginning of this chapter with the sub-headings "The transfiguration of Jesus considered as a miraculous external event", "The natural explanation of the narrative in various forms", and "The history of the transfiguration considered as a mythus". Each chapter follows the same method of critique.

In the introduction to the 4th edition of *Das Leben Jesu*, Otto Pfleiderer of University of Berlin marks out the project of Strauss as addressing the growing problem in the Church, where "the simple-minded believer cannot [separate] between the spiritual idea and the outward form of its representation, and to find in the former both the productive power and the permanent kernel within the outward husk".[207]

Strauss' project of separating the "kernel" of *Begriff* from the "husk" of *Vorstellung* was certainly not without its echoes from past hermeneuts to which attention should be paid.[208] For example, we see in Hegel's dialectical project a similar triadic methodology with the intellectual movement from thesis to the necessary antithesis and then on to synthesis. This systematic triadic form is represented in Strauss'

---

207 David Friedrich Strauss *The Life of Jesus, Critically Examined. 4th Edition.* Trans. George Eliot (New York: Swan Sonnenschein and Co., 1848,1898) p. xvi.

208 Christian Wolff, one of the more prolific of eighteenth-century philosophers, argued for a similar separation and re-interpretation in his chapters "On reading historical and dogmatic books" and "On interpreting the Holy Scriptures" found in *Vernünftige Gedanken.* As noted by Kurt Mueller-Vollmer, Wolff divided all writings into the categories of "historical" and "dogmatic" works. 'Historical' writings are to be judged on their completeness of the historical account they report as well as their "truthfulness and sincerity, since we no longer have access to historical truth once the events referred to are past". "Dogmatic" writings, on the other hand, are to be judged on the "strength of their arguments, their truth content, and the knowledge of the subject matter displayed". See Kurt Mueller-Vollmer, ed., *The Hermeneutics Reader* (New York: Continuum, 1997) pp. 54ff.

conception of history. As mentioned at the end of chapter 3, Hegel held the notion of Christ as "the mere example" of the unity of the divine and human nature which is the Absolute or Universal Spirit. As noted from *Lectures on the Philosophy of Religion*, Hegel holds that "the history of Christ is a history for the spiritual community because it is absolutely adequate to the idea" of the synthesis of the divine and human, and the previous temporal example of a Christ is "only the effort of Spirit to reach the determination implied in the implicit unity of the divine and human".[209] History for Strauss can be viewed as the *form* of this Absolute or Universal Spirit as articulated through time. With regard to the idea of Christ, extricating the kernel of the Absolute Spirit requires progressing from previously primitive or "crude" supernaturalism, coming into opposition with the "empty" form of Rationalism, and ultimately arriving at an enlightened or "true" *Begriff* within the *mythi* where the life of Jesus is merely the consciousness of the church objectified by the human spirit as divine.

Publication of *Das Leben Jesu* caused something of a firestorm in theological discourse. In the Preface to *David Friedrich Strauss and his Theology*, Horton Harris makes this observation: "Of all the nineteenth-century theologians, Strauss was the most notorious. No single theological work ever created such consternation in the theological world as Strauss' *Life of Jesus*. It split the century into two theological eras – before and after 1835".[210] In the conclusion of *Das Leben Jesu*, the Absolute Spirit that had traditionally been attributed as the one God-human embodiment in traditional orthodox christology was now to be seen not as an individual, but (in keeping with Hegel) as "Idea" within all of humanity collectively. In the concluding dissertation, Strauss makes the following assertion:

> If reality is ascribed to the idea of the unity of the divine and human natures, is this equivalent to the admission that this unity must actually have been once manifested, as it never had been, and never more will be, in one individual? This is indeed not the mode in which Idea

---

[209] G.W. Hegel, *Lectures on the Philosophy of Religion*. Trans. E.B. Speirs and J.B. Sanderson (London: K. Paul, Trench, and Co., 1895), III, p. 113.

[210] Horton Harris, *David Friedrich Strauss and his Theology* (London: Cambridge University Press, 1973) p. ix.

> realises itself; it is not wont to lavish all its fullness on one exemplar, and be niggardly towards all others – to express itself perfectly in that one individual, and imperfectly in all the rest: it rather loves to distribute its riches among a multiplicity of exemplars which reciprocally complete each other – in the alternate appearance and suppression of a series of individuals. And is this no true realisation of the Idea? Is not the idea of unity of the divine and human natures a real one in a far higher sense, when I regard the whole race of mankind as its realisation, than when I single out one man as such a realisation? Is not an incarnation of God from eternity, a truer one than an incarnation limited to a particular point in time?[211]

Strauss continues his thesis by sounding the replacing of traditional conceptions of a Christ with Humanity as the locus for complete union of creator and created:

> This is the key to the whole of Christology, that, as subject of the predicate which the church assigns to Christ, we place, instead of an individual, an Idea; but an idea which has an existence in reality, not in the mind only, like that of Kant. In an individual, a God-man, the properties and functions which the church ascribes to Christ contradict themselves; in the idea of the race, they perfectly agree. Humanity is the union of the two natures – God become man, the infinite manifesting itself in the finite, and the finite spirit remembering its infinitude... It is Humanity that dies, rises, and ascends to heaven, for from the negation of its phenomenal life there proceeds a higher spiritual life... by kindling with him of the idea of Humanity, the individual man participates in the divinely human life of the species... This alone is the absolute sense of Christology: that it is annexed to the person and history of one individual, is a necessary result of the historical form which Christology has taken.[212]

Strauss recognises that this radical shift in christology poses a challenge not only to those in the academy, but those in the pulpit as well. As he says, "how is the continuance of a ministry in the church possible when theology has reached this stage?"[213] In short, Strauss acknowledges the inevitablity for hypocrisy in the pulpit, although to say this would be the demonstration of what Strauss calls an "uncultivated mind":

---

211 David Friedrich Strauss, op. cit., pp. 779-780.
212 ibid., p. 780.
213 ibid., p. 781.

> The difference between the theologian and the church is regarded as a total one; it is thought, that in answer to the question, whether he believes in the history of Christ, he ought to say exactly, no; whereas he says, yes: and this is a falsehood... Hence it is an evidence of an uncultivated mind, to denounce as a hypocrite a theologian who preaches, for example, on the resurrection of Christ, since, though he may not believe in the reality of that event as a single sensible fact, he may nevertheless, hold to be true the representation of the process of spiritual life, which the resurrection of Christ affords.[214]

Basil Willey notes Strauss' "practical advice" to clergy in this way:

> What shall the clergyman do when he has seen the light, learnt the secret? Renounce his Orders and become a professor?... Stay in the church, then, and preach the identity of Christianity *and* philosophy? But no one will understand him. Keep his best thoughts for a few initiates, and preach the old doctrines with mental reservations? But the sense of his own hypocrisy will probably suffocate him. Strauss does not pretend to solve the problem or to give authoritative advice to the Robert Elsmeres.[215]

As a result of the protest surrounding the publication of *Das Leben Jesu*, Strauss was removed from his post at Tübingen and became increasingly sceptical of Christianity. Disappointed with the negative reception of *Das Leben Jesu*, Strauss rewrote and restated his argument for a wider audience in 1864, one-year after the publication of Ernest Renan's *Life of Jesus* in France.[216] In this restating, Strauss restructured his hypothesis into assertions, contending with great strength that the four Gospel writers had indeed fabricated what they wrote and that

---

[214] ibid., p. 782.

[215] Basil Willey *Nineteenth Century Studies: Coleridge to Matthew Arnold.* (London: Chatto and Windus, 1949) p. 227. Willey, of course, refers to the Robert Elsmere of Mrs. Humphrey Ward's novel.

[216] Ernest Renan had stated in regard to Strauss' *Das Leben Jesu* that "the historian finds it too devoid of facts; the critic, too uniform in its processes; the theologian, founded upon a hypothesis subversive to Christianity". Cited by A.S. Byatt in *George Eliot: Selected Essays, Poems, and Other Writings*, ed. A.S. Byatt (London: Penguin, 1990) p. 446.

Jesus was ultimately a deceiver and an impostor. In 1872, Strauss published *The Old and the New Faith* in which he completely divorced himself from orthodox Christian doctrine and remained "alienated from and out of sympathy with his associates" in the academy.[217]

Reception of *Das Leben Jesu* in England was also mixed, even within those circles sympathetic to German Higher Criticism. In a letter to William Coningham dated 1840, John Sterling makes the following positive assertion in regard to trends in German theological discourse in his time, four years prior to Marian Evans' translation of *Das Leben Jesu*:

> More than half of all German theology, for the last fifty years, has turned upon the controversy about the literal accuracy and plenary inspiration of the book we call the Bible... No English book gives a plausible share of this kind of information. After long and very painful resistance of mind, I was forced to admit, that if I am to follow honestly the best light afforded me, I must own there is error in the Scriptures, and that the denial of this is, in an adequately instructed man, a mere *lying for God*, - one of the most absurd and suicidal of all human superstitions.[218]

Matthew Arnold cited his criticism of Strauss' project thus:

> It is easy to be too systematic. Strauss had the idea, acute and ingenious, of explaining the miracles of the New Testament as a reiteration of the miracles of the Old. Of some miracles this supplies a good explanation. It plausibly explains the story of the Transfiguration, for instance. The story of the illuminated face of Jesus, - Jesus the prophet like unto Moses, whom Moses foretold, - might naturally owe its origin to the illuminated face of Moses himself. But of other miracles Strauss's idea affords no admissible explanation whatever. To employ it for these cases can only show the imperturbable resolution of a German professor in making all the facts suit a theory which he had adopted.[219]

---

[217] ibid.

[218] John Sterling, *Twelve Letters by John Sterling* ed. William Coningham (London: 1851) p.3.

[219] Matthew Arnold, 'God and the Bible', *Complete Prose Works of Matthew Arnold.* Cited in Rosemary Ashton, *The German Idea: Four English Writers and the Reception of German Thought 1800-1860* (London: Libris, 1980, 1994) p. 150.

But the *esprit de corps* was ready to receive Strauss into the circle of English readers despite Arnold's noteworthy critique. In 1841, John Sterling reflected to Ralph Waldo Emerson that it was a time in England where "Wordsworth and Coleridge were mystagogues lurking in caverns, and German literature was thought of with a good deal less favour than we are now disposed to show towards that of China". In a telling statement at the close of his reflections to Emerson, Sterling notes almost prophetically, "Thought is leaking into this country, – even Strauss sells".[220]

As noted previously, Scripture was now placed alongside other works of literature in what Goethe termed *Weltliteratur* where scripture was not so much devalued but, conversely, other literature was raised to the status of *the* meaning-making agent that was previously held exclusively by the Bible. As stated by Jasper, "... it is the Bible which yields the historical canon, both particular and symbolic, opening into the second tier, the 'supercanon' of the universal records of *Weltliteratur*, of all times and places".[221]

Stephen Prickett notes that the second half of the eighteenth century brought a

> complex and confused situation where ideas and models are constantly being taken, adapted and reused by biblical and literary critics with very little sense of the later separation that was to be imposed between the two by their more specialised descendants: what a German biblical critic, Hermann Usener, was to call in the 1880's a *Gletscherwall* – a 'glacier wall' – of academic partition.[222]

This *Gletscherwall* manifests itself by the beginning of the nineteenth-century as a pronounced divide between narrative as 'history' and narrative as 'fiction' that had become "much more clearly demarcated".[223] Yet the designation of what was 'history' and what was

[220] John Sterling, *A Correspondence between John Sterling and Ralph Waldo Emerson* ed. E.W. Emerson (Boston: 1897) pp. 59-60.

[221] David Jasper, *The Sacred and Secular Canon in Romanticism*, p. 22.

[222] Stephen Prickett, "Biblical Criticism and the Nineteenth-Century Novel", *The Critical Spirit and The Will to Believe* ed. David Jasper and T.R. Wright (London: Macmillan Press, 1989) p. 11.

[223] ibid.

'fictive' became more difficult to determine. In an article on 'Ancient and Modern Poetry' in 1822, James Marsh makes clear this distinction:

> Poetry and history are no longer one. Art and nature were divorced from each other, fiction ceased to have the power of truth, and the boundaries of the imagination did not, as of old, overpower the mind with religious awe and dread. Reason and philosophy gradually distinguished from each other the worlds of faith and imagination before so intimately blended, and as our sober ancestors turned all their poetry into religion, so we are in danger of turning all our religion into poetry.[224]

Marsh's use of *poetry* reflects the German understanding whereby *all* imaginative literature – that which is distanced from the claims of history – is considered poetry. But without historical grounding, what is the nature and form of truth? The attempt to respond to this question took on aesthetically differing forms in the beginning of the nineteenth century between Germany and England. Hans Frei in *The Eclipse of Biblical Narrative* notes that:

> In England, where a serious body of realistic narrative literature and a certain amount of criticism of the literature was building up, there arose no corresponding cumulative tradition of criticism of the biblical writings, and that included no narrative interpretation of them. In Germany, on the other hand, where a body of critical analysis as well as general hermeneutics of the biblical writings build up rapidly in the later half of the eighteenth-century, there was no simultaneous development of realistic prose and its critical appraisal.[225]

In reflecting upon Goethe's *Wilhelm Meister,* Friedrich Schlegel describes his work as being "all poetry – high, pure poetry. Everything has been thought and uttered as though by one who is both a divine poet and a perfect artist…"[226] This comment is not merely a reflection on Goethe's vocation of a writer of prose *and* poetry, but rather Schlegel's

---

224 James Marsh, 'Ancient and Modern Poetry', *North American Review* XV, vol. vi (1822) no. 1, pp. 130-31. Cited by Stephen Prickett, op. cit..

225 Hans Frei, *The Eclipse of Biblical Narrative* (New Haven: Yale University Press, 1974) p. 155.

226 Kathleen Wheeler, ed., *German Aesthetic and Literary Criticism: The Romantic Ironists and Goethe* (Cambridge: Cambridge University Press, 1984) p. 64.

theory of the novel that did not set apart genres from each other and believed in

> a theory of the novel which could be a theory in the original sense of the word; a spiritual viewing of the subject with calm and serene feeling, as it is proper to view in solemn joy the meaningful play of divine images. Such a theory of the novel would have to be in itself a novel which would reflect imaginatively every tone of the imagination and would again confound the chaos of the world...[227]

This re-reading of scripture alongside other texts left the reading subject of the eighteenth and nineteenth century in a world that was destabilised of its former foundational claims of selfhood found in the historicity of texts. The reading subject now exists in a world that forged Hölderlin's *Empedokles* or Goethe's *Wilhelm Meister* where readers must construct the foundational truth that is to be found within this literary space as well as construct their own subjective identity. Where the form of the subject after Augustine provided a clear exemplar of the form of God, now the shift to the ultimate subjectivity of self-as-self after the Enlightenment left the notion of "form" to be figured without a god as key image.

[227] Kathleen Wheeler, ibid., p. 64.

# Chapter 5

# Victorian Poetics and (Re)Writing Jesus

In nineteenth century Britain, the space of literature reached particular dynamism in William Wordsworth's *The Prelude.*[228] Throughout *The Prelude*, Wordsworth seeks to reconcile a sense of selfhood in relation to the *res cogitans* and *res extensa*:

> I looked for universal things; perused
> The common countenance of earth and sky:
> Earth, nowhere unembellished by some trace
> Of that first Paradise whence man was driven;
> And sky, whose beauty and bounty are expressed
> By the proud name she bears – the name of Heaven.
> I called on both to teach me what they might;
> Or turning the mind in upon herself
> Pored, watched, expected, listened, spread my thoughts,
> And spread them with a wider creeping; felt
> Incumbencies more awful, visitings
> Of the Upholder of the tranquil soul,
> That tolerates the indignities of Time,
> And, from the centre of Eternity
> All finite motions overruling, lives
> In glory immutable.[229]

Wordsworth is searching the expanse of earth and heaven with a "mind turned in upon itself" to find a sense of identity and, ultimately, his calling. It is in Book XI of *The Prelude* that Wordsworth sees that *the*

[228] I will be keeping my remarks to the 1850 edition of Prelude which had a much larger reading than the 1805 edition.

[229] William Wordsworth, *The Prelude – The Four Texts 1798, 1799, 1805, 1850* ed. John Wordsworth (London: Penguin Classics, 1995) Book III, lines 109-124, p. 109.

*search itself* is ultimately his vocation – "She, in the midst of all, preserved me still/ A Poet, made me seek beneath that name,/ And that alone, my office upon earth;/ And, lastly, as hereafter will be shown".[230] The traditional office of poet is too limiting for his task and he is seeking "beneath that name" and aligning himself with "Poets, even as prophets, each with each/ Connected in a mighty scheme of truth,/ Have each for his peculiar faculty,/ Heaven's gift, a sense that fits him to perceive/ Objects unseen before".[231] His task is that of a creator of that which he has been given

> ... clear sight
> Of a new world – a world, too, that was fit
> To be transmitted and to other eyes
> Made visible; as ruled by those fixed laws
> Whence spiritual dignity originates,
> Which do both gives it being and maintain
> A balance, an ennobling interchange
> Of action from without and from within;
> The excellence, pure function, and best power
> Both of the object seen, and eye that sees.[232]

This universe of "the object seen and the eye that sees" is for Wordsworth where:

> All that breathes and is, was chastened, stemmed
> And balanced by pathetic truth, by trust
> In hopeful reason, leaning on the stay
> Of Providence; and in reverence for duty,
> Here, if need be, struggling with storms, and there
> Strewing in peace life's humblest ground with herbs,
> At every season green, sweet at all hours.[233]

The unifying force of reason "in her most exalted mood" (XIV, 192) is the imagination of the poet. It is this "reason which indeed is reason"

---

230 ibid., Book XI, lines 346-349, p. 455.
231 ibid., Book XIII, lines 301-304, p. 505.
232 ibid., Book XIII, lines 369-378, p. 509.
233 ibid., Book XIV, lines 295-301, p. 527.

that balances the world *res cogitans* and *res extensa.* God only *animates* this world – the *framing* of this world is in the hand of the writer. In Book XIII Wordsworth reflects to the reader that this journey has been brought to a close within the space of *The Prelude* itself which tells the tale:

> And now, O Friend! this history is brought
> To its appointed close: the discipline
> And consummation of a Poet's mind,
> In everything that stood most prominent,
> Have faithfully been pictured; we have reached
> The time (which was our object from the first)
> When we may, not presumptuously, I hope,
> Suppose my powers so far confirmed, and such
> My knowledge as to make me capable
> Of building up a Work that shall endure.[234]

As noted by M.H. Abrams, *The Prelude* is "an involuted poem which is about its own genesis – a prelude to itself. Its structural end is its own beginning; and its temporal beginning… is Wordsworth's entrance upon the stage of his life at which it ends… [he] converts the wayfaring Christian of the Augustinian spiritual journey into the self-formative traveller of the Romantic educational journey".[235] *The Prelude* represents a self-forming universe where the context within which the writer is known (the fictive realm) is also that which he creates. Ultimately, Wordsworth's journey in *The Prelude* is a journey of discovery. This is a discovery of self in the act of creating itself – a reflectivity of the writer as the framer of subjectivity and context where subjectivity resides. It is a universe that is framed and "history brought to its appointed close". This universe is controlled by the creating writer as a sanctuary for his vision – a place where "a work that shall endure" can be maintained. *The Prelude* begins by seeking throughout the lived world for meaning and ends with a framing of the never-ending search itself. This was an epistemological shift that was nothing short of a revolution. As put succinctly by Earl Wasserman:

---

[234] ibid., Book XIV, lines 302-311, p. 527.

[235] M.H. Abrams, "The Design of The Prelude", *Norton Critical Edition of William Wordsworth's The Prelude* ed. John Wordsworth (London: W.W. Norton, 1979) p. 591.

> Until the end of the eighteenth century there was sufficient intellectual homogeneity for men to share certain assumptions... In varying degrees... man accepted...the Christian interpretation of history, the sacramentalism of nature, the Great Chain of Being, the analogy of the various planes of creation, the conception of man as microcosm... These were cosmic syntaxes in the public domain; and the poet could afford to think of his art as imitative of "nature" since these patterns were what he meant by "nature".
>
> By the nineteenth century these world-pictures had passed from consciousness... The change from a *mimetic* to a creative [*poiesis*] conception of poetry is not merely a critical or philosophic phenomenon;... Now,... an additional formulative act was required of the poet [artist]... Within itself the modern poem must both formulate its own cosmic syntax and shape the autonomous poetic reality that the cosmic syntax permits: "nature", which was once prior to the poem and available for imitation, now shares with the poem a common origin in the poet's creativity.[236]

## Figuring Jesus in the Victorian Novel

> We are told that God has spoken. *Where? In a book?* We have tried it and it *disappoints*; it disappoints, that most holy and blessed gift, not from fault of its own, but because it is used for a purpose for which it was not given.[237] (emphasis added)

After Wordsworth, the increasing rise in popularity of the novel in the 1800's can be viewed in light of Newman's query ("Where? In a book?") as to where subjective meaning may be located. Paradoxically, with the challenging claims levelled against scripture through Higher Criticism and brought into line with all *Weltliteratur*, the novel, interestingly enough, became a mirror of the nineteenth century subject's search for meaning in vulgar discourse. In many ways the novel became the inheritor of sorts to scripture's role in the making of

---

236 Earl Wasserman, *The Subtler Language* (Baltimore: Johns Hopkins University Press, 1968) pp. 10-11.

237 John Henry Newman, *An Essay on the Development of Christian Doctrine*, 1845 (London: Penguin, 1974) p. 175.

meaning. The novel, as noted by French critic Gustave Kahn, "is perhaps more like the *conte philosophique* than like the romance, in that it records a similar process of disillusionment; but while philosophical tales cast such disillusionment in ideological terms, novels treat it experientially, in the terms of quotidian reality".[238] Schoder notes that "the novel would then seem to be an essentially ironic fictional form, occupying a middle position between the non-ironic romance and the philosophical tale, which is ironic, but in ways often different from those of the novel... This irony [of the novel] falls under the heading of *tropes*, figures of speech; but the irony of the novel is rather a figure of thought, in the broadest sense".[239]

The ironic nature of the Victorian novel can indeed be seen in its very form.[240] First, the world of the novel is made of words in the historical realm that open imaginative dimensions in the fictive realm and are at once unreal and imaginary. There are no physical objects, no real people in any novel in relation to historical space and time. Even an autobiographical account is not the "actual" account of a life and is therefore fictive to some extent. Yet, the novel speaks as though it represents reality in opposition to the context of the reading subject. In a letter to Louise Colet dated 1853, Gustave Flaubert makes the following assertion:

> The day before yesterday, in the woods of Le Touquet, in a charming spot beside a spring, I found old cigar butts and scraps of *paté*. People had been picnicking. I described such a scene in *Novembre*, eleven years ago; it was entirely imagined, and the other day it came true. Everything one invents is true, you may be sure. Poetry is as precise as geometry. Induction is as accurate as deduction; and besides, after reaching a certain point one no longer makes any mistake about the things of the soul. My poor Bovary, without a doubt, is suffering and weeping at this very instant in twenty villages of France.[241]

Stendhal makes the following assertion of the novel's claim of reality in *The Red and the Black*:

---

[238] Cited by Maurice Z. Schoder, "The Novel as a Genre", *The Theory of the Novel* ed. Philip Stevick (London: Collins-Macmillan, 1967) p. 16.
[239] Schoder, ibid., pp. 20, 22.
[240] See Ian Watt's *The Rise of the Novel* and J. Hillis Miller's *The Form of Victorian Fiction.*
[241] Gustave Flaubert, "Letter to Louise Colet, 1853" in *The Victorian Novel: Modern Essays in Criticism* ed. Ian Watt (London: Oxford University Press, 1971), p. 390.

> A novel is a mirror carried along a high road. At one moment it reflects the blue skies, at another the mud of the puddles at your feet. The man who carries this mirror in his pack you will accuse of being immortal! Blame instead that high road upon which the puddle lies, or even more the inspector of roads who allows the water to gather and the puddle to form.[242]

There is an ironic turn in the supposed realism that characterises these nineteenth century comments on writing: there is truth in fiction and what is real is seemingly removed and to be recovered through the act of writing. As noted by Michael Riffaterre, "fiction establishes its truth status by the way language turns back upon itself, tautologically, to accomplish the expectations it sets up".[243] This "fictional truth" is for Riffaterre "a means of joining history, theory, and language to describe the principle of abstract conjecturality as a ground for representing the world…it is less the factuality of the event that matters… than its ability to stimulate reflection *on the represented event*, the event as text… which marks both the connectedness to the world and opacity of that link - its mystery".[244]

This "mystery" is played out at the lowest common denominator of the novel's form and structure - words. Words of/within a novel act as structure for related minds that form interpersonal relations. Yet these networks of relationships are synthetic, a condition understood by the reading subject, while at the same time established as self-evidenced authenticity by the text. Additionally, a pattern of related minds exists in the novel's form and structure as a temporal rhythm - beings exist in time whether fictive or historical. As noted by Paul Ricoeur in *Time and Narrative*, fictive time and historical time exist as "counterpoints" to one another, each acknowledging and simultaneously denying the existence of the other

---

242 Stendhal, "*The Red and the Black*, 1830, Volume II, Chapter 49" in *The Victorian Novel*, p. 389.

243 Michael Riffaterre, *Fictional Truth* (London: John Hopkins University Press, 1990) p. viii

244 ibid., pp. viii-ix.

with the idea of "fictionality" casting a poetic shadow upon reality's sole claim to temporality:

> Unreal characters, we might say, have an unreal experience of time. Unreal, in the sense that the temporal marks of this experience do not have to be connected to the single spatial-temporal network constitutive of chronological time... In this sense, from the epic to the novel, by way of tragedy and the ancient and modern forms of comedy, the time of fictional narrative has been freed from the constraints requiring it to be referred back to the time of the universe... Each fictive temporal experience unfolds its world, and each of these worlds is singular, incomparable, unique.[245]

In addition to this 'unreal reality' of time in fiction, there is also the real probability offered in this space that makes claims beyond that of recorded history. Additionally, M.H. Abrams notes that for Aristotle in his *Poetics*, the writer does not describe "the thing that has happened, but *a kind of thing that might happen*... Hence poetry [art] is something more philosophic and of graver import than history, since its statements are of the nature rather of universals, whereas those of history are singulars."[246]

These three questions - the question of realism, the question of intersubjectivity, and the question of time, function as **ironic turns** that fracture the reading subject's ability to find "certainty" in the text by opening gaps or *destabilised spaces* within the poetics. To close these gaps into dialectic certainty was no longer an option with the challenges brought to bear by Higher Criticism and the revisioning of the role of the text in relation to the construction of the subject. As Wordsworth and those who followed his lead found in their developing poetics as British writers in the eighteenth and nineteenth century, meaning was to be found in the opening of destabilised spaces or "gaps" within the text,[247] not in their closing off or, to use Luce Irigarary's term,

---

[245] Paul Ricoeur, *Time and Narrative*, Vol. 3 (Chicago: University of Chicago Press, 1988) p. 128.

[246] Cited by M. H. Abrams, *The Mirror and the Lamp* (Oxford: Oxford University Press, 1953) p. 36.

[247] Jacques Lacan uses the term *béance* (gap) to figure "the relation of the subject to the Other [which is] entirely produced in a process of gap". For Lacan, the subject is constituted and defined by a "gap" which leaves the subject divided or "split". See Jacques Lacan, *The Seminar. Book XI: The Four Fundamental Concepts of Psychoanalysis*. Trans. Alan Sheridan (London: Hogarth Press, 1977) p. 206.

"suturing". These unsutured spaces or "wounds" resist resolution and draw the reading subject into the position of reconciler through 'touching the wound' more than closing it. It is in this honest penetration into such wounded poetics where readers become the bridge between the claims made by the fictive world and the world within which they as reading subjects "live, move, and have their being". As I discuss in more depth in the concluding chapter, such poetics shows a christological quest that is ultimately a/christological by attempting to move beyond language tautologically and toward a poetics of Jesus that is the authentic presencing of subject and the sacred within one space and time.[248]

The prospect of the text being open and unsutured to the touch was as terrifying to writers of the period as much as it was a revelation. Alfred Lord Tennyson, in his poem *In Memoriam*, portrays what Lance Butler calls "the face of a seemingly abandoned universe".[249] The role of doubt is a key theme within Victorian literature for those who faced the shift in poetics as a rupturing of meaning rather than a portal to new possibilities:

> Behold, we know not anything;
> I can but trust that good shall fall
> At last – far off – at last, to all,
> And every winter change to spring.
>
> So runs my dream: but what am I?
> An infant crying in the night:
> An infant crying for the light:

---

[248] As I will discuss in more depth in the conclusion, I see this form of poetics as exemplified in George Eliot's early writing as she attempts to find the meeting of the subject and the sacred through the space of literature. An example of this form is figured in the Gospel of St. John in the post-Easter encounter of Thomas and the risen Christ – "A week later his disciples were again in the house, and Thomas was with them. Although the doors were shut, Jesus came and stood among them and said, "Peace be with you". Then he said to Thomas, "Put your finger here and see my hands. Reach out your hand and put it in my side. Do not doubt but believe". Thomas answered him, "My Lord and My God!" John 20: 26-28 NRSV. This will be expanded in my conclusion.

[249] Lance St. John Butler, *Victorian Doubt: Literary and Cultural Discourses* (London: Simon and Schuster, 1990) p. 9.

And with no language but a cry...

I falter where I firmly trod,
And falling with my weight of cares
Upon the great world's altar-stairs
That slope through darkness up to God,

I stretch lame hands of faith, and grope,
And gather dust and chaff, and call
To what I feel is Lord of all,
And faintly trust the larger hope.[250]

The question in the first line of the second stanza cited from *In Memoriam* found in lyric 54 succinctly frames the state that Victorian fiction found itself: "So runs my dream: but what am I?" As noted by J. Hillis Miller, "the development of Victorian fiction is a movement from the assumption that society and the self are founded on some super-human power outside them, to a putting in question of the assumption, to the discovery that society now appears to be self-creating and self-supporting, resting on nothing outside itself".[251] The waking from the "dream" that Tennyson speaks of is the horrific reality that, to paraphrase Shakespeare, all the world's a fiction and we are merely its writers. Isobel Armstrong states that "there is a fundamental anxiety in *In Memoriam* about the dissolution of language altogether. The breakdown of language is collateral with the obliteration of the regulative 'Type' in the external world".[252] Words themselves, shattered seemingly beyond repair in the wake of Higher Criticism, had left the reading subject in a world "with no language but a cry" and to "falter where I firmly trod". The very hands that once grasped after faith are now "lame" and groping, but only find "dust and chaff".

Speaking from his orthodox foundation in *Apologia Pro Vita Sua* of 1864, John Henry Newman categorises this "lame groping" of the Victorian age:

---

[250] Alfred Lord Tennyson, "In Memoriam – 1849", in *Norton Anthology of English Literature 6th edition.* M.H. Abrams, ed. (London: Norton, 1993) lyric 54, lines 13-20; lyric 55, lines 13-20 p. 1104.

[251] J. Hillis Miller, *The Form of Victorian Fiction* (London: University of Notre Dame Press, 1968) p. 30.

[252] Isobel Armstrong, *Language as Living Form in Nineteenth Century Poetry* (Sussex: Harvester Press, 1982) p. 173.

> To consider the world in its length and breath, its various history, the many races of man, their starts, their fortunes, their mutual alienation, their conflicts; their aimless courses, their random achievements, and acquirements, the impotent conclusion of long-standing facts, the tokens so faint and broken, of a superintending design, the blind evolution of what turn out to be great powers or truths, the progress of things as if from unreasoning elements, not toward final causes, the greatness and littleness of man, his far-reaching aims, his short duration, the curtain over his futurity, the disappointments of life, the defeat of good, the success of evil, physical pain, mental anguish, the prevalence and intensity of sin, the pervading idolatries, the corruptions, the dreary hopeless irreligion, that condition of the whole race, so fearfully yet exactly described in the Apostle's words, "having no hope and without God in the world", - all this is a vision to dizzy and appal; and inflicts upon the mind the sense of a profound mystery, which is absolutely beyond human solution.[253]

Newman himself acknowledges that the foundation for "making meaning" that was previously located in the Bible is gone and leaves an age "having no hope and without God in the world". As noted earlier, Newman frames the key question in this regard in *An Essay on the Development of Christian Doctrine*, "We are told that God has spoken. *Where? In a book?* We have tried it and it *disappoints*; it disappoints, that most holy and blessed gift, not from fault of its own, but because it is used for a purpose for which it was not given".[254] (emphasis added)

While Newman's concern that the Bible "disappoints" because it is used "for a purpose for which it was not given", the fundamental query remains: what *is* the Bible to be used for then? What has been left for it to do if it is stripped of its sacredness and must stand alongside all other *Weltliteratur*? In the nineteenth century, one response to this question is seen in the proliferation of fictional accounts of Jesus – Incarnation as derivative genre that is to exist only in and through the act of (re)writing. Here one recalls Derrida's statement with regard to Hegel as one who announced that

[253] John Henry Newman, *Apologia Pro Vita Sua*, 1864 (London: Fount Press, 1977) p. 278.

[254] John Henry Newman, *An Essay on the Development of Christian Doctrine*, 1845 (London: Penguin, 1974) p. 175.

> the horizon of absolute knowledge is the effacement of writing in the *logos*, the retrieval of the trace in *parousia*, the reappropriation of difference, the accomplishment of what I have elsewhere called the metaphysics of the proper. Yet all that Hegel thought... may be reread as a meditation on writing. Hegel is also the thinker of irreducible difference... the last philosopher of the book and the first thinker of writing.[255]

The actualisation of Derrida's claim with regard to the "end of the book and the beginning of writing" can be seen in the Victorian attempts to (re)write Jesus within the space of the novel at the time that George Eliot was beginning her fictional output.

Attempts to figure Jesus within the Victorian novel are numerous. Examples of poetic forms attempted in the Victorian period include these by contemporaries of George Eliot – J.A. Froude's *The Nemesis of Faith* (1849), Walter Pater's *Marius the Epicurean* (1885), and Mrs. Humphrey Ward's *Robert Elsmere* (1888). Each exemplifies differing approaches attempting the same goal within the nineteenth century – to frame a poetics that evokes (to cite *Marius the Epicurean*) that "one only way which leads to a true philosophy"[256] which the Bible once claimed to be. Each contributes a significant attempt to reach this end. *The Nemesis of Faith* situates the 'condition of things' in the form of fictional epistolary correspondence, thus conferring upon the crisis of Victorian 'doubt' a news-worthy quality. *Marius* is striving to re-stabilise the Christian faith as pure aesthetic source from which to draw upon merely for art's sake. *Robert Elsmere* re-imagines Jesus as a reluctant clergyman who, in the words of Anthony Trollope, has a "heart that still loves the old teachings which the mind will no longer accept".[257] Each is a representative attempt to fix a static concept of Jesus – an incarnational poetics – within the fictional space. In contrast, I will argue that George Eliot offers a different conception of such a poetics of Jesus – one that is not formed, fixed, nor exposed, but is constantly

---

[255] Jacques Derrida, *Of Grammatology*, trans. G.C. Spivak (Baltimore: Johns Hopkins University Press, 1976) p. 26. Also cited in Mark C. Taylor, *Deconstruction in Context*, op. cit., p. 2.

[256] Walter Pater, *Marius the Epicurean* 1885 (London: Penguin Classics, 1985) p. 256.

[257] Anthony Trollope, *The Clergyman who subscribes for Colenso*, from *The Clergymen of the Church of England* (Leicester: Leicester University Press, 1974) p. 128.

forming, transient, and strangely veiled within the poetic space.[258]

## J.A. Froude – *The Nemesis of Faith*

In J.A. Froude's *The Nemesis of Faith* (1849), the absence of faith in Jesus takes on a confessional quality as the novel protrays the failed cleric Markham Sutherland through letters and journal entries in a manner similar in poetics to Goethe's *Sorrows of Young Werther*. More than a life, this is to be a "history of Markham Sutherland" which is "painted" for the reader to see as well as to read.[259] As Froude writes in his Preface,

> The moral of human life is never simple, and the moral of a story which aims only at being true to human life cannot be expected to be any more so. I do not think this book would have seemed so obscure as it seemed, if it had not been overly readily assumed that religious fiction must be didactic. Religion of late years has been so much a matter of word controversy, it has suffered so complete a divorce from life, that life is the last place in which we look for it.[260]

Froude begins his novel by asserting that this is a "history" and yet goes on to speak of a "life". This is indicative of the tension arising from the publications of Strauss' *Das Leben Jesu* as well as Ernst Renan's *Vie de Jésus* published in 1863. As mentioned previously in chapter 4, Biblical Higher Criticism, in keeping with Hegel's project, challenged the exclusive borders surrounding the person of Jesus as a figure outside the realm of inquiry and placed him alongside all figures whose being is grounded within a poetics. "History" no longer had a privileged place in such discussions. Yet the form that was to replace "history" was often wanting in the rendering of a "life of Jesus". As stated by Ernst Renan in his critique of Strauss' rendering of Jesus in *Das Leben Jesu*:

---

[258] Delimiting texts which represent this period of literary output is extremely difficult. As noted, I will use these as representative, not exhaustive, of various poetic attempts to capture the issues surrounding Victorian "doubt" and the figuring of Jesus within fiction.

[259] J.A. Froude, *The Nemesis of Faith* (London: George Woodfall and Son, 1849) p. v.

[260] ibid., p. iii.

> The criticism of the details of the Gospel texts especially… done by Strauss [in] a manner which leaves little to be desired. … Strauss may be mistaken in his theory of the compilation of the Gospels; … his book has, in my opinion, the fault of taking up the theological ground too much, the historical ground too little…[261]

In order to speak of, let alone 'conceive' (to use Mrs. Humphrey Ward's term) of Jesus, the use of "Life" became synonymous with "History" as a means of escaping the rupture of History as a stable ground of being. As I have noted, this shift was an opening akin to Hölderlin's *Empedokles* where an opening rather than a closure was created regarding the ability of poetics to form Jesus. This "tumbling of terms" in the use of "history" and "life" where one is synonymous yet veils the other is evidenced in Eliza Lynn Linton's novel *The True History of Joshua Davidson, Communist*, one of the novels written during the later nineteenth century as a fictional life of Jesus in "modern facing".[262] Joshua Davidson is the son of a carpenter whose very name bears obvious resemblance to the Biblical Jesus – "Joshua David's son". As the story unfolds, Joshua comes to realise his 'calling' and sees the hope of humanity framed in a contemporary re-framing of Marxist philosophy. The notion of Jesus as a Communist stirred enough of a reaction to see the title later changed to *The Life of Joshua Davidson; or the Modern Imitation of Christ: A Theoretical Novel.* Now the character is more closely aligned with the Jesus of Thomas à Kempis as opposed to Karl Marx and this tale is a possible "life" rather than a "true history".[263]

This interchange of meaning between what was "True History" as opposed to a "Life" within the space of fiction is one of the concerns addressed in Froude's *The Nemesis of Faith.* From the start, Froude acknowledges that the fundamental problem with regard to religion and religious writing is that it "must be didactic". He goes on to state that his hope for *The Nemesis of Faith* was to show "a human soul [that] was suffering and struggling", not a history that is removed from such things, but a human soul readers felt was "making a direct statement of [his] own opinions". As he states,

[261] Ernest Renan, *The Life of Jesus*, 1863 (Amherst: Prometheus Books, 1991) p. 3.

[262] Eliza Lynn Linton, *The True History of Joshua Davidson* (London, 1872).

[263] See also "Weltliteratur and the Bible Critics" in David Jasper, *The Sacred and Secular Canon in Romanticism* and Rosa Luxemburg, *Socialism and the Churches* (1905).

> I wrote a Tragedy; I have been supposed to have written a Confession of Faith; and in the shifting and changing, the vacillation, uncertainty, and self-contradiction of an honest mind, in which the energy of character is disproportionate to the intellect, men have only seen either that I did not understand myself, or that I was afraid of my own conclusions, or that I wished to avoid the responsibility of maintaining them.[264]

Froude comes to this semi-autobiographical project in 1849 as one of the "foremost historians of the nineteenth century".[265] As a great admirer of Carlyle, he shared with Carlyle a notion of a "rightness" that permeated all things, or as A.N. Wilson states, "a moral fittingness in historical events".[266] But Christianity, as it was shown to Froude through the institutionalisation of the Church in the nineteenth century, did not disclose this fundamental belief. Quite the contrary. As is indicated throughout *The Nemesis of Faith*, Froude was greatly disheartened by the lack of intellectual integrity and the "sheer silliness" exhibited by the great Victorian champions of the faith. As a student of John Henry Newman while at Oriel College Oxford, Froude became disillusioned with the lengths to which Newman sought to protect Christianity from reason:

> Newman talked much to us of the surrender of reason. Reason, first of every thing, must be swept away, so daily more and more unreasonable appeared to modern eyes so many of the doctrines to which the Church was committed. As I began to look into what he said about it, the more difficult it seemed to me. What did it mean? Reason could only be surrendered by an act of reason. Even the Church's infallible judgements could only be received through the senses, and apprehended by reason; why, if reason was a false guide, should we trust one act of it more than another?[267]

In his *Short Stories on Great Subjects*, Froude recounts an occasion when he heard Newman preach in the University Church at Oxford in the

---

[264] J.A. Froude, *The Nemesis of Faith*, p. iv.
[265] A. N. Wilson, *God's Funeral* (London: Abacus Press, 1999) p. 127.
[266] ibid.
[267] J.A. Froude, op. cit., p. 157.

1830s. The subject of Newman's sermon was the Passion of Christ and, according to Froude, was delivered in a manner that was "calm and passionless as marble" with regard to the torture of the Cross and the agony of Golgotha. As Froude notes, no one listening could discount the emotional impact of the sermon:

> For a few moments there was a breathless silence. Then, in a low, clear voice, of which the faintest vibration was audible in the farthest corner of St. Mary's, he said, "Now I bid you recollect that He to whom these things were done was Almighty God". It was as if an electric shock had gone through the church, as if every person present understood for the first time the meaning of what he had all his life been saying.[268]

In many ways, this summation of Newman's sermon is the heart of the concern for Newman's alter ego Markham Sutherland in *The Nemesis of Faith*. As Sutherland chronicles his discomfort and eventual near-death at the hands of doubt, the reader is led, with the protagonist, on a search for such an "electric shock of meaning" that will prove convicting not only of heart, but also of reason. This "shock" we all seek after, according to the narrator in *The Nemesis of Faith,* is God: "We seek for God, and we are sent to find Him in the words and thoughts of other nations and other ages about Him – which are no longer His glorious garment, but a curtain which conceals Him".[269] Yet like Froude himself, the narrator of *The Nemesis of Faith* asserts that the present age is an age of existential facts – and only "facts" will satisfy the need of those who seek:

> Times are changed. This age is an age of fact – it believes only in experience – it is jealous and inquiring. It has rejected all these preternatural stories, and now clings only to the Bible. It halts here, for it is afraid of its conclusions. …And men feel this, and yet they dare not act upon it. *They cling to the old form, although God has abolished that form by withdrawing from their minds the power of profiting by it.* He has given them a new covenant into which they will not enter, and therefore religion is dead.[270]

---

[268] J.A. Froude, *Short Stories on Great Subjects.* (London: Longmans, Green & Co., 1894) iv, p. 286.
[269] J.A. Froude, *The Nemesis of Faith.*, ibid., pp. ix, x.
[270] ibid., p. xi.

The clearest manifestation of this "old form" that the narrator speaks of is found in the Church and its desire to ignore "the one great Bible which cannot lie" which is "the history of the human race" which tells us, if we are to read it well, that

> when in any nation religion is left corrupting in the form in which it is now with ourselves, that nation is near its end. The very same symptoms meet us steadily in the decline of every great people – an old faith, withered in its shell, yet which is preserved in false show of reverence, either from cowardice, or indolence, or miserable social convenience.[271]

Sutherland's crisis of subjectivity comes about in his realisation that as a cleric, he is a "man of a particular sort" who sees the end of the old "form", but is "unfortunately, something not more but less than men – men who have sacrificed their own selves to become the paid instruments of a system".[272] The borders of the "form" he acknowledges as dying are what he himself is formed by. We all, states Sutherland, must come to realise that our subjectivity is self-generating in that we "cannot dream [ourselves] into a character; [we] must hammer and forge"[273] our identities as a will to being. As the foundation of orthodox Christianity begins to crumble amidst challenges of the nineteenth century in Higher Criticism and the emerging claims of scientific inquiry, the place of the subject seems to be without a context within which and upon which to reside. The exclusive place the Bible held which placed it above inquiry had been removed. Once the question is raised, akin to pulling a thread on a jumper, the unravelling seems unending:

> But why do they believe it [the Bible] at all? They must say "because it is in the Bible". Yes, here it is. Other books we may sit in judgement upon, but not upon the Bible. That is the exception, the one book which is wholly and entirely true. And we are to believe whatever is there, no matter how monstrous, on the authority of God. He has told us, and that is enough. But how do they know He has told us? The

[271] ibid., p. xii.
[272] ibid., p. 3.
[273] ibid., p. 4.

> Church says so. Why does the Church say so? Because the Jews said so. And how do we know the Jews could not be mistaken? Because they said they were God's people, and God guided them.[274]

What the subject is left with is a never-ending series of questions after authority where each level of investiture is only provided by another questionable source, each question peels back another layer that will peel back upon inquiry like a proverbial onion that when peeled layer by layer will eventually render nothing but tears. As Sutherland later concludes, noting what would be described today as a hermeneutic circle, all (the subject) is left with is a whirlwind where "the Church proves the Bible, and the Bible proves the Church – cloudy pillars rotating upon air – round and round the theory goes, whirling like the summer wind-gusts"[275] akin to the ever-turning, widening gyre of W.B. Yeats' "Second Coming".

At times, Sutherland attempts to articulate his insecure place amidst this search for his own character in the dying of nineteenth century Christianity, but language itself seems to fail, degenerating into a stuttering call to being that becomes a fading echo waiting for a response. Without the "walls" of faith provided by the Bible, individuals such as Markham Sutherland no longer possess the "structure" to refract their calling out after their own subjectivity. As Markham states :

> I know, too, there are some excellent, oh, most excellent people, deep and serious people, who do not find the difficulties there at all which I find, and accept it all with awe and fear, perhaps, but still with a real, serious conviction that it is all true. Perhaps it is. And then I… I… am… am…[276]

But where does humanity turn when history, the "one great Bible" left to us after all other sources (such as religious faith, tradition, dogma), is exhausted? As suggested by Markham Sutherland in Letter 1 of *The Nemesis of Faith*, we are left only with ourselves and the ability to write:

> *I have nothing but myself to write about*, no facts, no theories, no opinions, no adventures, no sentiments, nothing but my own poor barren

[274] ibid., pp. 20, 21.
[275] ibid., p. 27.
[276] ibid., p. 14.

> individualism, of considerable interest to me, but I do not know why I should presume it will be so for you.[277]

This act of writing is realised as a dangerous one given that the act itself is an act of madness:

> Suppose I was to write a book, Arthur, and say I was inspired to write it – *a madhouse would be the best place for me*, because common sense would at once pass sentence on the pretension, and, if it did not, the poor book would be its own sentence.[278]

Yet without *the* book, Markham realises that we are still left with "writing" or in a more general sense, the *poiesis* that manifests itself as a poetics.

It is with this realisation that Sutherland merely retreats as *The Nemesis of Faith* continues. While he acknowledges to Arthur that "I can do nothing but write to you",[279] he turns away from true writing – *writing as poiesis* – to merely critique and review. He is locked into a spiral where all that he can do through his writing is reframe what has been. The possibility of a new world is silent. As Sutherland compares the lack of mythological resources that have given form to the great works of the past and the silence of the church, he is caught between the clashing of the Scylla of the possible and Charybdis of a dead past and is unwilling to move: "There are no faeries and no ghosts there any more; only the church bells and the church music have anything of the old tones, and they are silent, too, except at rare, mournful, gusty intervals".[280] Caught within this space, Sutherland sees not an opening but a desert where nothing is taking root and all is passing away:

> Yet is not that, too, all passing away, away beyond recall? The old monks are dead. The hermit-saints and hallowed relics are dust and ashes now. The faeries dance no more around the charmed forest ring. They are gone, gone even here. The creed still seems to stand; but the creed is dead in the thoughts of mankind. *Its roots are cut away, down*

---

[277] ibid., p. 2.
[278] ibid., p. 26.
[279] ibid., p. 29.
[280] ibid., p. 28.

> *where alone it can gather strength for life*... the aged faith of aged centuries will be exiled as the old was to the simple inhabitants of these simple places.[281]

Sutherland sees himself as a statue, akin to those venerated out of habit in worship, that is merely a symbol of stone unable to respond:

> The statues were sanctified and made the images of saints, the augur's colleges were rudely violated, and they who were still faithful were offered up as martyrs, or scattered as wanderers over the face of the earth, and the old gods were expelled from the old dominion – the divinity of nature before the divinity of man... Change is strong, but habit is strong, too; and you cannot change the old for new, like a garment.[282]

Sutherland does acknowledge that there are questions that need to be addressed, "garments" that need changing – but no writer, himself included, is willing to risk such a task. As he states in Letter V: "Books nauseate me; I seem to have learnt all that I can learn from books, or else to have lost the power of learning anything from them; and of all these modern writers there is not one who will come boldly up and meet the question which lies the nearest, or ought to lie the nearest, to our heart".[283] While he goes on to say that Carlyle is willing to "raise questions he cannot answer", Sutherland finds even his example "very helpless, I know it is; but there is no mending it, it must be. I wait for guidance, and my soul must have it, if I give it time".[284]

What Froude sees in *The Nemesis of Faith* is that "Life is change, to cease to change is to cease to live... let not your heart be silent on the dissolving of a faith".[285] Sutherland is trapped in a poetic spiral where he acknowledges the need to give voice to "the question which lies nearest... to our hearts", yet does not do so. The critique is reframed in numerous ways for the "lack" that is nineteenth century Christendom yet no alternative is offered, no re-imagining of a possibility. This ultimately results in an embrace of futility and a resignation to despair. He acknowledges that it is only in *poiesis* that he

281 ibid., p. 33.
282 ibid., p. 31.
283 ibid., p. 35.
284 ibid., p. 36.
285 ibid., p. 34.

can approach that which he hungers for, yet cannot make a "real living link" with that which will transform his critique into something beyond remarks:

> Oh! how I wish I could write. I try sometimes; for I seem to feel myself overflowing with thoughts, and I cry out to be relieved of them. But it is so stiff and miserable when I get anything done. What seemed so clear and liquid, comes out so thick, stupid, and frost-bitten, that I myself, who put the idea there, can hardly find it for shame, if I go look for it a few days after... to form a link, however humble, a real living link, in the electric chain which conducts the light of the ages! Oh! how my heart burns at the very hope.[286]

Christianity itself was fuelled by this 'real living link' according to Froude and it is the severing of this link that is at the heart of much of doubt. "When Christianity was first published", notes Sutherland in Letter X of *The Nemesis of Faith*, "the *imagination* of mankind presented the relation of heaven to earth very differently from what it does now".[287]

Where *The Nemesis of Faith* ultimately fails is in its unwillingness to move beyond this critique – acknowledgement of the problem and the reluctance to put forward an alternative. It is the unwillingness to "write" beyond this place and *into* a new "writing" that is also the undoing of Markham Sutherland in his illicit relationship with Helen Leonard. Mrs. Leonard attempts to break off the relationship she knows is damaging but is unable to change what has been set in motion. She sees writing as a means of change yet is unwilling:

> Twice she moved towards her writing-table: a note should go to Markham, and tell him, pray him, for both their sakes, to go away and leave her. Twice her heart failed. The third time the emotion rose it was strong enough to move her from her seat. And then insidious reason pressed up to urge a thousand arguments that it was far better

286 ibid., p. 45.
287 ibid., p. 69.

> he should stay. ... So sad, too, so lonely as he had been; and now his health so delicate... How could she? why should she, send him from her?[288]

Markham also sees the dilemma yet is silent, unable to write and therefore to move beyond the growing crisis that is this relationship: "When they met again at the tea table, all was not as it had been; such as that it never could be again. ...He had long left off writing, even thinking; that was over when he had ceased to be alone".[289] As the climax of Annie Leonard's death[290] comes as a result of fever caught while remaining "quite wet" for too long, it is only here that Markham returns to writing. For Markham, writing has come to be an act of extinction in that it does not offer new possibilities and is too late to serve as a salvific act:

> Markham sat down and wrote three notes; one to his banker with directions for the payment of a few bills left unsettled in the town, and desiring them to make over what remained of his money in their hands to some public charity. The second was to the people of his old lodging. His clothes, and anything else they had of his, they were to keep... He himself, he said, was going away, and it was uncertain when he might return. The last was to Helen: brief and scrawled with a shaking hand, and blotted with tears. It was only to say that he was gone...[291]

As the novel closes, we find that Markham is written out of existence not only by his own hand, but by those of his fictional world and ultimately by Froude himself:

> ... amidst the wasted ruins of his life, where the bare bleak soil was strewed with wrecked purposes and shattered creeds, with no hope to stay him, with no fear to raise the most dreary phantom beyond the grave, he sank down in the barren waste, and the dry sands rolled over

---

288 ibid., p. 177.

289 ibid., pp. 178, 179.

290 Froude recalls Goethe's *Elective Affinities* when the negligence of those who have abilities yet do not exercise them become culpable in the loss of the future. The drowning of the child in *Elective Affinities* is symbolic of this loss, whilst in *The Nemesis of Faith*, Froude chooses a more subtle loss with the child catching a fever.

291 ibid., pp. 207-208.

> him where he lay; and no living being was left behind him upon earth, who would mourn the day which brought life to Markham Sutherland.[292]

## Walter Pater – *Marius the Epicurean*

Where J.A. Froude's *The Nemesis of Faith* attempts to form a poetics that engages questions of Christianity yet only remains at the level of critique, Walter Pater's *Marius the Epicurean* represents the attempt to figure a poetics that seeks the answer to the *Zeitgeist* of Victorian doubt through a return to the Keatsian tautological edict – "Truth is Beauty, Beauty Truth" – in a framing of Christianity as source of pure art.

In her critique of *Marius the Epicurean*, Mrs. Humphrey Ward found the novel to be of "great psychological interest". Yet its treatment of Christianity was, in her estimation, merely "an almost *aesthetic* acquiescence" of the Christian faith and provided mere "exquisite moments" rather than any strong or sustained belief in Christianity itself and the *source* of its truth and reality.[293] This distinction regarding the teleological nature of Christianity (what is the end purpose of Christianity) is key to reading Walter Pater's only completed novel.[294] Where much of the discussion surrounding the ultimate concern of Christianity in the nineteenth century by Higher Criticism and novelists such as Mrs. Humphrey Ward and J.A. Froude centred upon *historicity as concern* regarding the "truth" found in Jesus and the Bible, Pater attempted to look *beyond the historicity* of Christianity for a reservoir of pure aestheticism – an aesthetic end in itself.

As Pater was writing *Marius the Epicurean*, he wrote to Violet Paget (the author Vernon Lee) in July of 1883 that his intention was "an Imaginary Portrait of a peculiar type of mind in the time of Marcus

---

[292] ibid., pp. 226-227.

[293] Michael Levey, "Introduction to *Marius the Epicurean*" in Walter Pater, *Marius the Epicurean* (London: Penguin Classics, 1985) p. 12.

[294] As Michael Levey notes regarding *Marius*: "Among the modest five volumes of writing which represent his output during his lifetime, it is outstanding not only for its scale and its highly complex aims but also for the fact that it is the only work of his conceived and executed as a whole. Normally he made up his books from essays, lectures and articles often printed previously in some form". ibid., p. 8.

Aurelius... I regard this present matter as a sort of duty... I think that there is a *fourth sort of religious phase* possible for the modern mind over and above those presented... [by you] in the *Contemporary*, the condition of which phase it is the main object of my design to convey". In 1887 Pater had published his collection of fictional studies entitled *Imaginary Portraits,* and *Marius* was to stand as a more fully actualised "portrait" whose central character's *bildung* was to move through the phases of unbelief that Vernon Lee had outlined in the article "The Responsibilities of Unbelief", published in the *Contemporary*. In this article, Lee creates a dialogue between three speakers who are the embodiments of Voltairean optimism, aesthetic pessimism, and what Michael Levey has termed "militant, humanitarian atheism".[295] In essence, Pater is arguing for yet another phase of the modern mind that goes beyond Lee's three categories. For Pater, this "fourth phase" is both an acquiescence of the previous three in temperament and belief that is ultimately drawn together in an appreciation of the 'form' of Christianity as a lived aesthetic. As he writes in *Marius*: "For what Christianity did many centuries afterwards in the way of informing an art, a poetry, of graver and higher beauty, we may think, than that of Greek art and poetry at their best, was in truth conformable to the original tendency of its genius".[296] This lived aesthetic was a "unique power of Christianity" for Pater that could stir "some wonderful new hope" through its unique vision of life "behind the veil" of life "as it has been exercised... in spite of many hindrances, and under the most inopportune circumstances".[297] While in 1866, Gerard Manley Hopkins, who was then a student of Pater's, notes that Pater had spoken to him in private "taking two hours against Christianity",[298] by 1886 this was not the case. Mrs. Humphrey Ward notes that before the publication of *Marius*, his views regarding Christianity had shifted and he had grown conscious of the "mystery of Christianity". He was haunted, she wrote, "by the something in it".[299]

In his "blending of all religions" in a search for meaning rather than merely a fictional reaction against the institutionalisation of the

---

295 ibid., p. 16.
296 ibid., p. 239.
297 ibid., p. 235.
298 Cited by Michael Levey, ibid., p. 16.
299 ibid.

Church and Higher Criticism in the nineteenth century, Pater seeks a different path through his poetic project. As Michael Levey notes:

> Instead of having to depict that fashionable nineteenth-century figure of fact and fiction (such as Amiel and Robert Elsmere) – the doubter of Christianity – Pater could have his figure's doubts directed at a variety of pagan beliefs. The Rome of his chosen date was where, as he was to write, "A blending of all the religions of the ancient world had been accomplished". In none would Marius find what he was seeking. That was romantically modern of him: disillusioned, alienated, "*un autre*", floating, detached from the society that bred him, yearning for something he failed to find in the old-fashioned religion of his childhood, in epicureanism or in stoicism. Just then, in that old, jaded civilisation a new hope had arisen.[300]

For Marius, the central character of Pater's novel set in Rome in the time following the death of Emperor Antoninus Pius in AD 161, the journey toward his own *bildung* is itself a journey of unveiling. As the narrator of *Marius the Epicurean* notes:

> Tis art's function to conceal itself: *ars est celare artem* – is a saying, which, exaggerated by inexact quotation, has perhaps been oftenest and most confidently quoted by those who have had little literary or other art to conceal; and from the very beginning of professional literature, the 'labour of the file', a labour in the case of Plato, for instance, or Virgil, like that of the oldest goldsmiths as described by Apuleius, enriching the work by far more than the weight of the precious metal it removed has always had its function.[301]

But this is an unveiling that is a unique occurrence within a lifetime for which all of one's endeavours are merely preparations:

> We wait for the great crisis which is to try what is in us: we can hardly bear the pressure of our hearts, as we think of it: the lonely wrestler, or victim, which imagination foreshadows to us, can hardly be one's self;

[300] Michael Levey, ibid., p. 17.
[301] Walter Pater, *Marius the Epicurean* 1885 (London: Penguin Classics, 1985) p. 90.

> it seems an outrage of our destiny that we should be led along so gently and imperceptibly, to so terrible a leaping-place in the dark, for more perhaps than life or death. At last, the great act, the critical moment itself comes, easily, almost unconsciously. Another motion of the clock, and our fatal line – the 'great climacteric point' – has been passed, which changes ourselves or our lives.[302]

It is this 'great climacteric point' that Marius searches for throughout the novel. Through his various philosophical gestations played out through the narrative, it is a hope to see beyond the veil of the 'real' world and to see the "original premise or starting point" that remains central. As Marius muses upon coming to Cornelius' house in the chapter "Two Curious Houses" in Part Fourth of the novel:

> For himself, it was clear, he must still hold by what his eyes really saw. Only, he had to concede also, that the very boldness of such theory bore witness, at least, to a variety of human disposition and a consequent variety of mental view, which might – who can tell? – be correspondent to, be defined by and define, varieties of facts, of truths, just '*behind the veil*', regarding the world all alike had actually before them as their original premises or starting point; a world, wider, perhaps, in its possibilities than all possible fancies concerning it.[303]

As Marius moves toward his "great climacteric point" at the end of the novel, Pater utilises images of death and earthquakes as means of "opening" the text and pulling back the veil of certainty in order to show what lies beyond. Marius notes the growth in a family burial plot of Cecilii and reflects on the encroaching presence of death among the land of the living:

> A narrow opening cut its steep side, like a solid blackness there, admitted Marius and his gleaming leader into a hollow cavern or crypt, neither more or less in fact than the family burial-place of Cecilii, to whom this residence belonged… Here, in truth, was the centre of the peculiar religious expressiveness, of the sanctity, of the entire scene. ... Yet this was certainly unlike any cemetery Marius had ever before seen; most obviously in this, that these people returned to the older fashion

[302] ibid., pp. 290-291.
[303] ibid., p. 225.

> of disposing of their dead by burial instead of burning. Originally a family sepulchre, it was growing to a vast *necropolis*, a whole township of the deceased, by means of some free expansion.[304]

It is in this place that Marius comes to see the Christian society that he has found himself a part of as a "strange new society" that existed as a "garden enclosed" and was the "fulfilment of all the preferences". Noting that the Christian society is willing to live among its dead by "disposing of their dead by burial rather than by burning", the veil between life and death remains thin – one always in repose to the other – the city of God among the city of the dead. As Marius concludes:

> Here, it might be, was, if not the cure, yet the solace or anodyne of his great sorrows – of that constitutional sorrowfulness, not peculiar to himself perhaps, but which had made his life like one long 'disease of the spirit'... Might this new vision, like the malignant beauty of pagan Medusa, be exclusive of any admiring gaze upon anything but itself? At least he suspected that, after beholding it, he could never again be altogether as he had been before.[305]

For Marius (as well as Pater), the vision of Christianity which comes after all searching is one that is "exclusive of any admiring gaze upon anything but itself." This is a "transforming" vision of "a reality of experience" that is regenerative for humanity yet ultimately closed off in its purest realisation. As Marius reflects:

> And what he found, thus looking, literally, for the dead among the living, was the vision of a natural, a scrupulously natural, love, transforming, by some new gift of insight into the truth of human relationships, and under the urgency of some new motive by him so far unfathomable, all the conditions of life. He saw, in all its primitive freshness and amid the lively facts of its actual coming into the world,

[304] ibid., p. 229.
[305] ibid., p. 234.

> as a reality of experience, that regenerate type of humanity, which, centuries later, Giotto and his successors, down to the best and purest days of the young Raphael, working under conditions very friendly to the imagination, were to conceive as an artistic ideal.[306]

At the end, Marius sees the pure vision of Christianity as the pure art which is at the heart of all great art. As mentioned previously, this is not a "cure" for his longing, but it is "the solace or anodyne of his great sorrows". Marius experiences peace in this solace, but is never to know the cure which he had longed for, possibly due to the fact that one was never available in Pater's conception.

It is at this point of having found this all-consuming and transforming vision of beauty as an end in itself that the world around him becomes unsettled (literally and figuratively) through a deconstructing earthquake:

> And it was no ordinary morning into which Marius stepped forth. There was a menace in the dark masses of hill, and motion-less wood, against the gray, although apparently unclouded sky... The Christian people of the town, hardly less terrified and overwrought by the haunting sickness about them than their pagan neighbours, were at prayer before the tomb of the martyr; and even as Marius pressed among them to a place beside Cornelius, on a sudden the hill seemed to roll like a sea in motion, around the whole compass of the horizon. For a moment Marius supposed himself attacked with some sudden sickness of brain, till the fall of a great mass of building convinced him that not himself but the earth under his feet was giddy.[307]

Pater attempts to open his poetics up at this point to "look beyond the veil" which is key to his protagonist's search for meaning. The close proximity of death to life, the sickness that surrounds all, and the instability of the very earth beneath their feet shows a universe that Pater holds to be on the verge of opening to some new possibility amidst its fragility, revelation coming to light as the veil of life and death becomes thin. Yet the failure of Pater's poetics in this vein is that he retreats into a closed stylistics that does not allow for anything beyond the very veil he wishes to lift. The novel ends with Marius'

[306] ibid., p. 235.
[307] ibid., p. 290.

passing into a Christian martyrdom that is bestowed upon him by mere happenstance and any search for what lies behind the veil that has been sought for through the narrative is abandoned. The reader is left with merely a portrait that is controlled and ultimately dies at the hand of the author – a "slim philosophical parable ends abruptly with a Sebastian martyrized by the *Zeitgeist*."[308] In this way, as U.C. Knoepflmacher notes in *Religious Humanism and the Victorian Novel*, "the quality of Pater's fiction is nondramatic, derivative, almost static. It is a fiction of an art critic. … Pater's imaginary portraits are as stationary and immobile as pictures in a gallery."[309] Not all saw Pater's attempt as a failure however. As W.B. Yeats reflected upon *Marius* in his letters:

> Three or four years ago I re-read *Marius the Epicurean*, expecting to find I cared for it no longer, but it still seemed to me, as I think it seemed to us all, the only great prose in modern English, and yet I began to wonder if it, or the attitude of mind which it was the noblest expression, had not caused the disaster of my friends. It taught us to walk upon a rope, tightly stretched through serene air, and we were left to keep our feet upon a swaying rope in a storm.[310]

Pater's former student, Oscar Wilde, wrote in his letter *De Profundis* to Alfred Douglas from prison that *Marius* was a reconciliation of "the artistic life with a life of religion in the deep, sweet, and austere sense of the word".[311] As Yeats and Wilde clearly acknowledge, *Marius* is truly a masterful work. Yet in the end, Pater's only novel remains an end in itself – an example of the reverence of aesthetics that is incapable of moving beyond its own space and resistant toward allowing for any fracture that could call beyond itself. Its attempt at a self-sustained artistic vision that is sealed into its own perfection in the end results in a closed tomb rather than a living tome. George Eliot, reacting to Pater's poetics, wrote that Pater "seems to me quite poisonous in…

---

308 U.C. Knoepflmacher, *Religious Humanism and the Victorian Novel: George Eliot, Walter Pater, and Samuel Butler* (Princeton: Princeton University Press, 1965) p. 163.
309 U.C. Knoepflmacher, ibid., p. 159.
310 W.B. Yeats, cited by U.C. Knoepflmacher, op. cit., p. 189.
311 Oscar Wilde, "De Profundis and Other Essays", cited by Michael Levey, op. cit., p. 9.

principles of criticism and false conceptions of life".[312] Just as Marius' ashes are buried within a closed tomb – a pagan buried as a Christian martyr – so does Pater close off the very questions of ultimate concern, meaning, the possible nexus of the self and the sacred just as he seems to be beginning to utter them.

## Mrs. Humphrey Ward – *Robert Elsmere*

In turning to Mrs. Humphrey Ward's *Robert Elsmere*, it is important to note that, as U.C. Knoepflmacher states, "the controversy over *Robert Elsmere* was symptomatic: the book's historic significance exceeded by far its intrinsic merits".[313] As a novel, *Robert Elsmere* is more 'fictionalised criticism' or a *roman à thése* that is content to utilise the genre of the novel to argue issues rather than create a work of "true" fiction – (albeit it was *the* best-selling novel of the nineteenth century). A decade before Mrs. Humphrey Ward published *Robert Elsmere*, George Eliot argued that her own writing, having turned from criticism to fiction at this point, was of the function that is "the *aesthetic*, not the doctrinal teacher – the rousing of nobler emotions, which make mankind desire the social right, not the prescribing of special measures".[314] *Robert Elsmere*, while not of the measure of the higher aesthetic that would "rouse the nobler emotions" George Eliot sought after through her poetics, is an important novel in comparison to George Eliot's works in a *negative* fashion – in what it **does not** achieve given the questions it raises with respect to what it attempts.

On one level, *Robert Elsmere*'s failure as a novel can be argued from to its form exhibiting mere Bunyan-esque allegory. This is due to the relative ease with which critics saw through the veil of the thin characters of Robert, Catherine, Rose Leyburn, Edward Langham, Henry Gray, Mr. Newcome, and the infidel Squire Wendover. In his review of the novel in *The Fortnightly Review* in May 1892, entitled "Amateur Christianity", W.H. Mallock points out the reasons for the success of the novel with the reading public but that, in the end, the

[312] George Eliot, *The George Eliot Letters*, ed. Gordon S. Haight (New Haven: Yale University Press, 1954, 1955), V, p. 455. Cited also in U.C. Knoepflmacher, *Religious Humanism and the Victorian Novel*, op. cit., p. 150 and Levey, op. cit., p. 20.

[313] U.C. Knoepflmacher, *Religious Humanism and the Victorian Novel: George Eliot, Walter Pater, and Samuel Butler* (Princeton: Princeton University Press, 1965) p. 4.

[314] George Eliot, *The George Eliot Letters*, VII, 44. Cited by U.C. Knoepflmacher, op. cit., p. 14.

novel itself is merely a vehicle for ideas:

> First, the amount of unformulated scepticism prevalent amongst the Christian public; secondly, the eagerness of this public to understand its own scepticism more clearly; and lastly, its eagerness to discover that, whatever its scepticism might take from it, something would still be left it, which was really the essence of Christianity. In other words, the popularity of *Robert Elsmere* is mainly the expression of the devout idea that the essence of Christianity will somehow survive its doctrines.[315]

Mallock argues primarily against the way in which Mrs. Humphrey Ward attempts to recast Christianity in what Knoepflmacher calls "drab Christian socialism" in the guise of the young Robert Elsmere, the clever Oxford-educated rector who embodies the questions raised against traditional Christian doctrine through Higher Criticism. He is 'foretold' before his character enters Book 1 as one who "belonged to another race – a race sprung from the soil and content to spend the whole of life in very close contact and very homely intercourse with their mother earth".[316] As the reader is informed,

> within the last twenty years, however, the few remaining survivors of the primitive clerical order … have dropped into their quiet unremembered graves, and new men of other ways and other modes of speech reign in their stead... And naturally the churches too have shared in the process of transformation. The ecclesiastical revival of the half-century has worked its will even in the remotest corners of the Cumbrian country, and soon not a vestige of the homely worshipping-places of an earlier day will remain.[317]

It is this "other order" of cleric that is foretold as the reader is introduced to Robert Elsmere. His physical description is "like a vigorous unfinished sketch"[318] one who is "drawn" but is not

---

[315] W.H. Mallock, "Amateur Christianity," *The Fortnightly Review*, LVII (May 1892) p. 678.
[316] Mrs. Humphrey Ward, *Robert Elsmere* 9th Edition (London: Smith, Elder, & Co., 1888) p. 16.
[317] ibid., p. 17.
[318] ibid., p. 22.

"finished;" something created but not necessarily creative. This is exemplified in the description of Robert as he walks through the countryside reciting the poetry of Wordsworth to himself:

> He stood there bathed in silent enchantment, an eager nature going out to meet and absorb into itself the beauty and peace of the scene. Lines of Wordsworth were on his lips; the little well-worn volume was in his pocket, but he did not need to bring it out; and his voice had all a poet's intensity of emphasis as he strolled along, reciting under his breath – 'It is a beauteous evening, calm and free,/ The holy time is quiet as a nun/ Breathless with adoration!'[319]

While having a "poet's intensity" he is not a poet, someone who recites rather than composes. This extends even to his speech made in Book VI on "The Claim of Jesus Upon Modern Life" at the North R – Club, in which his aim is to be the "reconceiving of Christ".[320] This is ultimately a *re-considering* rather than a "re-conceiving". Amidst Elsmere's efforts to "reconceive the Christ", Jesus remains merely a re-considered cleric who reminds the reader of a distant Christ in a distant era whose role in culture is not to be creative and therefore remains forever trapped in the context of society. The reality that Robert should not be a cleric is apparent to Robert's mother as she reflects on the nature of the cleric in nineteenth century England. She understands that the cleric is bound to exist only in relation to his essential context of society which devours "individuals" who "came and went, but the type [the cleric of tradition]… was always the same… Mrs. Elsmere had no yearning for a *clerical* son".[321]

It is when Robert is at Oxford that he becomes enamoured first with the scholastic life yet still considers becoming a cleric. In listening to Henry Gray's lay sermons, Robert begins to identify with larger questions of meaning. Yet what draws Robert into admiration of the speaker was Mr. Gray's ability to embody the pragmatic amidst the scholastic:

> Mr. Grey's treatment of these questions was clothed, throughout a

[319] ibid., p. 28.
[320] ibid., p. 496.
[321] ibid., p. 46. In contrast, this symbiotic relationship between the cleric and the society is clearly seen by George Eliot as will be seen in the next chapter.

> large portion of the lecture, in metaphysical language, which no boy fresh from school, however intellectually quick, could be expected to follow with any precision. It was not, therefore, the argument, or the logical structure of the sermon, which profoundly affected young Elsmere. It was the speaker himself, and the occasional passages in which, addressing himself to the practical needs of his hearers, he put before them the claims and conditions of the higher life with a pregnant simplicity and rugged beauty of phrase.[322]

It was here that Robert "recognised with a great burst of enthusiasm and astonishment, that, after all, Mill and Herbert Spencer had not said the last word on all things in heaven and earth". It is in listening to Mr. Grey that Robert's "imagination" becomes possessed "more and more... the system behind the sight took stronger and stronger hold upon him; he began to wish ardently and continuously to become a part of it, to cast in his lot definitely with it".[323]

What Mrs. Humphrey Ward attempts throughout the remainder of *Robert Elsmere* is to show what this "system behind the sight" is in relation to the fundamental claims of Christianity, and in particular, the nature of Christ in relation to "Christianity" in its nineteenth century manifestation. In a discussion with his tutor Edward Langham,[324] Robert comes against the possibility that the "system behind the sight" of Christianity may indeed be nothing more than a myth:

> "Well, after all," he said at last, very slowly, "the difficulty lies in preaching anything. One may as well preach a respectable mythology as anything else."
> "What do you mean by a mythology?" cried Robert hotly.
> "Simple ideas, or experiences, personified." said Langham, puffing away. "I take it they are the subject-matter of all theologies."
> "I don't understand you," said Robert, flushing. "To the Christian, facts have been the medium by which ideas the world could not otherwise have come at have been communicated to man. Christian

[322] ibid., pp. 58, 59.
[323] ibid., pp. 62, 63.
[324] Usually thought to be a fictionalised Walter Pater. See U.C. Knoepflmacher, "1888 and a look backwards" in *Religious Humanism and the Victorian Novel* (Princeton: Princeton University Press, 1965) pp. 3ff.

> theology is a system of ideas indeed, but of ideas realised, made manifest in facts."[325]

As Edward Langham reflects during this discussion, "the intellect had precious little to do with Elsmere's Christianity. He had got hold of all the stock apologetic arguments, and used them, his companion admitted, with ability and ingenuity. But they were merely outworks of the citadel. The inmost fortress was held something wholly distinct from intellectual conviction – by moral passion, by love, by feeling, by that mysticism, in short, which no healthy youth should be without".[326]

By the beginning of Book II (Surrey) where Robert, now married to Catherine, takes his first charge, we see the beginning of his eventual fall. Throughout Book II Robert wrestles with the notion brought forward by Langham that history is not created in a neutral medium, but through the recording of subjective testimony given by individuals such as Robert himself. As Langham challenges him to consider:

> History depends on *testimony*. What is the nature and the value of testimony at given times? In other words, did the man of the third century understand, or report, or interpret facts in the same way as the man of the sixteenth or the nineteenth? And if not, what are the differences, and what are the deductions to be made from them, if any? ... [T]he whole of orthodox Christianity is (dependent on testimony)![327]

Having spent numerous hours in Squire Wendover's library (which is later called "an Institute" showing the changing nature of such a collection – moving from a place of mere reading to that of criticism) Robert looks over the key works of the period that were challenging his orthodox views:

> Here were most of the early editions of the *Leben Jesu*, with some corrections from Strauss's hand, and similar records of Baur, Ewald, and other members or opponents of the Tübingen school. And so on, through the whole bookcase. Something of everything was there - Philosophy, Theology, History, Philology... A history of modern thinking Germany, of that 'unextinguished hearth' whence the mind of

---

[325] Mrs. Humphrey Ward, *Robert Elsmere*, p. 66.
[326] ibid.
[327] ibid., p. 199.

> Europe had been kindled for three generations, might almost have been evolved from that bookcase and its contents alone.[328]

In Book III (The Squire), we find the final blow to Robert's faith coming in the form of a book delivered to his home by Squire Wendover. Upon reading Wendover's *The Idols of the Marketplace* (an omnibus of Strauss-like critique of sorts), Robert sees his faith slipping away, exemplified in *The Idols of the Marketplace* which falls closed from his grasp:

> It was the first volume of *The Idols of the Marketplace*. ... The Pentateuch, the Prophets, the Gospels, St. Paul, Tradition, the Fathers, Protestantism and Justification by Faith, the Eighteenth Century, the Broad Church Movement, Anglican Theology – the squire had his say about them all. And while the coolness and frankness of the method sent a shock of indignation and horror through the religious public, the subtle and caustic style, and the epigrams with which the book was strewn, forced both the religious and irreligious public to read, whether they would or no. A storm of controversy rose round the volumes, and some of the keenest observers of English life had said at the time, and maintained since, that the publication of the book had made or marked an epoch...
>
> Not a sound in the house. Outside, the tossing moaning December night; inside, the faintly crackling fire, the standing figure. Suddenly it was to Robert as though a cruel torturing hand were laid upon his inmost being. His breath failed him; the book slipped out of his grasp; he sank down upon his chair, his head in his hands. Oh, what a desolate intolerable moment! Over the young idealist soul there swept a dry destroying whirlwind of thought. Elements gathered from all sources – from his own historical work, from the squire's book, from the secret half-conscious recesses of the mind – entered into it, and as it passed it seemed to scorch his heart.[329]

Exemplified in the "story within a story" told at the beginning of Book II by the "Ritualist clergyman" Mr. Newcome, the reader sees Robert come undone:

---

[328] ibid., p. 196.
[329] ibid., p. 280.

> Stroke by stroke, as the words and facts were beguiled from him, all that was futile and quarrelsome in the sharp-featured priest sank out of sight; the face glowed with inward light; the stature of the man seemed to rise; the angel in him unsheathed its wings. Suddenly a story… – a story of the purest Christian heroism told in the simplest way – came to an end...[330]

Likewise, the tale of *Robert Elsmere* is to be a "story of the purest Christian heroism told in the simplest way" where the reader is to be left with "a face glowing with inward light" but fails to do so. As an exercise in poetics, the characters Mrs. Humphrey Ward creates remain caricatures – living in constant relation to the issues they represent and embody but never truly alive. Ever tied to the context of society, the characters she writes into being acknowledge this limitation as seen in discourse surrounding fictional characters within *Robert Elsmere* and their attempts to write. In Book II, Robert speaks to Langham about writing a book:

> "Perhaps you don't know that I too am engaged upon a great work."
> "A great work – you?"
> Langham looked at his companion as though to find out whether his remark was meant seriously or whether he might venture to be cynical. *Elsmere writing! Why should everybody write books? It was absurd!* The scholar who knows what toll scholarship takes of life is always apt to resent the intrusion of the man of action into his domains. It looks to him like a kind of ridiculous assumption that any one *d'un coeur léger* can do what has cost him his heart's blood.[331] (emphasis added)

Later, in Book III, Robert suggests to Langham in relation to his "great work", that he has discovered a key issue with regard to the act of writing:

> The *form* taken by this training of his own mind he had been thus encouraged not to abandon, was, as we know, the study of history… As he told Langham, he just got below the surface of a great subject and was beginning to dig into the roots of it. Hitherto he had been under the guidance of men of his own day, of the nineteenth century

---

330 ibid., p. 164.
331 ibid., p. 197.

> historian, who refashions the past on the lines of his own mind, who gives it rationality, coherence, and, as it were, moderness, so that the main impression he produces on us, so long as we look at that past through him only, is on the whole an *impression of continuity*, of *resemblance*.
>
> Whereas, on the contrary, the first impression left on a man by the attempt to plunge into the materials of history for himself is almost always an extraordinary sharp *impression of difference*, of *contrast*. Ultimately, of course, he sees that these men and women whose letters and biographies, whose creeds and general conceptions he is investigating, are in truth his ancestors, bone of his bone, flesh of his flesh...
>
> Then he sees what it is makes the difference, digs the gulf. '*Science*,' the mind cries, '*ordered knowledge*.'[332]

Yet what Robert Elsmere the protagonist perceives, *Robert Elsmere* the novel fails to do. Robert is not a character who is allowed sharp "contrast" or "impression of difference." Rather, he merely "resembles" the manifestations of the Zeitgeist.

In the important chapter XL in Book VI entitled (ironically) "New Openings", we see Mrs. Humphrey Ward come closest to realising her aims of "reconceiving the Christ", yet ultimately closing off any "new opening" she had hoped to introduce. In this chapter, Robert has been invited to present a lecture to the North R – Club (also called "the Workman's Club") entitled "The Claims of Jesus on Modern Life". This is a society that is made up of "dock workers and gas fitters" whom Robert sees as the base from which "the religious movement of the future" will arise "in sufficient volume among the masses, where the vested interests of all kinds are less tremendous".[333] This club has been circulating handbills and pamphlets that satirise the Established Church and the notion of Christ as figured by the status quo, bearing such titles as *Faith and Fools* and *The Comic Life of Christ* that "contained a caricature of the Crucifixion [and] a scroll emanating from Mary Magdalene's mouth, in particular, containing obscenities which

---

[332] ibid., p. 276.
[333] ibid., p. 524.

cannot be quoted here".[334] In his outrage, Robert accepts an invitation to speak and hopefully put forth his re-visioned "claims of Jesus to Modern Life" on Good Friday. On Wednesday of Passion week, Robert reflects upon how the shape of humanity has misshapen the image of Christ:

> He had seen them with the bodily eye, and the fact had enormously quickened his historical perception. The child of Nazareth, the moralist and teacher of Capernaum and Gennesaret, the strenuous seer and martyr of the later Jerusalem preaching – all these various images sprang into throbbing poetic life within him. That anything in human shape should be capable of dragging this life and this death through the mire of a hideous and befouling laughter! Who was responsible?[335]

As Robert states to Catherine before giving his lecture, it is his hope to reverse this trend:

> "I want simply, if I can, to transfer to their minds that image of Jesus of Nazareth which thought, and love, and reading have left upon my own. I want to make them realise for themselves the historical character, so far as it can be realised – *to make them see for themselves the real figure*, as it went in and out amongst men – so far as our eyes can now discern it."[336] (emphasis added)

What is key here is this notion of re-casting an image of the "real figure" – a re-forming christology and a re-visioning of Jesus of Nazareth apart from the current "form", or to use John McIntyre's terminology, "shape of Christology". It is this notion that permeates Robert's concern – a concern not so much of doctrine, but rather of form and shape. As Catherine Elsmere notes, the "Historical Christ… will never win souls. If he was God, every word… would insult him. If he was man, he was not a good man!"[337] Robert understands this in part, choosing instead to conform what he sees as the central challenge – the "imaging" of Christ in the Modern World.

Part of this challenge is shown as Robert enters the lecture hall of the Workman's Club on Good Friday. As he enters, it is noted that

---

[334] ibid., p. 477.

[335] ibid.

[336] ibid., p. 480.

[337] ibid.

the walls of the hall are covered "at intervals with political portraits and a few cheap engravings of famous men, Jesus of Nazareth taking his turn with Buddha, Socrates, Moses, Shakespeare, and Paul of Tarsus".[338] These pictures serve as a verbal-visual key to what Mrs. Humphrey Ward in *Robert Elsmere* asserts as the core issue regarding Christianity's poor state in the later nineteenth century. What are the images before us? What are the "pictures" by which those of "human shape" begin to "shape" an image of Christ? As Robert states at the beginning of his lecture on "The Claims of Jesus on Modern Life", it is a claim of form that is made – a picture as opposed to words that needs to be re-cast with regard to Jesus:

> I shall aim at rousing in him such a state of feeling as may suddenly convince him that what is injured by writing of this sort is not the orthodox Christian, or the Church, or Jesus of Nazareth, but always and inevitably the man who writes it and the man who loves it! His mind is possessed of an inflaming and hateful image, which drives him to mockery and violence. *I want to replace it*, if I can, by one of calm, of beauty and tenderness, which may drive him to humility and sympathy. *And this, indeed, is the only way in which opinion is ever really altered – by the substitution of one mental picture for another.*[339] (emphasis added)

As Robert goes on to note that as we "go back to the root of things", we are called "to reconceive the Christ, to bring him afresh into our lives, to make life so freely given for man minister again in new ways to man's new needs". This is the task of "every great religion… in truth, a concentration of great ideas, capable, as all ideas are, of infinite expansion and adaptation… *To reconceive the Christ!* It is the special task of our age, though in some sort and degree it has been the ever-recurring task of Europe since the beginning".[340] Throughout the lecture, iconographic language is used to "reconceive the Christ" as a visual-verbal re-imagining. Images of both painting and sculpting are utilised as opposed to traditional language of dogmatic apologetics. In Mrs. Humphrey Ward's narrative, it is a compelling picture or image

---

338 ibid., p. 490.
339 ibid., p. 492.
340 ibid., p. 496.

that must emerge with regard to Jesus rather than a strong logocentric argument. As noted in the thoughts of Hugh Flaxman as he listened to the lecture: "and bit by bit, as the quick nervous sentences issued and struck, *each like the touch of a chisel, the majestic figure emerged*, set against its natural background, instinct with some fraction at least of the magic of reality, most human, most persuasive, most tragic".[341] In recounting his hopes for the lasting impact of his lecture, Robert later tells Catherine

> "You ask me," he would say in effect, "to prove to you that men can love, can make a new and fruitful use, for daily life and conduct, of a merely human Christ. Go amongst our men, talk to our children, and satisfy yourself. A little while ago scores of these men either hated the very name of Christianity or were entirely indifferent to it. To scores of them now the *name* of the teacher of Nazareth, the victim of Jerusalem, is dear and sacred; his life, his death, his words, are becoming once more a constant source of moral effort and spiritual hope. *See for yourself!*"[342] (emphasis added)

As with its chapter title "New Openings", Mrs. Humphrey Ward is also advocating a "new opening" that is a place not defined by the "very *name* of Christianity" but rather re-imagined around "the *name* of the teacher of Nazareth". Yet there is no opening to be found. The Jesus that is advocated throughout *Robert Elsmere* as the "reconceived Christ" is one trapped as well. Mrs. Humphrey Ward has merely traded doctrinal and ecclesiastical systematic constrictions for a static Christ that is more contextualised than the product of "true" fiction. As Robert asks his audience to consider the "reconceived Christ", it is a regressive act that does not fully return to a realistic present:

> Let me try, however feebly, and *draw it afresh* for you, that life of lives, that story of stories, as the labour of our own age in particular has patiently revealed it to us. Come back with me through the centuries; *let us try and see the Christ of Galilee and the Christ of Jerusalem as he was*, before a credulous love and Jewish tradition and Greek subtlety had at once dimmed and glorified the truth.[343]

Robert notes that "the world has grown since Jesus preached in Galilee

341 ibid., p. 497.
342 ibid., p. 505.
343 ibid., p. 496.

and Judea. We cannot learn the *whole* of God's lesson from him now – nay, we could not then!"[344] Yet the Jesus that is presented in *Robert Elsmere* is not one that has "grown" with the world. As Robert Elsmere is presented in *Robert Elsmere* as a "form" of Jesus reimagined, the reader is left with a figuring of Jesus that is strangely familiar to the very one being argued against. What Mrs. Humphrey Ward offers is merely an isolated clergyman trained in the established church who, in appealing to a Historical Jesus of the first century that contemporary Anglo-German scholarship of the period was acknowledging as impossible to fully capture, advocates one doctrinal system over another. While the compelling "picture" of Robert Elsmere shows an active "Social Gospel" alternative to static scholasticism in regard to the figuring of Jesus, it remains a derivative of the very system accused of being misguided and false. While claims that his "reconceived Christ" is one that is "risen" as the Easter Christ "in a wiser reverence and more reasonable love; *risen in new forms* of social help inspired by his memory, called afresh by his name! *Risen* – if you and your children will it – in a church or company of the faithful...,"[345] it is this proposed "new form" that lacks the "new openings" promised. In contrast to the poetics of George Eliot, Mrs. Humphrey Ward (as with other writers of her period) made critical assessment of the doubt within the Victorian age and, through fiction, sought to put a face to this assessment. Yet it was the very act of writing that, while freeing the questions of doubt from dialectics and systematic constraints, ultimately confined the very Jesus these writers sought to free or at least, in the words of *Robert Elsmere*, "conceive". In the case of Mrs. Humphrey Ward, it is merely trading an unimaginative dogma for an unimaginative failed cleric – both closed forms that encase rather than liberate. It is this factor that differentiated George Eliot's poetics from that of the other discussed in the Victorian era. As we shall see, hers is a poetics of open space and organicism that is more akin to Goethe and Hölderlin than to the writing of her own society. It is a poetics that in its very "a/structuring" comes closer to writing the "reconceived Christ" than Mrs. Humphrey Ward could achieve in her project.

---

[344] ibid., p. 497.
[345] ibid., p. 499.

# Chapter 6

## *Scenes of Clerical Life* – Images under Erasure

> They've gotten rid of the Christian God, and now they think they have to hold onto Christian morality all the more: that's *English* logic, we don't want to blame it on little moral females *à la* Eliot. In England, for every little emancipation from theology, you have to make yourself respectable again as a moral fanatic in the most frightening way. Over there, that's the *penance* one pays...
>
> Things are different for the rest of us. If you give up Christian faith, you pull the *right* to Christian morality out from under your feet. This morality is simply *not* self-evident: one has to bring this point home again and again, despite the English dimwits. Christianity is a system, a view of things that is conceived as a connected *whole*. If you break off a major concept from it, faith in God, you break up the whole world as well: there are no necessities left to hold onto anymore. Christianity presupposes that human beings do not know, *cannot* know, what is good and evil for them: they believe in God, who is the only one who knows it. Christian morality is a commandment; its origin is transcendent; it is beyond all criticism, all right to criticism; it is true only if God is truth – it stands and falls with faith in God.[346]

In his 1889 collection of sermonic indictments of the state of the Western world entitled *Twilight of the Idols* (subtitled "How to Philosophise with a Hammer"), Friedrich Nietzsche lists those he deems "responsible" for the fall of Western culture by name, and levels what he sees as the appropriate charges against them. Interestingly, George Eliot is included alongside Rousseau, Schiller, Dante, Kant, and John Stuart Mill. Nietzsche's charge against her, as cited in the above

[346] Friedrich Nietzsche, *Twilight of the Idols* (Cambridge: Hackett Publishing Company, 1997) p. 53.

quotation, is to have forgotten that "Christianity is a system, a view of things that is conceived as a connected *whole*. If you break off a major concept from it, faith in God, you break up the whole world as well: there are no necessities left to hold onto anymore". In one respect, Nietzsche's charge against Eliot is well deserved. Eliot is indeed unwilling to see the essence of Christianity grounded in a systematic rendering. As I have argued in the opening chapters of this study, Eliot was indeed concerned with the task of seeing the "possible" of Christianity (to use a phrase of Eliot's) that was not to be found in a system and is not, as argued by Nietzsche, "beyond all criticism". As Nietzsche correctly assets, Eliot is challenging the notion that Christianity was a system while at the same time maintaining a sense of the whole. How this "whole" is presented is key to Eliot's re-imagining of the "mystery beneath the real". Throughout her critical writing for the *Westminster Review* this is apparent. But it is in her turn toward fiction that this challenge reaches new and more profound dimensions.

David Carroll begins his discussion of George Eliot's *Scenes of Clerical Life* by stating that the so-called protagonists of the narratives are "at risk", not because of lack of coherence of character, but because of the destabilised context within which they ground their identity – "If stable character is based upon a coherent view of the world, then the clergyman protagonists of *Scenes of Clerical Life*, living in English provincial society during the first half of the nineteenth century, are at risk".[347] The "world" in which these clergy exist is in a constant state of erosion throughout the three stories that make up *Scenes*. With this context under-erasure, the rules that had governed the construction of self and the sacred erode as well. Eliot's three tales are a truth-telling of sorts – announcing through fiction the fracturing of assumptions that govern, to use Ricoeur's term, the "world of the text" and by association, the world of the reader. As Carroll notes, *Scenes of Clerical Life* show "radical discontinuities in communities which are themselves seriously divided".[348] Eliot's *Scenes*, ironically, do not show forth a coherent "scene" or image of a truth systematically realised. The "scene" that is exposed through Eliot's poetics is not one of solidity,

[347] David Carroll, *George Eliot and the Conflict of Interpretations* (Cambridge: Cambridge University Press, 1992) p. 38.
[348] ibid.

but a reality largely "filled" by *gaps* – fissures that are the true context of life and living such as those between the idealised church and real community, between the cleric and his true vocation, between the identity of women in truth and perception, and ultimately, between the reader and the narrator. In this destabilised world, what had been seen as stable is fractured and that which may be "hidden" or "veiled" is finally seen, albeit at times only in absence or "lack", as with Milly Barton and Tina Sarti, or notably the last story of the trilogy, "Janet's Repentance", in the mystery of the bruised and broken figure. The challenge that Eliot puts forward is a hermeneutic challenge – to read differently not only "the world of the text" but the world of the reader as well. Like Hölderlin's *Empedokles*, all tumble into a fire "divinely gleaming" where all is fracture and gaps are not the space between solidity, but the context itself. With an ironic turn, it is only in this destabilised world that Eliot can bring forward what she terms "the possible clothed in human form". As noted by Peter C. Hodgson,

> the fictional world of George Eliot… projects a new way of being that is poetically distanced from everyday reality even as it makes its way through the world of ordinary experience. The latter is not negated but opened up and transformed by the power of projection, which is able to make a break, a new beginning, in the midst of the old and familiar. The reality status of what is poetically envisioned is that of the *possible*. The possible is not the illusory, a product of wishful thinking, nor is it the merely ideal in the sense of a mental fantasy; rather it is the real transfigured, fulfilled as to its possibilities.[349]

It is in the space of fiction and not in her previous work in criticism that Eliot is able to begin "poetically envisioning the possible". This "possible" for Eliot is not to be accomplished within the confines of a comprehensive synthetic theory, which was in David Carroll's phrase, the "Victorian Holy Grail".[350] Eliot's oft quoted remarks to positivist Frederic Harrison in a letter dating 1876 affirms her reticence in this regard. She describes her fictional writing to Harrison as simply "a set of experiments in life – an endeavour to see what our thought and emotion may be capable of – what stores of motive, actual or hinted as possible, give promise of a better life after which we may strive to keep

[349] Peter C. Hodgson, *Theology in the Fiction of George Eliot* (London: SCM Press, 2001) p. 149.

[350] David Carroll, ibid., p. 16.

hold of something more than shifting theory".[351] She asserts this further to Harrison by stating that she will not "adopt any formula which does not get itself clothed for me in some human figure and individual experience, and perhaps that is a sign that if I help others to see at all it must be through that medium of art".[352] This path was evident during her period of critical writing prior to her fictional work as editor of the *Westminster Review*. In her praise of the philosopher Gruppe in her essay "The Future of German Philosophy" Eliot notes Gruppe's desire to join together the abstract and concrete, analytical and synthetic in order to fulfil the true task of philosophy in the future: "it must renounce metaphysics: it must renounce the ambitious attempt to form a theory of the universe, to know things in their causes and first principles... [taking not] the high *a priori* road... [but the humble] *a posteriori* path".[353] This is her desire as well – to announce a way of *seeing* and ultimately *living* that is more than mere understanding through her offering an aesthetic "clothed in human figure and individual experience" to "help others to *see* through the medium of art". *Scenes of Clerical Life* is the beginning of Eliot's attempt to present the gaps and discontinuity of an organic fictional world "clothed in human figures". Through her use of paradox and discontinuity that creates a coherent yet continuously deconstructing world, Eliot allows the face of the sacred to be seen in human form that is deeply incarnational and takes on a very christological bent. Where other writers might opt to hold this incarnational nexus static, Eliot's poetics continues to unveil and remember, deconstructing and creating anew. Peter Hodgson puts Eliot into a hermeneutic tradition that seeks such a recovery:

> The whole of post-Enlightenment theology, from Schleiermacher and Hegel through Troeltsch, was a sustained effort to reconstruct the central convictions of Christian faith about God, world, humanity, Christ, sin and redemption in forms appropriate to modern philosophy,

[351] George Eliot, *The George Eliot Letters*, ed. Gordon S. Haight, 9 vols. (New Haven: Yale University Press, 1954-78) IV, p. 300.
[352] ibid.
[353] ibid., p. 11.

> science, and culture. In her own way George Eliot was engaging in a similar demythologising effort.[354]

But the difference for Eliot that was "her own way" was in putting forth "central convictions" in a form "clothed in human figure" and not merely dogmatic or credal rendering. What Schleiermacher and Hegel sought in the genre of philosophy, Eliot sought in the act of fiction. While I agree with Hodgson's suggestion that Eliot was indeed engaging in a reconstruction of essential convictions common and in some ways similar to the Christian faith (albeit not orthodox, but more akin to the Liberation theologians such as Gustavo Gutierrez and Rosemary Ruether), she was not striving merely to replace the former theologies with a new one. This would have been merely "the dismantling of orthodoxy" only to lead to "new forms of hubris".[355] In a letter to her friend the phrenologist Charles Bray in 1857 in which she objects to his *The Philosophy of Necessity* as an attempt to provide an overtly systematic rendering of God, she states that we are "totally [unable] to find in our own nature a key to the Divine Mystery... I could more readily turn Christian...than embrace a Theism which professes to explain the proceedings of God".[356]

Her writings were indeed concerned with the same things that concern theologians, although her form and ultimate aims were noticeably different. As Hodgson notes,

> [T]heology itself is a kind of fiction that creates imaginative variations on what history offers as real in order to bespeak the mystery beneath the real, and... it approaches this mystery in terms of how redemptive transformations come about in ordinary human life... [Theology and Art] 'make up things,' but they do so for purposes of illuminating reality, not escaping from it into a fantasy world. They are constrained but not constricted by empirical fact since they draw upon the full range of human experience and potentiality (emotional, psychological, ethical, aesthetic, religious); what they produce must be congruent with history but not necessarily derived from it.[357]

This comparison is concurrent with Eliot's move into fiction. Yet

---

354 Peter C. Hodgson, *Theology in the Fiction of George Eliot,* pp. 148-49.
355 David Carroll, op. cit., p. 14.
356 ibid.
357 Peter C. Hodgson, op. cit., p. 149.

unlike most theology which tends to begin with the universal in the search for a systematic approach to the ultimate, her writing continued to begin with the particular. I suggest that her task is a search for a new a/christology and her writing more a new "gospel" than a new "theology". Eliot's quest for the sacred or divine was a seeking after the particular nexus of the sacred in and throughout humanity – which is something more akin to Strauss' intended aims in *Das Leben Jesu* than Feuerbach's *The Essence of Christianity*. Feuerbach's aim was to show that the antithesis of divine and human is altogether illusory. For Feuerbach, it is nothing else than the antithesis between the human nature in general and the human individual specifically, and "all religious cosmogonies are products of the imagination" with the Incarnation merely being a symbol of the dialectical meeting of the abstract and concrete. Strauss, on the other hand, was attempting to hold on to and ultimately re-cover the actual and particular meeting of the divine and humanity. This was also Eliot's desire – the recovery of the real and particular "Divine Mystery" that was not to be unlocked merely with a "key" of a system, but that which must be described and displayed as one recounts a life in the fullness of time, which is also the task of gospel. In this way I argue that Eliot, in *Scenes of Clerical Life*, is announcing an incarnational poetics that requires "a phenomenological hermeneutic"[358] similar to that found in Martin Heidegger, Paul Ricoeur, and Jacques Derrida. In a phenomenological hermeneutic, interpretation must be focused at the intersection of the two directions of language, that is, neither exclusively with the writer's text nor with the reader, but in the encounter between the two. Secondly, any attempt to reduce or remove the tensional aspect of poetic discourse will impose an arbitrary closure on it. Interpretation must maintain the tensional character of the text. Additionally, the act of interpretation must bring forth the historicity of the writer's text, and the historicity of the reader, so that the interpretative encounter can engage two spheres of discourse. In this way, the act of interpretation itself must be dialectical and take onto a higher level of conceptual meaning the meaning of the reader. At its core, this mode of interpretation is never

[358] Mario J. Valdes, *Reflection and Imagination: A Ricoeur Reader* (Toronto: University of Toronto Press, 1991) p. 15.

completed, for the aim cannot be to deplete the text (or life for that matter) of its dynamism. The aim must be to arrive at a temporary statement that participates in a tradition of commentary on texts.[359]

As Ricoeur states in *Hermeneutics and the Human Sciences*, the hermeneutic act is ultimately an act of "depth semantics" whereby the text

> seeks to place us in its meaning, that is – according to another acceptation of the word *sens* – in the same direction. So if the intention is that of the text and if this intention is the direction which it *opens up for thought*, then depth semantics must be understood in a fundamentally dynamic way. I shall therefore say: to explain is to bring out the structure, that is, *the internal relations of dependence* which constitute the situation of the text; to interpret is to follow the path of thought opened up by the text, to place oneself *en route* towards the *orient* of the text.[360] (emphasis added)

## Heidegger Reads Eliot – the "Possible" of Poetics

George Eliot's wariness of any comprehensive synthetic theory that seeks to apprehend the "mystery beneath the processes" is in line with the phenomenological approach of Martin Heidegger, particularly his reflections on the nature of literature and its role in the disclosure of the sacred. Both Heidegger and Eliot argue for an overturning of traditional modes of criticism by announcing a profound reversal – theory must be read *through* the lens of poetics and not the other way around. Additionally, both Heidegger and Eliot are profoundly concerned with the role literature plays in the veiling and exposing of the sacred. In this way, a discussion of Heidegger's concerns are worthy to note in looking at Eliot's poetics.

As noted by Martin Schäfer, Heidegger's discussion of literature and the sacred appear *together* when he begins to discuss each of them with great significance.[361] Heidegger's lectures in the winter of 1934/35 consists of a close reading of the poet Friedrich Hölderlin published as

---

[359] ibid., pp. 15, 16.

[360] Paul Ricoeur, *Hermeneutics and the Human Sciences: Essays on Language, Action and Interpretation*. Ed., trans., and introd. J.B. Thompson. (Cambridge: Cambridge University Press, 1981) pp. 161-62.

[361] Martin Schäfer, "The Sacred: A Figureless Figure: On Heidegger" Paper presented at the Conference on Theology and Criticism at John Hopkins University, March 4-7, 1999.

*What is called Thinking?*[362] For Heidegger, reading Hölderlin means experiencing something completely "other" in relation to the then modern traditions of Western thought. In his view, Hölderlin takes the risk of journeying beyond the domain of Western systematic thought and, as Heidegger puts it, to ask through his act of writing "the question that has yet to be asked". This of course is the famous Heideggerian notion of *Dasein* as opposed to beings, which – although indicated in pre-Socratic thinking – begins to disappear in Plato's philosophy and ultimately throughout the history of Western philosophy. According to Heidegger, this loss of the question of *Dasein* prevents humanity from *being* in the world *as being-in-the-world*, the "being there" that is *Dasein*. As a consequence, humanity not only merely inhabits "world", but views "world" as a thing which can be used and controlled - a "tool". What Heidegger is arguing throughout his philosophical project is toward that which results not in the location of being, but results merely in the proliferation of theories that have led to alienation and dislocation within civilisation. This is in keeping with Eliot's remarks to her friend Sara Hennell in a letter dated 1857 where she states "I feel every day a greater disinclination for theories and arguments about the origin of things in the presence of all this mystery and beauty and pain and ugliness, that flood one with conflicting emotions".[363] Poetics, in a sense, provides a lens rather than a grid through which we may once again recover what Ricoeur termed "the internal relations of dependence"[364] without the screen of "theories and arguments", allowing for a "telling of the simple story" and also the recasting of the world into a transformed "possible". (It is interesting to note the symbolism in Eliot's journal where she notes, "Tuesday, Sep. 22. Began to write 'The Sad Fortunes of the Reverend Amos Barton', which I hope to make one of a series called 'Scenes of Clerical Life'. Wednesday - Went into the city and bought a microscope)".[365]

---

[362] Martin Heidegger, *What is Called Thinking?* trans. J. Glenn Gray, 1958 (New York: Harper and Row, 1968).

[363] George Eliot, *The George Eliot Letters*, ed. Gordon S. Haight, 9 vols. (New Haven: Yale University Press, 1954-78) II, p. 341.

[364] See Paul Ricoeur, *Hermeneutics and the Human Sciences* (Cambridge: Cambridge University Press, 1981) pp. 182ff.

[365] George Eliot, *The Journals of George Eliot* – ed. Margaret Harris and Judith Johnston

Western thinkers, as Heidegger puts it, have attempted to overcome the oblivion of Being by retracing the *thought* of Being in the forgetful world in which we "live and move and have our being".[366] Hölderlin, however, seeks to name the space of the sacred which is a *poetical* naming that opens up the sphere in which the *thought* of being can ultimately take place (*Der Denker sagt das Sein. Der Dichter nennt das Heilige*). [367] Heidegger considers this sphere that Hölderlin seeks, the sphere of the sacred, to be that very sphere in which Being is regained from its oblivion. It is a space of *Uneigennützigkeit* or "unselfishness",[368] where the things named by poetics are *let be what they are* without being placed within a synthetic matrix of what Eliot calls "theories and arguments". The sacred resides in the sphere in which one is posited beyond one's own control. Here the possibility of Dasein's authenticity can be experienced: the positing of the simple fact that there is *something* rather than *nothing* allows for the possibility of *being*. The sacred is then the realm where things have come wholly back into their Being in a form of self-possessedness, *ins Heile*. Ultimately, poetics then becomes the foundry for being, and the writer/poet – in naming the space – is the founder (*Der Dichter ist der Begründer des Seyns*).[369] Heidegger recognises this in Hölderlin's poetics as exemplified in *Empedokles* and other works.

In this way, form dissolves into negativity where that which was embodied is dispersed into and throughout the conceptual. This progression resembles the stages of knowing argued by Spinoza whom Eliot had translated. In his *Ethics*, Spinoza puts forth a three-fold theory of knowing which begins with fragmentary, particular perceptions, moving to a level of adequate ideas and generalisations, and if followed to its ends, will ultimately achieve a mystical, intuitive knowledge of particular things in relations to their place and purpose within the cosmic order. Neither boundary nor form are found for the locating of the subject or the sacred but a complete dissolving of categories in this Hölderlin-like "flame", which is not extinguished nor is the fissure through which it came upon the subject closed.

For Heidegger, reading Hölderlin means being confronted with

---

(Cambridge: Cambridge University Press, 1998) p. 63.

[366] Acts 17: 28 in which the Apostle Paul cites Epimenides in his *Cretica*.

[367] Martin Schäfer, op. cit.

[368] ibid.

[369] ibid.

the sacred space of a possible "gathering together" to come amidst the gap. But Heidegger was not attracted to Hölderlin because of the literary possibilities. To Heidegger, literature as such has nothing in common with the sacred, i.e. the realm of Being, but it has far more in common with theology. For Heidegger, theology is the very expression of the oblivion of Being. As Heidegger aptly stated, *Das Heilige läßt sich überhaupt nicht 'theologisch' ausmachen, denn [...] immer dort, wo die Theologie aufkommt, [hat] der Gott schon die Flucht begonnen* ("Wherever theology comes up, the god has been on the run for quite a while").[370] In this way, Heidegger is arguing that Being and the sacred have vanished when a figured god, a highest being, is delimited into text and considered to be the most powerful thing in a great chain of beings. It is *the questioning after* the Being of all these beings (*das Sein des Seienden*) that is the task of poetic writing.[371] When a text is made, the most one can hope for is theology – talking about that which one has ceased to seek. Heidegger goes on to note that the history of Being's oblivion thus accumulates in the act of ontotheology, an ontology that is entirely theological. This is where literature is theology and theology is literature and both ultimately fail in choosing to figure Being and the sacred amidst images, metaphors, and tropes – which to Heidegger's mind is language that belongs to the realm of ontotheology and thus to the oblivion of Being and the sacred.

In *The Sad Fortunes of Rev. Amos Barton*, Eliot's narrator makes reference to the over-importance placed upon "text" in reference to preaching:

> "Rather a low-bred fellow, I think, Barton," said Mr. Pilgrim, who hated the Reverend Amos… "They said his father was a Dissenting shoemaker; and he's half a Dissenter himself. Why, doesn't he preach extempore in that cottage up here, of a Sunday's evening?"
>
> "Tchaw!" - this was Mr. Hackit's favourite interjection – 'that preaching without book's no good, only when a man has a gift, and has the Bible at his fingers' ends... But our parson's no gift at all that way; he can preach as good a sermon as need be heard when he writes it down. But

370 Cited by Martin Schäfer, ibid.

371 ibid.

> when he tries to preach wi'out book, he rambles about, and doesn't stick to the text; and every now and then he flounders about like a sheep as has cast itself, and can't get on'ts legs again. You wouldn't like that, Mrs. Patten, if you was to go to church now?"[372]

In Mr. Hackit's pronouncement regarding Amos Barton's failings as a preacher, his attempts to "preach wi'out book… and doesn't stick to the text" are considered noteworthy, even for Mrs. Patten, although she is known not to attend church at all. That the text is adhered to is *the* important question, above even that of attendance where such deviations would actually be heard. In the concerned minds of the Shepperton community, Eliot figures within the text of *Sad Fortunes of Rev. Amos Barton* a fear of the loss of "text" as a key with which one can divine the Divine. As noted in *Amos Barton*, a desire to hold onto a tradition of systems, "finished by keeping 'terms' at Cambridge, where there are able mathematicians, and butter sold by the yard, is not apparently the medium through which Christian doctrine will distil as welcome dew on withered souls".[373] There is a need to have "a flexible imagination that can take …a leap"[374] beyond such restrictions of a closed system in order to begin approaching the true nature of Being and ultimately the face of the sacred.

Turning to the role of literature and poetics, it is interesting to note that, in the end, Heidegger considers literature more a problem than a solution. This is pointed out in the Heideggerian lectures on Nietzsche, which accompany his readings of Hölderlin in 1934. Nietzsche's saying "God is dead" is the key-word of Heidegger's analysis of the disease of humanity and it is this saying which restructures both Heidegger's interpretation of Hölderlin and his call for a return to seeking for the sacred. For Heidegger, the literary aspects in Nietzsche's writing actually distorts rather than clarifies its philosophical content. By way of contrast, as noted by Martin Schäfer, Heidegger ultimately sees Nietzsche as a *dichtender Denker*, "a poeticising thinker"[375] whereas Hölderlin is a *denkender Dichter*, "a thinking poet".[376]

---

[372] George Eliot, *Scenes of Clerical Life*, 1857 ed. Jennifer Gribble (London: Penguin Books, 1998) p. 13.
[373] ibid., p. 28.
[374] ibid., p. 27.
[375] Schäfer, op. cit.
[376] ibid.

Heidegger accepts Nietzsche as a writer of literature, but he finds problems in his conclusions. In reference to Nietzsche's statement that God is dead, Heidegger argues that merely stating the death of God is not enough to rid us of the now-remaining ontotheological schema. On the contrary, Heidegger's opinion is that this schema still exists in Nietzsche and it does so more powerfully than ever before in the entire history of Being. The Nietzschean *Übermensch* merely takes over the vacant seat of the newly killed god. In the Übermensch's "will to power", Heidegger finds *a will of will*: a will that only wills itself and that accomplishes its self-will in that it finds its own power mirrored in the "imprints" it leaves in the world. This "will to will" or "will *of* will" is always on the move, will always outdo itself, and will return in new forms, new stamps, new imprints and, ironically, new literature.[377]

The only thing that is constant in this steady flow of forms is the self-positing fact that there is a form that keeps attempting to master chaos. Or to use a term Heidegger himself comes up with to describe this movement, what masters the eternal flow is the *"Freiheit der Gestalt"*, the freedom of something which should find a translation between figure and statue.[378] In this way, the freedom *of* form, or rather the freedom *to* form, does not free from the ontotheological. The never-ending invention of new forms will rather repeat the ontotheological endlessly as Coleridge's Ancient Mariner tells his tale, renewed evermore "like night, from land to land" in some ever new "strange power of speech".[379]

In light of this eternal return of forms of language, there is to be no resolution to what Nietzsche set out to overturn – merely another book among others. We are back where we began. Heidegger readily identifies Nietzsche's Zarathustra, the *Gestalt* in the centre of this piece of literature, with his creator. The figure of Zarathustra would then be the very expression of the philosopher's figurative power that distorts the potential of his thought. Eliot is also very conscious of this

---

377 Martin Heidegger, *What is Called Thinking?* trans. J. Glenn Gray 1958 (New York: Harper and Row, 1968) pp. 68ff.

378 Schäfer, op. cit.

379 Samuel Taylor Coleridge, "The Rime of the Ancient Mariner" (1798) – *Norton Anthology of English Literature, Vol. 2 – 6th Edition* (London: W.W. Norton and Company, 1993) line 586, p. 345.

possibility and the "will to power" that can distort the "telling the simple story". As the narrator is quick to note in *Sad Fortunes of Rev. Amos Barton*:

> … you will say [reader]… Surely you are misrepresenting the facts.
>
> Heaven forbid! For not having a fertile imagination, as you perceive, and being unable to invent thrilling incidence for your amusement, my only merit must lie in the faithfulness with which I represent to you the humble experience of an ordinary fellow-mortal. I wish to stir your sympathy with commonplace troubles – to win your tears for real sorrow: sorrow such as may live next door to you – such as walks neither in rags nor in velvet, but in very ordinary decent apparel.[380]

Here Eliot strikes the key issue that is to be the ultimate task of writing – not the forming of forms – but *Dichtung*, the telling of "truth". This is what Heidegger sees in Hölderlin apart from Nietzsche. What Heidegger distinguishes from literature as *Dichtung*, first of all Hölderlin's *Dichtung*, has nothing to do with writing and it is not ultimately- as Heidegger asserts throughout *The Origin of the Work of Art* – aesthetics itself. *Dichtung* is a gift of truth or, as Heidegger puts it, authenticity in, for, and beyond itself. *Dichtung* takes place as the event which brings Ricoeur's "the world of the text" and "the world of the reader", which is opened up by it, into Being. *Dichtung* or "Truth" is the shock of being in the world. And if language is the "house of Being", as Heidegger puts it, it is *Dichtung* or "Truth" that gives form to this home, yet also displaces it at the same time. But the sort of poetics Heidegger has in mind does not display the artist's figurative skills. For Heidegger, Hölderlin's poetic language is a language of the name. The world named in this language is thus opened up to what Heidegger calls a "people". And at the same time this language immediately falls prey to the oblivion of Being when being used in daily intercourse. But the autonomy of the aesthetic sphere keeps it from definite decline. For Heidegger poetic language is a language spoken only for the sake of language itself. Poetic language is not instrumentalized as a sign for the purpose of communication in the way it happens to language in everyday life. Although according to Heidegger's history of Being the world of ancient Greece begins with

[380] George Eliot, *Scenes of Clerical Life*, p. 59.

the stories told by Homer, Heidegger does not consider the Homeric myths to be the origin of this world. A people's language and a people's world do not originate in mythology but rather it is poetics that arise *within* language as a necessary event, because it is only when poetics as self-sufficient language arises that Being, and thus the sacred, can be announced and thereby "be". The "poetic dwelling" on earth, which Heidegger's lectures on Hölderlin in *What is called Thinking?* reveal, does not mean a return to a life sheltered by myth. This "poetic dwelling" is the shock of the emptiness left by the lack of the sacred.

This is not, however, a return to a Romantic notion of the power of mythology. This is an affirmation of what modernity has termed the autonomy of the aesthetic sphere. The realm of the aesthetic secularises the enclosed space of the ancient sacred in which the gods used to appear. The sacred can be experienced when language is spoken for its own sake. According to Heidegger, Hölderlin's poetry manages to catch a trace of the sacred because it actually reflects the impossibility of forcing an epiphany into Being. Hölderlin constantly seeks after the very lack of sacred names in modern humanity. For Heidegger the trace of the sacred is thus to be found in the very fragility of the Hölderlinian word. This word is deprived of the only function it has in the modern world: its employment of a communicative sign. What retraces the sacred in Hölderlin would be nothing but the silence that comes into Being by his words. Heidegger finds in this silence of the sacred (or rather "sacred silence") a *mourning* of language, which is also the mourning of the sacred in the double sense of the genitive through Hölderlin's mourning for the vanished gods of ancient Greece and Christianity. According to Heidegger, this act of mourning will never be accomplished as a Freudian work of mourning which overcomes its lost object. Neither will this mourning lose itself by clinging to this object in a melancholic fashion. Heidegger presents the act of sacred mourning, as the act of letting the vanished gods be what they are: vanished. With the absence of epiphany and *parousia*, Hölderlin's poetry keeps a sacred space open in which a god could show up, to use George Eliot's phrase, as "the possible". Heidegger's sacred is the transcendental spacing in which epiphany could happen without being produced by human will. The sacred therefore signifies the absence of religion without offering a new one. The sacred is the absence or failure of the name, never a metaphor or a trope, which a writer would be able to create, let alone master.

Eliot shows this sense of mourning throughout *Scenes of Clerical Life*. The loss of Milly Barton proves to be the salvation of Amos. As she begins to fade under "the heaviness of trouble… gentle, uncomplaining Millie – whose delicate body was becoming less fit for all that had to be done between rising up and lying down"[381] awakened in Amos and the community around him the "possible" of true community. At her death, mourning evokes true empathy:

> … Amos, for the first time, felt that he was alone - that day after day, month after month, year after year, would have to be lived through without Milly's love. Spring would come, and she would not be there; summer, and she would not be there; and he would never have her again with him by the fireside in the long evenings. The seasons all seemed irksome to his thoughts; and how dreary the sunshiny day that would be sure to come! She was gone from him; and he could never show her his love any more, never make up for omissions in the past by filling future days with tenderness.
>
> O the anguish of that thought, that we can never atone to our dead for the stinted affection we gave them, for the light answers we returned to their plaints or their pleadings, for the little reverence we showed to that sacred human soul that lived so close to us, and was the divinest thing God had given us to know.[382]

This sense of mourning, carried over into "Mr. Gilfil's Love Story" which begins with Mr. Gilfil's sense of loss, embodied as a locked room to which he had the key – a room that is the Vicarage now inherited from Amos Barton:

> But there was a chamber in Shepperton Vicarage which told a different story from that bare and cheerless dining room – a chamber never entered by any one besides Mr. Gilfil and old Martha the housekeeper… the blinds of this chamber were always down, except one-quarter, when Martha entered that she might air and clean it. She always asked Mr. Gilfil for the key, which he kept locked up in his bureau… Such was the locked-up chamber in Mr. Gilfil's house: a sort

[381] George Eliot, *Scenes of Clerical Life*, p. 60.
[382] ibid., p. 71.

> of visible symbol of the secret chamber in his heart, where he had long turned the key on early hopes and early sorrows, shutting up for ever all the passion and the poetry of his life.[383]

This sense of mourning and emptiness is passed down through the stories as a constant. In the end of each tale, we are met with death and loss – a space is opened and mourning is present. As the narrator of "Mr. Gilfil's Love Story" notes, humanity is in a state of constant erosion as "poor mortals [who] are often little better than wood-ashes":

> ...there is small sign of the sap, and the leafy freshness, and the bursting buds that were once there; but wherever we see wood-ashes, we know that all that early fullness of life must have been. I, at least, hardly ever look at a bent old man, or a wizened old woman, but I see also, with my mind's eye, that Past of which they are the shrunken remnant, and the unfinished romance of rosy cheeks and bright eyes seems sometimes of feeble interest and significance, compared with that drama of hope and love which has long ago reached its catastrophe, and left the poor soul, like a dim and dusty stage, with all its sweet garden-scenes and fair perspectives overturned and thrust out of sight.[384]

This opening left by death and later remembered in mourning is not filled - whether it is sorrow for the death of Milly Barton, the sad turns of fate upon Tina Sarti and Maynard Gilfil's love, or the injustice in the life of Janet Dempster at the hands of her husband - the reader is left without true closure. Gaps and fracture have been exposed, but where is wholeness then to come from? For Heidegger, this is the space that awaits the coming of the sacred and the coming of the subject. This is what I believe Eliot means by "repentance" within the context of her third story, entitled "Janet's Repentance". Repentance is the return to authentic being (*metanoia*) through a waiting amidst the fissure opened for and through the sacred. It is a place of destabilising of context and character as a turning toward the "possible". It is a place where language fails to fix certainty and its power to name is lost. At the end

[383] ibid., p. 88.
[384] ibid., p. 87.

of chapter XXIV of "Janet's Repentance", we see this in Janet's sitting beside the bed of her husband, Robert, as he fades into death, thus ending this relationship of abuse which she has been veiled behind:

> Suddenly a slight movement, like the passing away of a shadow, visible in his face, and he opened his eyes full on Janet.
> It was almost like meeting him again on the resurrection morning, after the night of the grave.
> "Robert, do you know me?"
> He kept his eyes fixed on her, and there was a faintly perceptible motion of the lips, as if he wanted to speak.
> But the moment of speech was for ever gone… the thick veil of death fell between them, and her lips touched a corpse.[385]

After the passing of her husband, Janet seeks confession for wrongs she has done (indulging in drink, slandering Mr. Tryan's name) and confides in Mr. Tryan whom she sees to be a truly kind and understanding person. As she goes out into the night, she experiences an opening into the place of the sacred:

> So she went out into the dewy starlight… walked on quickly till she turned into the fields; then she slackened her pace a little, enjoying the sense of solitude which a few hours before had been intolerable for her. The Divine Presence did not now seem far off, where she had not wings to reach it; prayer itself seemed superfluous in those moments of calm trust. The temptation which had so lately made her shudder before the possibilities of the future, was now a source of confidence; for had she not been delivered from it? Had not rescue come in the extremity of danger? Yes; Infinite Love was caring for her. She felt like a little child whose hand is firmly grasped by its father, as its frail limbs make their way over the rough ground; if it should stumble, the father will not let it go.[386]

As the narrator describes Janet's awakening at this point, she describes entering into the sacred as one whose soul is baptised:

> That walk in the dewy starlight remained for ever in Janet's memory as one of the baptismal epochs,when the soul, dipped in the sacred

[385] ibid., p. 328.
[386] ibid., p. 337.

> waters of joy and peace, rises from them with new energies, with unalterable longings.[387]

Yet this is not something to be named, only marked by "unalterable longings". Like the sacred name as put forward by Hölderlin, naming of the sacred will fail to dominate. Heidegger's reading of Hölderlin can be read to aim at nothing less than an attempt at repeating this failure or at least experiencing its "shock" in mourning and "unalterable longing". It is the writer who stands in this troubling gap, as Empedokles forever falling into the fire "divinely gleaming", stands between his people and the absent god. But rather than close this fissure by trying to dominate or control, the writer's true vocation is to prevent such closure by continually reopening this sacred space in-between them - *das Zwischen des Heiligen* as Heidegger calls it; in-between the lost gods and the possibility of the gods to come;[388] in-between the withdrawing gods and remaining humanity, and in-between all singular human beings. Each of these human beings falls back onto his/her fragile *Being-unto-death.* Being-unto-death undermines an instrumentalisation of the world and thus opens up the possibility of being with others. The world of the sacred spacing of in-between thus closely resembles the world Heidegger has outlined in *Being and Time* as the world of *Eigentlichkeit*, as *the world of proper being.* Since the poetic act has to open up this ever-fracturing space of the in-between, it is first of all the poet who is threatened by the failure of this act. The uncontrollable turning of the name turns against the poet *as* poet. In the first lecture on Hölderlin, Heidegger talks about a pain of Being which is also a pain of the sacred and moreover it is the writer's pain: the pain which keeps the fissure open, ultimately given the vocation of "writing the *pain* of naming the failure" instead of failing to name. In *The Origin of the Work of Art*, written at the same time as his lectures on Hölderlin, Heidegger uses a word for this openness of the fissure – this sacred space opened up by the shock of *Dichtung* or "Truth" is called *Gestalt* – "figuring".

Figuring serves as borderline to the safety-zone in which the failure of the name is turned into the name of failure and in which at

387 ibid.

388 Schäfer, ibid.

the same time one can get rid of the figurative language of the ontotheological. The keeping of the name and the deletion of figural speech in Hölderlin's *Dichtung* are accomplished by enclosing this *Dichtung* in the figure as such: the *Gestalt*. It is a form of poetic madness that breaks in when this figurative borderline dividing the metaphors from the names, and the names from destruction, is transgressed.

The *Gestalt* of the sacred is never there but always a trace to withdraw and at the same time a shock to come. It is *the gift of form* rather than the Nietzschean *power to form*. The Heideggerian figuring of the sacred brings, though hidden, an imprint or type that draws the line separating that which remains whole – the holy – from that which becomes scattered in every day life – the profane. A withdrawal and retreat of the figurative in language, of its metaphors and tropes, is sign of the sacred, and at the same time this withdrawal retraces the original figure as the *Gestalt*. The stability of the *Gestalt* keeps the domination of the failure of the name from failing. The imprint of the *Gestalt* is never there but always yet to come and already gone. This is analogous to what, in the graphical sense, Derrida means by "writing" in his earlier work, particularly *Of Grammatology*. Heidegger is acutely aware of the problem of *Gestalt*. He defines the sacred spacing as a "trace" instead, i.e. the very word Derrida will later take up as a synonym for writing and the term used by Levinas. What safeguards the purity of language in poetry is now madness itself: Not the Hölderlinian madness transgressing the borderline of *Gestalt*, but – Heidegger uses Trakl's poetic term, which is of course not to be taken metaphorically – a *sanfter Wahnsinn*, a "gentle madness".[389] This madness is madness because it sweeps language away by its own destructive power of naming. This madness is gentle because in sweeping language away it also effects the gathering of language in poetic naming. Heidegger tries to think this sweeping away and this gathering of speech in one, at once, as gentle madness. Thus he tries to get rid of the last ontotheological figure haunting his own discourse: the *Gestalt*, which was to keep open the sacred in-between. "Gentle madness" can be seen as an alternate, catastrophic name for the sacred: a madness which loses the sacred at the very point it gains it, and vice versa. But if one wants to call the sacred in-between held open by *Gestalt* a gathering of a people amidst *poiesis*, one would have to describe this gathering primarily as a fragile

---

[389] Schäfer, ibid. See also lecture IX in Martin Heidegger, *What is Called Thinking?*, pp. 88ff.

network opened up by failed readings. To Heidegger, Hölderlin's *Dichtung* conveys nothing but the incommensurable shock of the "un-understandable", and it conveys the sacred only in that it does so. The people's community Heidegger has in mind would be held together by nothing but everybody's failure to read. This theme is carried forward by Eliot as she challenges the reader in her next novel, *Adam Bede* and its now-famous chapter XVII "Where the Story Pauses A Little". Here, the reader is asked to "see" rather than merely read, marking her acknowledgement of the failure of reading alone to provoke and awaken the "possible" that is "clothed in human form".

# Chapter 7

# *Adam Bede* – Poetics of the Possible and Learning to "See"

So that ye may have
*Clear images before your gladden'd eyes*
Of nature's unambitious underwood
And flowers that prosper in the shade. And when
I speak of such among the flock as swerved
Or fell, those only shall be singled out
Upon whose lapse, or error, something more
Than brotherly forgiveness may attend.[390]

*Adam Bede* is an exercise in bringing "clear images" before the reader's "gladden'd eyes". George Eliot opens her story by citing this passage from Wordsworth's *The Excursion*, of which *Adam Bede* can be seen as a prose echo. In the poem by Wordsworth, a pastor mourns his dead parishioner Ellen, who is buried next to her dead baby and is described as "a virtuous women, in pure youth", "delivered to distress and shame" by a lover who breaks his promise of fidelity and leaves her alone when she becomes pregnant. It is interesting that of all the portions of *The Excursion*, this is the stanza which George Eliot chooses to reference, one that is an admonition *to see clearly images that are before the reader.* Given this agenda by George Eliot from the outset, I would like to propose a reading of *Adam Bede* that observes the iconographic signifiers of her narrative and *sees* them for what they are. In this regard,

[390] William Wordsworth, *The Excursion* (1814), book VI, lines 651-658. Cited on the title page of the original printing of *Adam Bede* by William Blackwood and Sons in 1859. Reprinted in *Adam Bede* (Oxford: Oxford Classics, 1996) p. 2.

I will be utilising Mieke Bal's definition of "iconographic signifier" as that which the artist utilises to

> help the reader recognise the preceding visual tradition, which in turn refers to the verbal text; in the second case the recognition is directly related to the text and works with the text's verbal devices. [We utilise] the term "iconographic sign" for the sign that travels the visual-verbal route. The sign based upon the solely verbal reference then falls under the more encompassing concept of intertexuality and exemplifies the subcategory of pre-textual thematic reference.[391]

As noted by Valentine Cunningham, "the distinction of *Adam Bede* is to tell a story, and also tell about telling a story. This is a novel about obscure lives, and also about *how* to be a novel about obscure lives".[392] More than "reading" in a traditional sense, George Eliot wants the reader to "see" the world by "viewing" well. In this way there is more to "reading" *Adam Bede* than merely acknowledging the words on the page. This is an attempt at creating a bridge between the visual and the verbal accounts of reality to bring forward that which is without language and yet has meaning.

*Adam Bede* is a sentient novel, fully aware of the story it is portraying and equally aware that it is being "read" by the reading subject. Akin to Samuel Johnson's statement in "Preface to Shakespeare", Eliot takes seriously the edict that "the end of writing is to instruct".[393] Additionally, this is a narrative that finds part of its genesis as a reported history, told to Eliot by her Aunt. Eliot's choice not to record her Aunt's tale, but to tell it herself moves this narrative to a form that is neither fiction nor fact, yet is more than both. As noted by Cunningham:

> It's *My* Aunt's Story – a narration of George Eliot's own, her own design, her particular narrative blend, the product of a real, live author, one who is neither dead nor disappeared (in those curious formulas of

391 Mieke Bal, *Reading "Rembrandt": Beyond the Word-Image Opposition,* (Cambridge: Cambridge University Press, 1991) p. 184.

392 Valentine Cunningham, 'Introduction to *Adam Bede*,' in George Eliot's *Adam Bede* (Oxford: Oxford Classics, 1996) p. viii.

393 Samuel Johnson, "Preface to Shakespeare" cited in M.H. Abrams, op. cit., p. 19.

> Roland Barthes and Michel Foucault), the written sum of all her intentions, beliefs, philosophies, her various discourses (as they say), her assumptions about how lives and stories should go. It's also My *Aunt's* Story – a historically rooted narration, a story steeped in the real, datable, historical world of real lives, actual locales, living persons and tractable bits of religious history and social circumstance. Again, it's also My Aunt's *Story* – a story, emphatically a story; a poeticization, a rhetoricization, a fictionalising of a history and a philosophy. This is a text obedient and susceptible to the constraints and conventions of numerous available narrative forms past and present.[394]

## Iconographic Reading – Chapter XVII and Dutch Realism

Eliot strives in her poetics to show that there are certain laws that apply in both the fictive and historical realities, utilising the alignment of the two worlds as a reciprocal testimonial to the truth of each – each "world" backs up the claims of the other. For example, life has cause and effect in both the world of *Adam Bede* and the world of the reader and actions do have their consequences, albeit the difference between choice and determinism is often blurred. In Chapter XVI "Links", the Rector, Mr. Irwine, speaks to Arthur Donnithorne of the "Nemesis" that is the "unpitying" nature of consequences due to one's "deeds":

> A man can never do anything at variance with his own nature. He carries within him the germ of his most exceptional action: and if we wise people make eminent fools of ourselves on any particular occasion, we must endure the legitimate conclusion that we carry a few grains of folly to our one ounce of wisdom... Our deeds carry their terrible consequences... consequences that are hardly ever confined to ourselves. And it is best to fix our minds on that certainty, instead of considering what may be the elements of excuse for us.[395]

Eliot shifts from the fictive realm of her created characters to address the reading subject directly in Chapter XXIX "The Next Morning". These actions or "deeds" reflected upon in the fictive dimension in

[394] Valentine Cunningham, op. cit., p. xxxvi.
[395] George Eliot, *Adam Bede*, pp. 172 -73.

Chapter XVI "Links" that determine one's subjectivity and are "hammered home in narrative reflections"[396] by the narrator to the reader amidst the narrative:

> Our deeds determine us, as much as we determine our deeds; and until we know what has been or will be the particular combination of outward with inward facts, which constitutes a man's critical actions, it will be better not to think ourselves wise about his character.[397]

The nature of determinism and causality is questioned in both the fictive and historical reality and this synchronicity gives a testimony to the truth of each realm's claim: the fictive supports the historical and the historical supports the fictive.

The claims of subjectivity are also supported in such a manner. In the case of Dinah Morris, her identity is self-creating and self-sustaining as evidenced in her resolute assertion: "I am Dinah Morris", As Cunningham notes,

> this is clearly an 'I' worth attending to, whatever we might have thought before of mill-girls, rural eloquence, provincial intelligence, and Nonconformist religious sincerity. The banished, muted, disregarded selfhood of the Victorian margin crowds thus on to the centre-stage, in an arranged renovation of sympathy and imagination that has the male, scathing, educated and uneducated Anglican audience awed into silence.[398]

The query in the opening sentence of *The Impressions of Theophrastus Such*, "it is my habit to give an account to myself of the characters I meet with: can I give any true account of my own?",[399] is responded to in Dinah Morris' declaration of identity: we can make an account of ourselves and in many respects are the only ones who can. The first person singular of Dinah Morris stands against any other characterisation of her – she is who she is because she says so. (This

[396] Valentine Cunningham, p. xxx.
[397] George Eliot, op. cit., p. 313.
[398] Valentine Cunningham, op. cit., p. xix.
[399] George Eliot, *The Impressions of Theophratus Such* (1879) (London: Everyman Press, 1995) p. 3.

has particular resonance in Dinah Morris as the incarnate "I am" who is the new Adam, as shall be discussed in further depth.) In this way, George Eliot through the narrative of *Adam Bede*

> … exactly mirrors, and thus mightily animates and energises, the struggle by whole segments of English society and geography to be heard and seen in Victorian England, to be taken seriously, to be known for themselves, and to have their selfhood, their identity, their name recognised, in the pages of the English Novel… For George Eliot, being realistic and true to life will result in a fiction whose plot exemplifies, inexorably, some such laws of the material and human world.[400]

Identity and the "selfing" of the subject are central to Eliot's textuality. In Chapter XVII of *Adam Bede,* Eliot repeatedly refers to the "reader" directly – acknowledging that the one who reads the story is to be identified *and* to be identifying oneself. While Hölderlin in *Empedokles* only longed for the reader to complete the hero's journey, Eliot calls out specifically through direct discourse to the reader, binding one to the fictive encounter as a member in the cast of characters and expanding the identity of the reading subject to a mythic level. As noted by Cunningham:

> … it is also the case that George Eliot had, and just as foundationally, been influenced by the argument that for a narrative to have any force of a religious or sacred nature – for it to be great in the way she wanted – it would have to amalgamate the historical and the philosophical with the poetic so as to comprise the mythic. This was the line of argument adopted by David Friedrich Strauss about the Bible.[401]

Yet while it was an argument adopted by Strauss, it was not truly actualised. In this way Eliot picks up where the 'Concluding Dissertation' of Strauss failed - to realise a "true fiction" of the life of Jesus that serves as *a poetic frame* through which to view life. Addressing the reader, Eliot makes this note:

> But you must have perceived long ago that I have no lofty vocation, and that I aspire to give no more than a faithful account of men and

[400] Valentine Cunningham, ibid., pp. viii, xxx.
[401] ibid., p. xxxv.

> things as they have mirrored themselves in my mind. The mirror is doubtless defective; the outlines will sometimes be disturbed; the reflection faint or confused; but I feel as much bound to tell you, as precisely as I can, what that reflection is, as if I were in the witness-box narrating my experience on oath.[402]

M.H. Abram states that "as late as the middle of the eighteenth century important critics continued to illustrate the concept of imitation by the nature of a looking glass".[403] In Goethe's *Die Leiden des jungen Werthers*, this "mirror" is located within the artist reflecting the Ideal onto the blank page:

> … I feel the presence of the Almighty Who created us in His own image, and the breath of that universal love which sustains us, as we float in an eternity of bliss… I often think with longing, Oh, If only I could express it, could breathe onto paper all that lives so warm and full within me, that it might become the mirror of my soul, as my soul is the mirror of the infinite God![404]

In this dimension of Goethe's rendering, the reading subject is invited into a house of mirrors – the writer's soul mirroring the Ideal mirrored from God which is mirrored onto the page to be mirrored onto the reader. Yet Eliot's poetic mirror "is doubtless defective; the outlines will sometimes be disturbed; the reflection faint or confused". She is aware that what is being offered before the reader is not a mimesis, but a *disturbed outline* which frames and focuses the reader's attention for viewing reality. Given the scope of her project as suggested by the choice of title *Adam Bede,*[405] George Eliot utilises her narrative project to suggest a "viewing" of humanity and history via this narrative frame.

---

[402] George Eliot, *Adam Bede* – 1859 (Oxford: Oxford Classics, 1996) p. 175.

[403] M.H. Abrams, *The Mirror and the Lamp* (Oxford: Oxford University Press, 1953) p. 32.

[404] Johann Wolfgang Von Goethe, "The Sorrows of Young Werther" from *Goethe: The Collected Works Volume 11,* ed. David E. Wellbury (Princeton: Princeton University Press, 1988) p. 6, (entry of 10th May 1771).

[405] "Adam Bede" brings together the references to "Adam", who in the biblical account of Genesis is the first created human, and Venerable "Bede" whose *Ecclesiastical History of the Church* is an ancient accounting of the "history" of the church.

With regard to "framing", I refer to Jonathan Culler's assertion that

> since the phenomena criticism deals with are signs, forms with socially-constituated meanings, one might try to think not of context but of *the framing of signs*: how are signs constituted (*framed*) by various discursive practices, institutional arrangements, systems of value, semiotic mechanisms... The expression *framing the sign* has several advantages over context: it reminds us that framing is something we do; it hints of the framing up ('falsifying evidence beforehand in order to make someone appear guilty')... and it eludes the incipient positivism of 'context' by alluding to the semiotic function of framing in art, where the frame is determining, setting off the object or event as art, and yet the frame itself may be nothing tangible, pure articulation.[406]

By the creation of visual-verbal signs, George Eliot recovers that which can be lost and submerged and *frames* it for the reader, both undoing institutional arrangements that hinder a proper "reading" and, at the same time, offering a re-imagined poetics through which to view life. In Chapter XVII, "In Which the Story Pauses A Little," George Eliot states that her thesis is "to tell my simple story, without trying to make things seem better than they were; dread nothing, indeed, but falsity, which, in spite of one's best efforts, there is reason to dread. Falsehood is so easy, truth so difficult".[407]

To illustrate this thesis, George Eliot goes on to use an illustration *of* illustration:

> The pencil is conscious of a delightful facility in drawing a griffin – the longer the claws, and the larger the wings, the better; but the marvellous facility which we mistook for genius, is apt to forsake us when we want to draw a real unexaggerated lion.[408]

In this way George Eliot "draws" an iconographic sign that travels the visual-verbal route. "Falsehood" is not explained by Eliot as much as it is *portrayed* through the act of visual poetics which subvert written language and thereby frees text through this act of intertexuality in grafting the *verbal* to the *visual* – in order to understand "falsehood",

---

406 Jonathan Culler, *Framing the Sign: Criticism and Its Institutions* (Oxford: Blackwell, 1988) p. ix.

407 George Eliot, *Adam Bede*, p. 177.

408 ibid.

one must *see* as well as understand it. Visual poetics forces the reader to ask what the visual counterpart of a word is. "Falsehood" in this instance is tethered with an *image* – a mythical griffin – which creates a sense of "density" through the verbal-visual tethering. "Density" in this instance refers to that which is defined by Nelson Goodman as conveying a bridged intertexuality of visual and verbal:

> [*Density* is] the fundamental inseparability of individual signs, as opposed to discreteness. This view eliminates at once difference between discourse and image... the same density that characterises visual texts obstructs the propositional clarity of verbal texts... This recognition means that the difference between verbal and visual texts is no longer one of the status and delimitation of the signs that constitute them. And the visual model, apparently predominant, overwhelms the concrete particularity of the signifier, giving rise to the "cloudiness" in each medium... language is as dense as pictures.[409]

The use of visual poetics allows for an expansion of meaning and ultimately a density that makes visible that which can (and often does) get overlooked. What is possible is the framing of that which language cannot display. The sign based upon the solely verbal reference then falls under the more encompassing concept of intertexuality and exemplifies the subcategory of pre-textual thematic reference.

As a reference to this act of intertexuality between the verbal and visual, George Eliot proceeds to refer the reader in Chapter XVII to the works of the sixteenth century Dutch Realists:

> It is for this rare, precious quality of truthfulness that I delight in many Dutch paintings, which lofty-minded people despise. I find a source of delicious sympathy in these faithful pictures of a monotonous homely existence, which has been the fate of so many more among my fellow-mortals than a life of pomp or of absolute indigence, of tragic suffering or of world-stirring actions... "Foh!" says my idealistic friend, "what vulgar details!"[410]

---

[409] Mieke Bal, op. cit., pp. 13-14. Citing the notion of "density" in reference to Nelson Goodman's *Languages of Art: An Approach to a Theory of Symbols* (Indianapolis: Hackett, 1976).

[410] George Eliot, *Adam Bede*, p. 177.

Dutch Realism created a remarkable shift in sixteenth-century art through its seeming lack of discrimination regarding the detail considered germane to a given work.[411] No detail could be considered irrelevant – a stray dog, a fallen tree branch, an overturned water bucket. Each item must be considered if the whole is to be truly framed. No sign is therefore neutral and is valued to the sense of wholeness for the composition. Furthermore, as the verbal calls to the visual, a desire in illustration is provoked into a tension between verbal and visual. This provoked moment, where sign is now the event of the visual and verbal exchange, creates "framing". Moving this notion to reading and writing text, one can engage is what Bal terms "iconographic reading":

> [Iconographic reading] is a discursive mode of reading because it subordinates the visually represented element to something else, thus privileging the symbol at the expense of the icon, while displacing the indexicality that allowed this semiosis in the first place. *Iconography means, literally, writing by means of images.* It is this challenge to the unwarranted assumption that visual art is iconic and verbal art symbolic that turns the iconographic mode of reading into a powerful critical tool, a tool that can be used to undermine the opposition between word and image.[412]

Bal is referring to a "reading" of paintings in this instance, yet the principle remains the same for the "reading" of text. Iconographic reading allows for a powerful release from both language and image and approach a reclaiming of what is lost when each (language and image) are isolated into distinction from the other.

In the case of *Adam Bede*, the reader is prompted to view/read the narrative and recognise the "density" of the underlying story that can so easily be overlooked – the role of women, the question of class, the forgotten rural life, the face of God. In this way, George Eliot

---

411 Hugh Whitemeyer makes an extensive study of George Eliot's knowledge of the visual composition in *George Eliot and the Visual Arts* (New Haven: Yale University Press, 1979). In speaking of her use of portraiture in relation to her character development, Whitemeyer holds that Eliot in *Scenes of Clerical Life* and *Adam Bede* was "primarily concerned to show that looks do mirror personality," that there are, as G.H. Lewes put it, "subtle connections between physical and mental organisation," p. 45.

412 Mieke Bal, op. cit., p. 178.

juxtaposes the evoked against the narrated story (for example, the image of humanity's Fall from Grace against the image of Hetty Sorrel's fall in the garden of Hayslope, the image of Jesus against the image of Dinah Morris) in order to let them interact and to let the tensions between the stories produce new meanings. As Bal notes, "Iconographic reading tends to obliterate the other story because stories are sometimes so generally known that reader/viewers have difficulty realising to what extent the visual work responding to the story signifies its own story".[413] This is similar to John Ruskin's use of *ut pictura poiesis* throughout *Modern Painters* where painting and writing are used together as hermeneutic lens for the interpretation of true "poetry". According to Ruskin, "Painting is properly to be opposed to *speaking* and *writing*, but not to *poetry*. Both painting and speaking are methods of expression. Poetry is the employment of either for the noblest purposes".[414] For Ruskin, it is in bringing works of art together – the visual and the textual – that allows for "Great art… produced by men who feel acutely and nobly…some sort of expression".[415] As George Landow notes, "It is thus particularly appropriate that a work [*Modern Painters*] which had been undertaken to defend the value of painting should have referred to the principle of *ut pictura poiesis*, for throughout the Renaissance and eighteenth century, poetry and painting had been juxtaposed as a means of defending the prestige of the visual art".[416]

## (Wo)men in the Garden

George Eliot offers an interesting (re)reading of the Genesis account of humanity's Fall in the Garden of Eden. As opposed to offering a dualism between the sexes that results in a view of women as a gender of weaker flesh that bending to Satan's lure, and in humanity's expulsion from the Garden of Eden, Eliot disturbs this rendering by

[413] ibid., p. 207.
[414] John Ruskin, *The Works of John Ruskin* ed. E.T. Cook and Alexander Wedderburn (London, 1903-1912) Vol. 5, p. 31.
[415] ibid., p. 32.
[416] George P. Landow, *The Aesthetic and Critical Theories of John Ruskin* (Princeton: Princeton University Press, 1971) p. 43.

showing *two* women in the Garden of Hayslope: Hetty Sorrel and Dinah Morris. They are portrayed as humanity in the first and second Adam, respectively, yet embodied in the female. Gender guilt is further overturned in this action through the secondary "Eves" of Arthur Donnithorne and Adam Bede who also show the extremes of damnation and grace. In this way fallen and obedient characters represent *humanity* rather than *gender* so that neither male nor female holds exclusive claim to sin or salvation. But it is a story told primarily through Hetty and Dinah - for it is their story which is most "visible" in this accounting. While the novel is entitled *Adam Bede*, it is that which is veiled beneath this title, namely the female characters, who are ultimately the centre of the reader's concern. In this new accounting of the narrative of the Fall, we are asked to "see" a side that had no language to be told – namely the choice, and lack of choice, of women.

Dinah and Hetty are mirrors of each other and humanity itself throughout the unfolding narrative of *Adam Bede.* Hetty wants to cast her past life behind her; but her "narrow bit of an imagination" only leads her to make "ill-defined pictures" of the future.[417] Dinah's sympathetic intuition, on the other hand, is based on her awareness of biblical history, and yet Hetty "for any practical result of strength in life, or trust in death, (had) never appropriated a single Christian idea or Christian feeling".[418] She is guided only by her current sensual responses. As noted by U.C. Knoepflmacher, parallels can be drawn between Milton's Eve in *Paradise Lost*[419] and the portrait we are offered of Hetty Sorrel in *Adam Bede.* In *Paradise Lost*, Eve's appetite is aroused "by the smell/ So savoury of that Fruit" as she approaches the Tree of Knowledge.[420] Similarly, Hetty is stimulated by the "sweet languid odours of the garden at the Chase" where she will lose her innocence.[421] Milton's Eve wants to be immortal, to rise in station. She fancies herself heightened "through expectation high/ Of knowledge, nor was God-head from her thought".[422] Hetty, later, "without knowing what she should do with her life,... craved the means of living as long as possible; and when we desire eagerly to find something, we are apt to

417 ibid., p. 154.

418 ibid., p. 384.

419 John Milton, "Paradise Lost" 1667 in *Norton Anthology of English Literature 6th edition.* Vol. 2, M.H. Abrams, ed. (London: Norton, 1993).

420 John Milton, ibid., Book IX, lines 740-741, p. 1583.

421 *Adam Bede*, p. 136.

422 John Milton, op. cit., Book IX, lines 789-790, p. 1584.

search for it in hopeless places",[423] flutters between "memory and dubious expectation" as she passes the gates of the forbidden Fir-Tree Grove:

> That was the foreground of Hetty's picture; behind it lay a bright hazy something – days that were not to be as the other days of her life had been. It was as if she had been wooed by a river-god, who might at any time take her to his wondrous halls below a watery heaven.[424]

Milton's Eve indulges in a pagan worship of the tree from which she has eaten. Arthur mythologizes the wood in which he seduces Hetty as a "sacred grove" immune to time:

> His arm is stealing round the waist again, it is tightening its clasp; he is bending his face nearer and nearer to the round cheek, his lips are meeting those pouting child-lips, and for a long moment time has vanished. He may be a shepherd in Arcadia for aught he knows, he may be the first youth kissing the first maiden, he may be Eros himself, sipping the lips of Psyche – it is all one.[425]

Yet this "garden" is not fashioned by Keats. George Eliot is quick to show the reader that this sublime moment is but a figment of Arthur's imagination. The novelist's mythological references are every bit as ironic as those Milton uses to describe Adam and Eve's lovemaking after the Fall. If Adam and Eve soon feel ashamed in their nakedness, Arthur, too, becomes uncomfortable, suddenly conscious that "something bitter had begun to mingle itself with the fountain of sweets".[426] Adam and Eve are reminded of God's rule; Arthur is reminded of time. As Knoepflmacher notes, Arthur "pulls out his watch and wonders 'how late it is'. He hopes that his watch is too fast. It is later than he thinks".[427]

---

[423] *Adam Bede*, p. 380.
[424] ibid., p. 136.
[425] ibid., p. 137.
[426] ibid., p. 138.
[427] U.C. Knoepflmacher "On *Adam Bede*" in Ian Watt *The Victorian Novel: Modern Essays in Criticism* (London: Oxford University Press, 1971) pp. 274-275.

Hetty and Arthur stand and fall together in symbiosis through the choices they make. With the evoking of visual poetics, George Eliot calls to mind in the fir grove of Hayslope a mythical place *outside* the normal order of things – a fantasy akin to that of Keats, filled with wondrous halls found in Arcadia and rivers teeming with river-gods. These images are clear and vivid. So much so that the reader who passes out of the world of Hayslope and into the mythical land of Hetty and Arthur's creation clearly note that this is *not* Eden, but an imagined fantasy that evaporates under the density of the more compelling reality of Hayslope, the "true fiction" of time and place. This is where Eden is to be – amidst the dairy maids, real shepherds, and common people of the land. This is not an Eden populated by idealised Greek shepherds who are known only through poetry, but is a realist composition in the midst of real life. In this way, fiction gives way to a "truer" fiction.

Arthur notes in the realisation of time ("how late it is"), in his attempt to create sublimity, that this Arcadian grove is a fiction that will not last and "something bitter" has indeed entered into his fantasy. But there are no serpents in this garden nor is evil mediated by a third party – the bitterness that arises is found between the two momentary lovers and they alone. Humanity is to own its destiny and its choices. But the traditional narrative of the Fall is further overturned. The tempter of the garden, Arthur Donnithorne, freely escapes and lives seemingly above moral law. Where the Adam of Milton's *Paradise Lost* leaves the garden to head toward the hope of salvation, Hetty Sorrel as the fallen "Eve" of Hayslope leaves her encounter in the garden as a character under erasure. Hetty is left to her "objectless wandering, apart from all love… clinging to life only as the hunted wounded brute clings to it".[428] She wishes to disappear, vanish, to "wander out of sight, and drown herself where her body would never be found, and no one should know what became of her"[429] which stirs an image that compels one to "see" Goethe's *Elective Affinities* played out anew. Throughout the narrative of *Adam Bede*, the reader is aware that Hetty is not truly alone in her Fall and that Arthur is living beyond the moral code by denying his relationship with her. In this way George Eliot puts before the reader the claim that guilt is never black and white, and that one person's fall from grace is surely tied to a larger circle. Arthur is exposed in the end, but remains to live another life. Hetty's fate does not contain this

---

428 *Adam Bede*, p. 389.

429 ibid., p. 383.

option. It is shown that Hetty is not fully to blame for the events that lead to her demise, yet neither is she fully absolved from them. In the end justice is rendered more to some than to others and with differing consequences. In the garden of good and evil there are no pure victims nor are there pure villains. For Eliot, choices that are made are always part of a community, never in isolation. The plight or salvation of humanity is not to be found in finding one at fault, be it a gender or a class, but in acknowledging the interwoven nature of all people who ultimately share triumphs and defeats together in seen and unseen ways. It is the unseen that concerns Eliot and it is that which she not only describes but displays through the frame of *Adam Bede.*

## A Poetics of Jesus in *Adam Bede*

Another compelling overturning of narrative in *Adam Bede* is with regard to the image of Jesus, the "new Adam". As I have noted in previous chapters, George Eliot felt distraught during her translation of Strauss' *Das Leben Jesu.* She felt that Strauss had lost "the beautiful story" in his attempt to re-imagine the life of Jesus through his treatise. Fiction was a primary space where "the beautiful story" was re-imagined outside of nineteenth century higher criticism. Multiple attempts had been made to re-write a "life of Jesus" within the Victorian *zeitgeist.* As mentioned in chapter 5, poetics arising in novels such as Mrs. Ward's *Robert Elsmere*, Froude's *The Nemesis of Faith*, Pater's *Marius the Epicurean* and others strove to place this "story of stories" in a context germane to the day. *For George Eliot, the issue was not to re-write the old Gospel tale as repetition as much as it was a returning of the narrative to its humanity in the refiguring act of "true fiction" that is Gospel as writing.* The humility, grace, and mercy of Jesus that Strauss blithely dismantled in his Hegelian project was to be returned by George Eliot with a fusing of image and word that gave a greater density to this "beautiful story" than Strauss was capable of. Also, by creating a tension between the orthodox understanding of Jesus within Victorian England and the "true fiction" that was "the beautiful story" that was lost to Higher Criticism, George Eliot not only challenged the traditional images, but framed the tradition itself in a viewing within the framing of her poetics. To exemplify this in the case of visual poetics, we must look at the iconographic images that Eliot figures in *Adam Bede* employed from Dutch Realism, and specifically, the rendering of Jesus by Rembrandt.

In 1635 Rembrandt completed a sketch entitled *Last Supper, after Leonardo da Vinci*. The copy looks like a simple sketch, most likely to help the copyist memorise the work and reflect on the possibilities its composition offered. This sketch serves as a representative work of the painter's renderings of Jesus. As noted by Mieke Bal:

> What the sketch has in common with the composition of da Vinci's fresco is in the first place the isolation of the Christ figure, surrounded by the disciples who are ostensibly busy doing other things. In this respect, the "Rembrandt" sketch is closer to the fresco than to the Birago copy through which presumably "Rembrandt" read it. The static character of Christ is opposed to the down-to-earth commerce of the others. If the disciples of the left can be interpreted as listening and responding to the master with the exception of the figure next to Christ, those at the far right are definitely not attending to him. They are arguing among themselves, maybe plotting, maybe responding in their own way; Christ, in contrast, is not engaged with any of them. Christ is thus suspended from the narrative of talk, of worldly futility. He is absorbed... He is also emphatically alone. His hands, from a narrative standpoint, are engaged in the gestures of teaching; but his absorption undermines the teaching. It separates him from the others (who are clearly not listening anyway), as does the halo around his head.[430]

It is interesting to note that Rembrandt never went to Italy and therefore never saw the original da Vinci fresco which his sketch emulates. What is evident here is that imitation or *mimesis* was not the most important goal for Rembrandt. Instead, sharing the *framework* of da Vinci's fresco rather than work itself provided Rembrandt with a language of signs that the "reader" will acknowledge even if not overtly. Rembrandt's sketch although "written" in da Vinci's language, is not identical to the work from which language was borrowed, nor was it trying to be. This exemplifies "the difference between language and utterance, between system and actual signs"[431] which underscore the framing project of the iconographic.

Referring back to the Rembrandt sketch of *Last Supper, after*

---

[430] Mieke Bal, *Reading "Rembrandt"*, p. 201.
[431] ibid., pp. 431-432.

*Leonardo da Vinci*, one can observe that behind Christ's head is *another* head – that of a woman, leaning toward Christ with attentiveness. This is a clear shift from the "narrative" of da Vinci although the *composition* is strangely coherent in Rembrandt's sketch, as if this "person" has been there all along. Bal makes the following remarks:

> Since this is merely a sketch, nothing would be easier than to ignore it. For example, it can be easily dispensed with as an earlier but rejected attempt at drawing Christ's head. The pointed finger of the bald man next to Jesus can be directed toward Jesus or toward one of the figures on the other side, and the strangely unreal second head does not need to be a women's head, although it alone has long, curly hair. Moreover, that second head can be taken as a proleptic allusion to Judas, who will later come up to kiss Jesus, thus identifying himself as the traitor. So one would think we need not worry about this second head, although the depiction of this Judas as a woman is remarkable.[432]

It is noted by Bal that women-in-excess are, as she states, "quite 'Rembrandtesque': They are readable, never mind how enigmatic they may otherwise be".[433] Here, this shadow woman seems to be uninvited as one only able to listen and not partake. To the "reader", this figure is compelling in that she is the only one who seems to be attending to what Christ is saying. In this way, the "reader" is led to wonder what she hears as one who is so close, what she feels as one who listens but only from outside the circle. Moreover, the "reader" is taken to *her* place at the table, which is what Bal terms "*excurse*" – that figuring within compositional form which leads the reader/viewer out of the story entirely. In this case, the "reader" is drawn away from the distracted table, and into the space where the absorptive Christ figure has gone. As Bal surmises, Rembrandt's sketch *Last Supper, after da Vinci* "tells us no more; it just suggests the sheer possibility of an 'elsewhere'."[434]

Rembrandt utilises da Vinci's compositional template of *The Last Supper* fresco in a 1638 painting entitled *Samson posing the Riddle to*

---

[432] ibid., p. 201.
[433] ibid.
[434] ibid.

*the Wedding Guests.* Painted three years after the sketch *Last Supper, after da Vinci*, here is a work of strikingly similar composition with a completely different subject: the episode of Samson's wedding in which Samson proposed the riddle to the wedding guests taken from Judges 14:12-20. Bal notes that

> Since the subject [of *Samson posing the Riddle to the Wedding Guests*] is so different from the sketch, it is not sufficient to use the iconographic mode of reading to identify the subject matter itself. Yet, in spite of the tradition of wedding painting, it is compelling to relate the *Samson* to the Leonardo rather than to works, say, like Brueghel's *Peasants' Wedding* (ca. 1560), which is closer in subject but different in composition.[435]

This is an important difference between *compositional* and *figural* iconography: we cannot use the iconographic mode of reading to identify theme, but we can use it to identify a very relevant meaning, to make the two subjects speak to each other, and to see how, for example, Rembrandt through the *Samson* painting appropriates unseen pre-texts - both Leonardo and the Gospel narrative – for its own ends. This approach for Bal "requires a semiotic attitude that abhors meaninglessness. Not all viewers will share this attitude, but those who do cannot leave the similarity of composition to accident".[436] Putting the sketch *Last Supper, after Leonardo da Vinci* into play with *Samson posing the Riddle to the Wedding Guests* shows a heritage that is truly striking and provocative. The compositional structure of the Leonardo fresco *frames* both works. Yet the shift that has taken place in the three years between the sketch *Last Supper* to the painting of the *Samson* is even more striking. Where the women in the Last Supper sketch is in *excurse,* she is now portrayed as filling the space of Christ in the *Samson.* Bal makes the following comparisons:

> The women is as isolated as Christ. She is not, as he was, engaged in a stillness outside of time and of the world, for she is not the son of God. But she, too, is lonely and about to die. Christ's inward gaze was directed to no one in particular; the bride's gaze is also directed outside of the story that the others are busy acting out; but whereas Christ's gaze is inward, the bride's is outward, toward the viewer. Thus she

[435] ibid., p. 202.
[436] ibid.

> steps out of a diegetic situation that is as frightening and as threatening as Susanna's situation when she is trapped by the Elders.[437]

Other textual similarities are also evident between these works of Rembrandt as we put them into play. The woman's head in the *Samson* is adorned with the curls of the head behind Christ in the *Last Supper* sketch, as if the woman, still hidden there, has stepped forward to tell her story of sacrificial death. Of course, no halo surrounds her head, but the figure in the background tapestry is just a little bit lighter around her head than elsewhere. This shows a truly ironic turn in Rembrandt's compositional choice:

> The irony here is one of shifting, of displacement, of turning the highest subject into a low one - the genre scene. But the displacement does not effect the women at the centre. She remains separated from the promiscuous scene, isolated in this way just as she is diegetically and pictorially isolated. In addition, there is no confusion, no extension of the reference to "the Biblical" in general. The sign is compositional, but no less precise and delimited... In *Samson's Wedding*, a specific moment of the one pre-text – of the Leonardo and, through it, of the Gospel - is seen to be used to compose the framework of the painting in which other pre-text – the Judges episode – is then made to fit. The context, the contemporary habit of typological interpretation, is used in a way that makes a highly sympathetic representation plausible.[438]

This compositional shape that is iconographically implied between the works brings about a tension between narratives. This provokes what Bal terms as a "double, differential reading, which juxtaposes the evoked against the narrated story, in order to let them interact and to let the tensions between the stories produce new meanings".[439] This reading radically challenges assumed foundational narratives by allowing differing subjects to occupy identical compositional reality. This goes to the heart of the reading event, where signs and signifiers are replaced by the item that is absent and only alluded to by language.

---

[437] ibid., p. 203.
[438] ibid., pp. 205-206.
[439] ibid., p. 207.

In *Adam Bede*, George Eliot evokes a similar compositional form through a visual poetics of Dinah Morris. In chapter II entitled "The Preaching" (note the definite article), Eliot calls to mind the biblical accounting of Jesus' Sermon on the Mount. Yet it is not Adam to which the title refers, but Dinah Morris who is central to the compositional structure of the scene and the Adam upon whom George Eliot bestows the "title" of new Adam. Like Jesus, she too is marginalized despite her prophetic gifts due to her common heritage as merely the "niece to Poyer's wife", one who is a "Methodisses" - those who are prone to go "stark starin' mad wi' their religion".[440] She is a compelling figure, at odds with tradition as a woman in "quaker-like costume" and draws a crowd of "stronger curiosity" to the village Green. As noted by a stranger in the crowd, she is merely a "sweet woman... but surely nature never meant her for a preacher".[441] She is described as one of "no particular beauty, beyond that of expression" whose eyes "looked so simple, so candid, so gravely loving..".[442] Her hand is stretched out "towards the descending sun" and her head is covered with a "net".[443] She is placed in the centre of the crowd by the composition of the narrative who gather around, listening but distracted throughout her sermon. In the sermon itself, Eliot gives visual cues that are to "see" a portrait of Christ as one reads the sermon voiced through the compositional centre of Dinah Morris:

> "*See*!" she exclaimed, turning to the left, with her eyes fixed on a point above the heads of the people – "*see* where our blessed Lord stands and weeps, and stretches out his arms towards you." .... In a pleading reproach, turning her eyes on the people again. "*See* the print of the nails on his dear hands and feet. It is your sins that made them! Ah, how pale and worn he looks! He has gone through all that great agony in the garden... And he is upon this earth too; he is among us; he is there close to you now; I *see* his wounded body and his look of love."[444] (emphases added)

With these visual cues George Eliot evokes the following image: a crowd that is gathered around a central figure whose gaze is turned

---

[440] *Adam Bede*, p. 16.
[441] ibid., p. 23.
[442] ibid.
[443] ibid.
[444] ibid. p. 30.

outward. The central figure is set apart even though placed compositionally in the centre. This central figure has their arms extended to show the palms of hands where one is to 'see' "the print of nails" that can be imagined and a covering about the head. The crowd is present yet not attentive to the one they gather around. Through her evoking of visual images tethered to verbal description, George Eliot has given density to this scene that is compositionally compatible with Rembrandt's works that utilise the compositional language of various pre-texts – namely da Vinci and ultimately the Gospel accounts. As noted with Rembrandt, who stands central to the tradition of Dutch realism which George Eliot addresses in chapter XVII, this compositional iconography allows for a double, differential reading that juxtaposes the evoked image of Jesus figured by da Vinci's compositional template against the narrated story of *Adam Bede*, in order to let them interact and to let the tensions between the stories produce new meanings. With this compositional iconography framing the text, both *imago* and *verbum* are challenged. This tension challenges assumed foundational narratives and allows for differing subjects to occupy identical compositional reality. As mentioned before, this goes to the heart of the reading event, where signs and signifiers are replaced by the item that is absent and only alluded to by language. So compelling is this image presented in chapter II that upon reading *Adam Bede*, Queen Victoria had this scene commissioned in 1861 as a painting by Edward Henry Corbould entitled "Dinah Morris preaching on Hayslope Green". In looking at the painting, the compositional form of the scene transcends the visual poetics into an image true to da Vinci and Rembrandt's compositional heritage and calls back to both the narrative of *Adam Bede* and ultimately, the deeper narrative of Jesus. The words indeed become flesh in this vivid rendering of image which gives further density to the verbal. The compositional iconography in *Adam Bede* allows for an image made word that allows images to speak beyond the limits of language. It is this possibility that is central to Eliots' poetics and key to a poetics of Jesus. As demonstrated in *Adam Bede*, Eliot evokes a "new Adam" that is neither "new" nor "Adam", yet an visual-verbal paradox arises that overturns assumptions through an intertexuality of the visual and the verbal. In a poetics of Jesus, narrative overturns narrative and allows for possibilities of new subjects, formerly unseen, to inhabit traditional compositional forms.

# Chapter 8

# *The Mill on the Floss* – Transfigurational Writing as Incarnation

In his book, *Fact and Feeling: Baconian Science and the Nineteenth-Century Literary Imagination*, Jonathan Smith summarises the state of affairs regarding the interplay between scientific and aesthetic discourse in the nineteenth century as follows:

> The nineteenth-century debate over scientific method included much more than a discussion of the logical process of scientific discovery. It could not avoid basic epistemological questions about reality and the relationship between observer and observed; it evaluated the nature and value of scientific knowledge vis-à-vis other forms of knowledge, including supposedly more intuitive form like religion and poetry.[445]

Smith exemplifies the growing nineteenth century split between science and aesthetics in citing the following passage from critic Edward Dowden (1877):

> Any inquiry at the present day into the relations of modern scientific thought with literature must in great part be guided by hints, signs, and presages. The time has not yet come when it may be possible to perceive in complete outline the significance of science for the imagination and emotions of men, but that significance is large and deep we cannot doubt. Literature proper, indeed, the literature of *power*, as DeQuincey named it, in distinction from the literature of knowledge, may, from point of view, be described as essentially non-scientific, or even antiscientific. To ascertain and communicate facts is

[445] Jonathan Smith, *Fact and Feeling: Baconian Science and the Nineteenth-Century Literary Imagination*, (Madison: University of Wisconsin Press, 1994) p. 5.

> the object of science; to quicken our life into a higher consciousness through the feelings is the function of art. But the knowing and feelings are not identical, and a fact expressed in terms of feelings affects us as other than the same fact expressed in terms of knowing, yet our emotions rest on and are controlled by our knowledge.[446]

In contrast to Dowden's attempts to define and thereby differentiate scientific and aesthetic discourse are the words of John Tyndall. A contemporary of Thomas Henry Huxley, Tyndall's 1868 address entitled "Scientific Use of the Imagination" proclaims the need for both the scientific *and* aesthetic view of life for a united view of life:

> … the world embraces not only a Newton, but a Shakespeare – not only a Boyle, but a Raphael – not only a Kant, but a Beethoven – not only a Darwin, but a Carlyle. Not in each of these, but in all, is human nature whole. They are not opposed, but supplementary – not mutually exclusive, but reconcilable.[447]

This was a period when scientific discourse had yet to become so specialised in nomenclature as to prohibit general recognition. Recent scientific discoveries and theories were alongside the novel in public discourse. Yet, as evidenced by the previous statements, the tension was growing more intense, and scientific and aesthetic discourse were quickly becoming polarised options, rather than necessary companions, in providing a language of meaning in Western culture. In the introduction to *The Foundations of a Creed*, George Henry Lewes makes the prophetic comment, "the great desire of this age is for a Doctrine which may serve to condense our knowledge, guide our researches, and shape our lives, so that Conduct may really be the consequence of Belief".[448]

---

[446] Edward Dowden, "The Scientific Movement and Literature", *Studies in Literature: 1789-1877, 6th ed.* (London: Kegan Paul, 1892) p. 85.

[447] John Tyndall, "Scientific Use of Imagination," *Fragments of Science, 6th ed., 2 vols.* (New York: Burt, n.d.) vol. 1, p. 494. As noted by Smith in *Facts and Feelings*, this particular passage does not appear in the earliest versions of the address.

[448] G.H. Lewes, *Problems of Life and Mind. First Series: The Foundations of a Creed, 2 vols.* (London, 1874-75), vol. 1, p. 2.

## The *Bildung* of Organicism and a Poetics of Jesus

Of those who realised the need for a "Doctrine to shape our lives" and responded to the challenge given by George Henry Lewes in *The Foundations of a Creed*, none was so close in ideological proximity than Lewes' partner, Marian Evans, known widely by this time through her *nom de plume* as George Eliot. Eliot is well documented as reading widely among the scientific theories of the day. She refers in her letters to Herbert Spencer, whose 1857 essay, "Progress: Its Law and its Cause", argued that "the law of organic development from homogeneity to heterogeneity governed all the spheres of natural and social science from physiology through to astronomy, anthropology, and philology".[449] Geologist Sir Charles Lyell, mentor to Charles Darwin and author of *Principles of Geology* (1830-33), proved intriguing to Eliot with his theory of Uniformitarianism which is an attempt to explain the former changes of the earth's surface by reference to causes present to observation. As Lyell states, "the history of the earth's surface can be accounted for using the same forces we see around us now – erosion, uplift, sedimentation, volcanic phenomena, etc. Operating at similar rates and intensities".[450] In short, one need only observe the here and now of a river's course, a lake's stillness, a tree's seasonal changes, or even the form of the smallest pebble and one can see the same forces at work that have been at work since the beginning of the world. This age is the same that has been and the same that will be to come. Essentially, things throughout nature are *as they are* and in the process, ever so slowly, of further becoming that which they will always be. In essence, Lyell was utilising a much older language than the seemingly new vocabulary of evolutionary thought – he was employing a view of *transfiguration* rather than evolution.

Uniformitarianism, as noted by Shuttleworth, "undermined ideas of natural fixity and theories of catastraophism, which had sought to reconcile evidence of the earth's changes with ideas of an unchanging natural order".[451] This influence of Lyell is exemplified in Eliot's article, "The Progress of the Intellect", where Eliot utilises a geological analogy

---

[449] Sally Shuttleworth, *George Eliot and Nineteenth-Century Science*, (Cambridge: Cambridge University Press, 1984) p. 13.

[450] Jonathan Smith, op. cit., p. 95.

[451] Sally Shuttleworth, op. cit., p. 14.

to explain her idea of the laws of uniform development that govern human development – "A correct generalisation gives significance to the smallest detail, just as the great inductions of geology demonstrate in every pebble the working of laws by which the earth has become adapted for the habitation of man."[452]

As one looks at the growing interest in evolutionary thinking during the nineteenth century, it was with the publishing of Charles Darwin's *On the Origin of Species*[453] that this form of dialectic was given its largest audience. Having been published during her writing of *The Mill on the Floss*, as noted by Smith, "within a month of its appearance she and Lewes had read it".[454] Darwin's theory of natural selection expressed a new dimension to the notions of organic functional interdependence. Unlike ideas espousing the *fixity* of species, Darwin continued the thinking of Lamarck and others by showing species development as well as that of the individual organism itself occurring through a process of ordered differentiation. In his closing lines from *On the Origin of Species*, Darwin observes:

> It is interesting to contemplate an entangled bank, clothed with many plants of many kinds, with birds singing on the bushes, with various insects flitting about, and with worms crawling through the damp earth, and to reflect that these elaborately constructed forms, so different from each other, and dependent on each other in so complex a manner, have all been produced by laws acting around us.[455]

It is known that neither Lewes nor Eliot saw Darwin's treatise as a particularly new direction in thought, rather a mere extension of current thinking in the doctrine of development expressed through other theorists. In a letter written to Barbara Bodichon, Eliot notes upon reading *Species* that the book left "a feeble impression compared with

---

[452] ibid., p. 13.
[453] Charles Darwin, *On the Origin of Species by Means of Natural Selection, or The Preservation of Favoured Races in the Struggle for Life.* ed. John Burrow (London: Murray, 1859). Hereafter referred to as *On the Origin of Species.*
[454] Jonathan Smith, op. cit., p. 122.
[455] Charles Darwin, *On the Origin of Species by Means of Natural Selection*, ed. John Burrow from the 1st edition, (London, 1859; Harmondsworth, 1968) p. 459.

the mystery that lies underneath the processes".[456] As noted by Lewes in a review of Darwin's theories in *Fortnightly Review* (April 1868): "The laws of Natural Selection may indeed be said to be only a larger and philosophic view of the law of Adaptation which Lamarck had imperfectly conceived".[457] Thus, in a review of the harmony of scientific and aesthetic discourse during Eliot's period, Shuttleworth remarks that

> the natural and social sciences formed an inter-related network. Thus Buckle, reviewing the science of his own period, observed that "the followers of Bichat are associated in geology with the doctrine of uniformity; in zoology with that of the transmutation of the species; and in astronomy, with the nebular hypothesis". Each of these scientific theories challenged conceptions of a fixed order, offering in their place an historical explanation of development. All demanded a similar stance to the world. This fact was well understood, not only by members of the scientific community, but also by the general public...[458]

Accessing a need, as noted earlier, for "a Doctrine which may serve to condense our knowledge, guide our researches, and shape our lives", Lewes puts forward his own conception – Organicism. As the underlying principle of his *Problems of Life and Mind*, Lewes defines organicism in the *Fortnightly review* as being

> distinguishable by its consistent carrying out of the hypothesis that the organic phenomena grouped under the terms Life and Mind are activities not of any single element, in or out of the organism, but activities of the whole organism in correspondence with a physical and social medium.[459]

In essence, life is defined in organicism as the interaction between an organism and its medium. Questions with regard to the essence of a being (in the case of organicism, the organism) are to be resolved, not through a subsequent systematic deconstruction of the organism into component elements. Rather, one must look instead at the organism as a *whole being* in the context of the environment (or medium) that the

---

456 Cited by Rosemary Ashton, *George Eliot: A Life* (London: Penguin, 1996) p. 239.

457 Cited by Sally Shuttleworth, op. cit., p. 16.

458 ibid.

459 G.H. Lewes, "Spiritualism and Materialism", *Fortnightly Review*, 19 (1876) p. 479.

organism exists within; observation *in context* rather explanation through systematic deconstruction is at the heart of organicism. As an organising theory, Lewes proposed an approach that went beyond binary oppositions of subject and object, mind and body, body and soul. For Lewes, atomistic and overtly systemic views tended to divide and categorise rather than explain and observe. In addressing the lack of unified theory for mind and body, Lewes asserted that "if the upholders of Organicism have not extended to the Mind the principles adopted with respect to Life, the stream of thought in modern psychological research has, I think, all pointed in this direction".[460] Mind, for Lewes, was the collected functions "of the whole organism in correspondence with a physical and social medium",[461] not merely those hidden segmented activities of the internal life proposed by German thinkers such as Freud and Schopenhauer.

It is well documented that George Eliot embraced her partner's views and held them in high regard:

> George Eliot found in Lewes' work a model of organic life that could encompass her changing assessment of the real foundations of organic unity. Lewes' theory suggested that both social and psychological life might be dominated less by harmony and control than by contradiction and disorder; for functional interdependence does not necessarily imply harmonious union. While Lewes only stated his theoretical assumptions, however, George Eliot explored fully in her novels their social and psychological implications.[462]

For Eliot, while organicism provided a theory, she was searching for something more – *a language*. This was also the case throughout nineteenth-century thought where

> the status of organic theory itself… should be seen less as a single idea than as a language. Within the confines of one structural framework, it offered multiple possibilities of interpretation. As a general conceptual model, however, it can be associated with the changes that occurred in social and scientific philosophy once the eighteenth-century

[460] ibid., p. 481.
[461] ibid., p. 716.
[462] Sally Shuttleworth, op. cit., p. 22.

> mechanistic cosmology was displaced. In all fields and from all perspectives, organic theory was linked to an increasing interest in history as a developmental process, and in notions of interaction and interdependence.[463]

It was in her developing a transfer of Lewes' views on organicism and her wide reading of various theorists into the aesthetic realm that we begin to see Eliot's reactions to an overly systematic epistemology as that being offered by Darwinism. In an article published in *The Leader* (1855) entitled "The Future of German Philosophy", George Eliot wrote: "the age of systems is passed... System is the *childhood* of philosophy; the manhood of philosophy is investigation".[464]

More specifically, Eliot opposed any system of philosophy that was purely systemic and supposedly grounded upon *a priori* claims. In reaction to Leibnitz and Kant, she states the following:

> The chief argument in favour of *a priori* ideas, as insisted on by Leibnitz and Kant is that they can never be arrived at by induction; that induction may lead to the general but never to the universal, and that, nevertheless, this idea of universality is found in speech and in thought with the mark of necessity. But this argument will not bear a rigid examination. The language of all peoples soon attains to the expressions *all, universal, necessary*, but these expressions have their origin purely in the observations of the senses; they are simply a practical expedient, and are valued only under certain well-known and presupposed conditions. To isolate such expressions, to operate with them apart from experience, to exalt their relative value into an absolute value, to deduce knowledge from them alone, and to make them a standing point higher than all experience – this, which is what Parmenides and all speculative philosophers since him have done, is an attempt to poise the universe on one's head, and no wonder if dizziness and delusion are the consequence.[465]

Eliot had read the key German scholars of the nineteenth century and was conversant in current thought surrounding Higher Criticism. As previously mentioned, having translated Strauss' *Das Leben Jesu* and Feuerbach's *Essence of Christianity*, Eliot had established herself, along

---

[463] ibid., p. 23.

[464] Cited by Rosemary Ashton, *The German Idea.* ( Libris: London, 1994) pp. 150-151.

[465] George Eliot. *Essays of George Eliot*, ed. Thomas Pinney. New York. 1963. Cited by Rosemary Ashton, op. cit., p. 151.

with Thomas Carlyle and Samuel Taylor Coleridge, as one of the key ambassadors of German thinking in England. Yet her strong tendency toward organicism made it difficult to embrace the rigid systematicians of German Idealism, notably Leibnitz and Kant.

Yet it was more in Germany than England that Eliot would find writers that exemplified her desire to integrate her scientific and aesthetic temperaments and ultimately provide the catalyst for her style as a novelist. As noted previously, one key figure was Johann Wolfgang von Goethe. Unlike the "German system-mongers" she criticises, Eliot repeatedly praises Goethe for not being "led by Schiller into embracing the Kantian [or any *a priori*] philosophical system".[466] In this regard, Eliot held Goethe as "eminently the man who helps us to rise to a lofty point of observation, so that we may see things in relative proportions".[467] In contrast to Kant's mathematical theory of nature,[468] Goethe attempted to frame an understanding of nature that was differentiated from an understanding based upon systematics. In *Maximen und Reflexionen* he states that "physics must be divorced from mathematics. It must be completely independent, and try to penetrate with all its loving, reverent, pious force into nature and its holy life, quite regardless of what mathematics accomplishes and does".[469]

As noted in chapter 3, Goethe drew a conception of morphology (a phrase which Goethe himself coined) that was a move beyond the rigidity of classification of type[470] toward a conception of *nature as process*. In this regard,

---

[466] Rosemary Ashton, *The German Idea*, p. 167.

[467] George Eliot, "The Natural History of German Life", *Westminster Review* (July 1856).

[468] "I assert that in any particular theory of nature we can find only so much of real science as we can find mathematics... A pure theory of determinate natural objects is possible only through mathematics; and... hence any theory of nature will contain only so much of real science as it permits the application of mathematics". From Kant's 1786 Preface to his *Metaphysische Anfangsgrunde der Naturwissenschaft.* Cited in Ernst Cassirer, *Rousseau, Kant, Goethe* (Princeton: Princeton University Press, 1945) p. 62.

[469] ibid., p. 63.

[470] Goethe had read Linnaeus' system of nature whereby understanding of nature is achieved when "we have succeeded in arranging it (nature) in the pigeonholes of our concepts, dividing it into species and genera, into families, classes, and orders". ibid., p. 69.

> For Goethe such an enterprise [merely *labelling* natural cause and effect] was not enough. According to him, what we grasp in this way are only the products, not the *process* of life. And into this life process he wanted, not only as a poet but also as scientist, to win insight; in it he saw what was greatest and highest.[471]

Eliot agreed with Goethe in asserting that one must look beyond the cataloguing of type in order to gain an appreciation of the whole. As previously stated, Goethe held that "... Classes, genera, species and individuals are related as instances to a law; they are contained in it, but they do not *contain* or *reveal* it".[472] In the chapter entitled, "The Purpose Set Forth" from *On Morphology*, Goethe writes the following:

> In observing objects of nature, especially those that are alive, we often think the best way of gaining an insight into the relationship between their inner nature and the effects they produce is to divide them into their constituent parts... these attempts at division also produce many adverse effects when carried to an extreme. To be sure, what is alive can be dissected into its component parts, but from these parts it will be impossible to restore it and bring it back to life. This is true even in inorganic substances, to say nothing of things organic in nature... The Germans have a word for the complex of existence presented by a physical organism: *Gestalt* [structured form]. With this expression they exclude what is changeable and assume that an interrelated whole is identified, defined, and fixed in character. / But if we look at all these *Gestalten*, especially the organic ones, we will discover that nothing in them is permanent, nothing is at rest or defined - everything is in a flux of continual motion. This is why Germans frequently and fittingly makes use of the word *Bildung* (formation) to describe the end product and what is in process of production as well.[473]

As previously mentioned, organicism for Eliot provided more than a unified theory of development, it provided a language of sorts with which to describe observations in an aesthetic medium that had scientific weight. Yet it was in Goethe's writing that this theory and language of organicism found its possible form in a *poetics* where

---

471 ibid.

472 ibid., p. 93.

473 Goethe, *Scientific Studies, Vol. 12, The Collected Works* (Princeton: Princeton University Press, 1988) pp. 63-64.

scientific observation catalysed into aesthetic genesis. In Eliot's journals and letters, it is well documented that she and Lewes spent considerable time reading Goethe's work, particularly during Lewes' work on *Life of Goethe*. In her essay "The Morality of Wilhelm Meister" Eliot exemplifies the truthfulness of Goethe's approach to writing in response to concerns that Goethe was immoral in his writing of *Lehrjahre*:

> But is *Wilhelm Meister* an immoral book? We think not; on the contrary, we think that it appears immoral to some minds because its morality has a grander orbit than any which can be measured by the calculations of the pulpit and of ordinary literature.[474]

This "grander orbit" was for Eliot a willingness in Goethe's poetics toward the morphological rather than systematic – a forming poetics that would never truly "form". This was a poetics of spaces and gaps where what was not seen "in the pulpit and ordinary literature" is seen by both the loss of context and the absence of presence. Her poetics, as previously asserted, sought to open gaps before the reader which allowed for both the "possible" of the sacred and the framing anew of that which traditionally is lost through the act of writing rather than freed. As seen in *Adam Bede*, Eliot sought to overcome the divide of the visual/verbal dichotomy by provoking to the "reader" to "see" and overturn narratives that may be closed to interpretation through provoking a continuous dialogue between word-image signs, provoking a double, differential reading that juxtaposes the evoked image against the narrated story, in order to let them (both image and word) interact and to let the tensions between the stories produce new possibilities. As we look at *The Mill on the Floss*, Eliot utilises her poetics as a means of framing the transfigurational and displaying the depth of subjectivity that is unchanging yet always transfiguring.[475]

---

[474] George Eliot, "The Morality of Wilhelm Meister", *The Leader* (21 July 1855), *Essays*, pp. 144-45.

[475] In using the term "tranfigurational" I am recalling the "figuring" of "transfiguration" in the account of Jesus' transfiguration in the Gospel of St. Matthew: "After six days Jesus took with him Peter, James, and John the brother of James, and led them up a high mountain by themselves. Here he was transfigured before them. His face shone like the sun, and his clothes became as white as the light… while he

## *Imitatio Jesus/Imitatio Maggie* – Writing into Tranfigurational Flowing

> A wide plain, where the broadening Floss hurries on between its green banks to the sea, and the loving tide, rushing to meet it, checks its passage with an impetuous embrace... How lovely the little river is, with its dark, changing wavelets! It seems to me like a living companion while I wander along the bank and listen to its low, placid voice, as to the voice of one who is deaf and loving.[476]

In the beginning of *The Mill on the Floss*, Eliot introduces one of the key figures in the novel – that of the "context" that exists before the "characters". Ultimately, it is the "true context" of those things that are timeless and ever-changing that Eliot reveals to the reader. As the reader enters the narrative, the narrator (akin to Riehl) gives a present-time rendering of the surroundings. The Floss is introduced as "a living companion", personified and thus set out as the first "character" in the narrative. It has a "low, placid voice, as the one who is deaf and loving". With the context presented as living it is fully present unlike the systems that writers such as Darwin sought to explain and delimit such a context. These static systems will never be present and alive and be forever past. Martin Buber makes such a distinction in *I and Thou*:

> The I of the primary world-I-It, that is, the I faced with no Thou, but surrounded by a multitude of "contents" has no present, only the past. Put in another way, in so far as man rests satisfied with the things that he experiences and uses, he lives in the past, and his moment has no present content. He has nothing but objects.... true beings are lived in the present, the life of objects is in the past.[477]

In a later portion of *The Mill on the Floss*, the narrator attributes similar anthropomorphic qualities to the surroundings, noting how "the awful Eagre, come up like a hungry monster, or to see the Great Ash, which had once wailed and groaned like a man – these things would always be

---

was speaking, a bright cloud enveloped them, and a voice from the cloud said, "This is my Son, whom I love; with him I am well pleased. Listen to him." Matthew 17: 1-3, 5 NRSV.

476 George Eliot, *The Mill on the Floss* (London: Penguin, 1860) p. 3.

477 Martin Buber, *I and Thou*. trans. Ronald Gregor Smith (Edinburgh: T & T Clark, 1959) p. 13.

just the same...".[478] The reader notes early in the novel that there is an unchanging, timeless quality to certain things such as the Floss ("these things would always be the same"):

> The rush of the water and the booming of the Mill bring a dreamy deafness which seems to heighten the peacefulness of the scene. They are like a great curtain of sound shutting one out from the world beyond. .../Now I turn my eyes towards the Mill again and watch the unresting wheel sending out its diamond jets of water. That little girl is watching too; she is standing on just the same spot at the edge of the water ever since I paused on the bridge.[479]

In this introduction to Maggie Tulliver, the space of temporality is collapsed in reference to the Floss – past and present seem to co-exist. What is also evident in this introduction of the timelessness of the Floss is its function as a temporal bridge that extends beyond past and present – always flowing and moving with no beginning and no end. Here we see the influence of Eliot's readings of Lyell's Uniformitarianism in this personification of the unchanging quality of things. The narrator makes mention that the sound of the Floss and the booming of the Mill "are like a great curtain of sound shutting one out from the world beyond". This is seen in Maggie's love of the Mill as a place apart from existence in the world of "everyday life":

> Maggie loved to linger in the great spaces of the mill, and often came out with her black hair powdered to a soft whiteness that made her dark eyes flash out with new fire. The resolute din, the unresting motion of the great stones, giving her a dim delicious awe as at the presence of an uncontrollable force – the meal forever pouring, pouring – the fine white powder softening all surfaces and making the very spider-nets look like a fairy lacework – the sweet pure scent of the meal – all helped to make Maggie feel that the mill was a little world apart from her outside everyday life. [480]

---

[478] *The Mill on the Floss*, p. 37.
[479] ibid., p. 4.
[480] ibid., p. 26.

The quality of the Floss in its timeless presence creates an "other-worldliness" about it and in this way we begin to have the Floss presented as Other – one that is unchanging yet moving, present yet timeless. When Maggie and Tom venture out to the Round Pool, aspects of Eliot's Uniformitarianism are shown as well:

> They were on their way to the Round Pool - that wonderful pool which the floods had made a long while ago; no one knew how deep it was, and it was mysterious too that it should be almost a perfect round, framed in with willows and tall reeds so that the water was only to be seen when you got close to the brink.[481]

Maggie Tulliver is portrayed in many respects as a *mimesis* of these qualities. Mrs. Tulliver comments on her being "out of time" and akin to the Floss when she is looking for Maggie early in the novel:

> … Mrs. Tulliver, rising and going to the window, "I don't know where she is now, an' it's pretty nigh tea-time. Ah, I thought so – wanderin' up an' down by the water, like a wild thing." [482]

Mrs. Tulliver makes continual references to Maggie as "this small mistake of nature"[483] that in some regards must be tamed. The narrator reflects on the fact that Maggie and Tom were "still very much like young animals" who must eventually learn to grow out of their "impulsiveness of the lower animals, but conduct [themselves] in every respect like members of a highly civilised society".[484] In this regard, Maggie personifies the theory of Organicism in that she is to be observed more than she is to be understood. Mirroring Eliot's value of the whole over the atomistic view of parts before the whole as a path for the ascertaining of meaning, Maggie describes her disgust with the notion of making a patchwork quilt:

> "Oh, mother," said Maggie in a vehemently cross tone, "I don't want to do patchwork."
> "What! Not your pretty patchwork, to make a counterpoint for your aunt Glegg?"

---

481 ibid., p. 37.
482 ibid., p. 9.
483 ibid., p. 9.
484 ibid., pp. 35-36.

> "It's foolish work," said Maggie with a toss of her mane, "tearing things to pieces to sew 'em together again."[485]

Maggie's nature *as* nature is shown. She is seen as having a "mane" like the "wild thing", and in this, finds foolishness in "tearing things to pieces to sew 'em together again". We see the organicism of Maggie further illustrated in comparison to Yap, the Tulliver's family dog:

> Maggie's phiz. which nature had seemed to have moulded and coloured with the most decided intention. But that same nature has the deep cunning which hides itself under the appearance of openness, so that simple people think they can see through her quite well, and all the while she is secretly preparing a refutation of their confident prophecies.[486]

As with the *Bildungsroman* of Goethe's *Wilhelm Meister*, George Eliot through *The Mill on the Floss* challenges the very form of writing itself:

> The "content" of the *Bildungsroman* instantly becomes a question of form, precisely because the content is the forming-of-content, "*Bildung*" – the formation of the human as the producer of itself as form. [487]

Throughout *The Mill on the Floss*, Maggie's development is one of *transfiguration* rather than one of evolution – she becomes more and more illuminated as to who she always was. She is one who is "moulded and coloured" rather than seen as added to and thereby essentially changed. As opposed to the Hegelian-laden theory of Natural Selection that Charles Darwin puts forth in *On the Origin of Species*, the *Bildung* of Maggie is one, not of drastic changes, but of gradual and persistent definition akin to Jean Baptiste Lamarck. Again, as with Charles Lyell, Eliot is seeing the gradual progress of figuration more as an act of clarification of essential and base essence rather than one of explosive and radical changes. Unlike Darwin, who neglected in *Species* what Eliot saw as "the mystery that lies under the processes",[488]

---

[485] ibid., p. 10.
[486] ibid., pp. 29-30.
[487] Marc Redfield, op. cit., p. 42.
[488] Cited by Rosemary Ashton, *George Eliot: A Life* (London: Penguin, 1996) p. 239.

the organicism of St. Oggs on the Floss is one that displays these mysterious processes through the gradual formations of form, content, and import together into *what they are* rather than a synthesis of thesis and antithesis that is abstracted and without *spiritus*.

Key to this understanding is Thomas à Kempis' classic, *Imitatio Christi – The Imitation of Christ.* Eliot had read and re-read this devotional classic and given copies of it to friends during the writing of *The Mill on the Floss.* In book 3 of *The Mill on the Floss* entitled "The Valley of Humiliation", which begins with the downfall of the Tulliver family, Maggie is shown turning to religious writing for strength and moral guidance:

> The old books, Virgil, Euclid, and Aldrich - that wrinkled fruit of the tree of knowledge - had been laid by, for Maggie had turned her back on the vain ambition to share the thoughts of the wise... She read so eagerly and constantly in her three books, the Bible, *Thomas à Kempis*, and the *Christian Year* (no longer rejected as a 'hymnbook')... [489]

At the end of the novel in the portion which follows her confession to Dr. Kenn in book 6 entitled "The Final Rescue", Maggie draws upon her earlier reading of a particular portion of *Imitation of Christ* which is on facing life as one preparing to die found in chapter 23 of book 1 entitled "Of Meditation on Death". As à Kempis writes, "Each morning remember that you may not live until evening; and in the evening, do not presume to promise yourself another day. Be ready at all times, and so live that death may never find you unprepared"[490] and

> Prepare yourself to endure many trials and obstacles in this vale of tears; for such will be your lot wherever you are, and you will encounter them wherever you conceal yourself. It must needs be so; nor is there any remedy or means of escape from ills and griefs; you must endure them.[491]

She recalls these mediations as she seeks to gain her strength to face God – 'the Unseen Pity' – in the disgrace stemming from her being carried away in the Floss with Stephen Guest. Recalling *Imitation of*

---

[489] George Eliot, *The Mill on the Floss.* (London: Penguin, 1860) p. 298.

[490] Thomas à Kempis, *The Imitation of Christ.* Trans. and introd. Leo Sherley-Price (London: Penguin Books, 1952) I. 23. pp. 53ff.

[491] ibid., II. 12. p. 87.

*Christ*, Maggie resolves the following:

> I will bear it, and bear it till death... But how long it will be before death comes! I am so young, so healthy. How shall I have the patience and strength? Am I to struggle and fall and repent again? Has life other trials as hard for me still?
>
> With that cry of self-despair Maggie fell on her knees against the table and buried her sorrow-stricken face. Her soul went out to the Unseen Pity that would be with her to the end. Surely there was something being taught her by this experience of great need; and she must be learning a secret of human tenderness and long suffering that the less erring could hardly know? "Oh God, if my life is to be long, let me live to bless and comfort." [492]

This statement – "Oh God, if my life is to be long, let me live to bless and comfort" – are the last words of Maggie prior to the realisation of the flooding of the Floss. They also are a profound summary of George Eliot's *lebenphilosophie* and the central theme of à Kempis' *Imitation of Christ.* In contrast to the reaching after scientific thought, Eliot recovers this 15th century devotional theme of Thomas à Kempis that makes such statements as:

> A humble knowledge of oneself is a surer road to God than a deep searching of the sciences. Yet learning itself is not to be blamed, nor is the simple knowledge of anything whatsoever to be despised, for true learning is good in itself and ordained by God; but a good conscience and a holy life are always to be preferred.[493]

In this way Eliot seeks to recover that which has been neglected amidst evolutionary theory and return to what John Hick termed as the 'language of love' that comes before theory – more than the progress and the scientific, Maggie will choose to embrace the timeless and humane. In the end, as noted by à Kempis, "a good conscience and a holy life are always to be preferred."

---

[492] *The Mill on the Floss*, p. 528.

[493] Thomas à Kempis, op. cit., I.23, p. 31.

Throughout *The Mill on the Floss*, Eliot evokes the timeless nature of things through the figuring of sacramental imagery. Maggie's life, likened to the Floss, is like water itself as observed by Mrs. Tulliver: "They're such children for the water, mine are," she said aloud, "without reflecting that there was no one to hear her."[494] In certain respects, one can here the echoes of Feuerbach's discussion of Baptism in *Essence of Christianity* which Eliot translated only five years prior to her work on *The Mill on the Floss*:

> Baptism should represent to us the wonderful but natural effect of water on man. Water has, in fact, not merely physical effects, but also, and as a result of these, moral and intellectual effects on man... What was denied by Grace has been granted by Nature... In the stream of water the fever of selfishness is allayed. Water is the readiest means of making friends with Nature. The bath is a sort of chemical process, in which our individuality is resolved into the objective life of Nature... water is the element of natural equality and freedom, the mirror of the golden age. ... in water we declare: Man can do nothing without Nature... It needs only that the ordinary course of things be interrupted in order to vindicate to common things an uncommon significance, *to life, as such, a religious import.*[495]

The qualities of water exemplify Eliot's "otherness" of nature in regard to the Floss. When Mr. Tulliver is speaking with Mr. Moss regarding Wakem's damming up the Floss, Mr. Tulliver reflects:

> ... water's a very particular thing – you can't pick it up with a pitchfork. That's why it's been nuts to Old Harry and the lawyers. It's plain enough what's the rights and the wrongs of water, if you look at it straightforward; for a river's a river, and if you've got a mill, you must have water to turn it; and it's no use telling me, Pivart's erigation and nonsense won't stop my wheel; I know what belongs to water better than that.[496]

---

494 *The Mill on the Floss*, p. 102.

495 See chapter XXV "The Contradiction in the Sacraments" in Ludwig Feuerbach, *The Essence of Christianity* trans. George Eliot (New York: Prometheus Books, 1989) pp. 236ff. See also Rosemary Ashton, *George Eliot: A Life* (London: Penguin, 1996) pp. 162-163.

496 *The Mill on the Floss*, p. 156.

Regarding the Mill changing ownership, Mr. Tulliver remarks to Luke: "There's a story as when the mill changes hands, the river's angry; I've heard my father say it many a time. There's no telling whether there mayn't be summat in the story, for this is a puzzling world".[497] The "otherness" of the Floss demands to maintain its alterity, becoming "angry" when not consulted regarding changes and not submitting to attempts to shape it, even to the point of resisting material formality so that one "can't pick it up with a pitchfork". With regard to the Other, Emmanuel Levinas makes this observation:

> Western philosophy coincides with the disclosure of the other where the other, in manifesting itself as a being, loses its alterity. From its infancy philosophy has been with a horror of the other remains other – with an insurmountable allergy. It is for this reason that it is essentially a philosophy of being, that the comprehension of being is its last word, and the fundamental structure of man. It is for this reason that it becomes philosophy of immanence and of autonomy, or atheism.[498]

Throughout the novel, one of the sub-plots is the legal battle between Mr. Tulliver and Mr. Wakem for possession of the Floss. Assuming that the Floss is something that can be owned, the battle wages on till Mr. Tulliver, consumed with a hunger for revenge regarding his rights to the Floss, dies with a curse on his lips for Wakem. At the other extreme, Mr. Deane remarks to Tom the growing irrelevancy of the Floss given the progress of industrialisation through the use of steam:

> 'You see, Tom,' said Mr. Deane at last, throwing himself backward, 'the world goes on at a smarter pace now than it did when I was a young fellow... The looms went slowish, and fashions didn't alter quite so fast... Everything was on a lower scale, sir - in point of expenditure, I mean. It's the steam, you see, that has made the difference; it drives on every wheel double pace, and the wheel of fortune along with 'em. [499]

---

497 Ibid, p. 268.

498 Emmanuel Levinas, "La Trace de L'Autre" trans. A Lingis in *Deconstruction in Context: Literature and Philosophy*. ed. by Mark C. Taylor (Chicago: University of Chicago Press, 1986) p. 346.

499 *The Mill on the Floss*, p. 405.

The Floss is neither something to own, nor something that is irrelevant. As noted by Levinas, these polar oppositions have lead to a philosophy in our age that is primarily immanent and ultimately devoid of alterity. In *The Mill on the Floss*, these options, while voiced, are not those of the Floss itself, but those who seek to control and ultimately delimit the "possible".

This notion is reflected in insights of Heidegger with regard to his reading of Hölderlin's poetry regarding rivers in contrast to the technological domination of German rivers and streams - not only through the construction of dams and canals - but those who are sought to be controlled through the very act of 'naming'. As Heidegger notes in *What is called Thinking?*, what makes Hölderlin's poetry different from the work of other poets is his willingness to name so as to "unname in the act of naming." According to Heidegger, naming for Hölderlin seems to pinpoint the rivers as that natural phenomenon which makes dwelling on earth possible for man in a world without gods. But these rivers (Heidegger uses the Rhine as an example) are not only named as the natural phenomena that they are, but also as *the streams of language.* Calling rivers "streams of language" does not make a metaphorical use of the named river, but it rather names the nature of naming: Naming the nature of naming is "naming nature" instead of naming. Naming nature instead of naming naming is naming the *impossibility* of naming – both in nature *and* naming. It names the *in-between* of nature and language: the opening up of a world which is only there *through* language but which is not effected *by* language. This would be the event of creating or acknowledging *a space in language*, in which it would no longer (or not yet) be possible to distinguish between nature and culture. It is the gift of opening whereby that which is a "home-founding world" and a "home-founding language" can, at the same time, find one (world-language) opened up by the other. As Heidegger notes, this turning of the sacred name (the act of unnaming naming) is not a trope in the rhetorical sense. This evoking of that which unnames naming it is not a trope that can be controlled and thus be employed by an artist. *It is what it is.*

In the end, Heidegger is arguing that it is a *necessity* of language (and of nature) which is at stake here. This necessity can never be controlled (as Eliot shows with the action of the Floss) and is thus always on the brink of failure, that is, on the brink of breaking down and opening one to the brink of madness. Naming nature as the failure of the name always threatens to take over the naming of the failure itself.

This fragile state is exemplified in and through the unknown moods of the Floss that are reflected in the life of Maggie. It too has a course that will eventually be shown in full, but is often hidden before the present observer. As pointed out by the narrator towards the end of the novel:

> But you have known Maggie a long while and need to be told, not her characteristics, but her history, which is a thing hardly to be predicted even from the completest knowledge of characteristics. For the tragedy of our lives is not created entirely from within. 'Character,' says Novalis in one of his questionable aphorisms '-character is destiny.' But not the whole of destiny… Maggie's destiny, then, is at present hidden, and we must wait for it to reveal itself like the course of an unmapped river; we only know that the river is full and rapid, and that for all rivers there is the same final home.[500]

Strains of *Wilhelm Meister's Lehrjahre* can be heard in this observation of Maggie. As in his reflection at the end of his apprenticeship, Wilhelm hears from his "interrogator" that "Perhaps… we should now be less at variance in regard to Destiny and Character". [501]

It is in the end that we see both the culmination and circularity of Eliot's world of St. Oggs on the Floss. "Oh God, where am I? Which is the way home?"[502] is the cry that marks the beginning of the end for Maggie as she is taken away by the flooding of the Floss.[503] She realises that in this encounter with the flood that "more and more strongly the energies seemed to come and put themselves forth as if her life were a stored-up force that had been spent in this hour, unneeded for any future".[504] In contrast to the aimless drifting that she and Stephen Guest engaged in upon the Floss, here the Floss and Maggie forge a nexus and act as one. In this way, the Floss, as a manifestation

---

[500] ibid., p. 411.
[501] Johann Wolfgang von Goethe, *Wilhelm Meister's Apprenticeship Vol.1*, p. 60.
[502] *The Mill on the Floss*, p. 530.
[503] In the milieu of the flood, it is an interesting order of questions: other ("Oh God"), self ("where am I"), and place ("Which is the way home").
[504] ibid., p. 531.

of poetic madness, illuminates and gives context to Maggie in its swelling and consumption, something not owned nor ignored. What can be seen here is *writing that writes beyond its own ability to figure*– a poetics that rises and recedes of its own unnamed accord – a poetics that ultimately transfigures and is no more, yet is what it is at last and always shall be. This is a poetic alterity where writing itself is Other. As noted by Levinas:

> The manifestation of the other is, to be sure, first produced in conformity with the way every signification is produced. The other is present in a cultural whole and is illuminated by this whole, like a text by its context. The manifestation of the whole ensures this presence and this present; they are illuminated by the light of the world. The comprehension of the other is thus a hermeneutics and an exegesis. The other is given in the concept of the totality to which it is immanent, and which… our own cultural initiative, the corporeal linguistic, or artistic gesture, expresses and discloses… the other does not only come to us out of a context, but comes without mediation; he signifies by himself… His presence consists in coming unto us, *making an entry*.[505]

This "entry" is reflected in the response to the swelling flood as a *poiesis*:

> In the first moments Maggie felt nothing, thought of nothing, but that she had suddenly passed away from that life which she had been dreading; it was the transition of death, without its agony – and she was alone in the darkness with God.[506]

Yet even in the midst of "the huge mass" of the Floss "hurrying on in hideous triumph",[507] Maggie does not dissolve nor lose her identity through being drowned. Rather, it is in this process that she experiences a *lichtung*, a Heideggarian opening/clearing of authenticity in poetics – a "lighting" that is transfiguration. Her "clarity" brings forth the final reconciliation of her life, namely the reunion with Tom. After St. Oggs begins life anew after the flood, Maggie is not lost, rather she becomes timeless as her name being etched into stone on her grave - a name that is now as timeless as the Floss itself. She has been

[505] Emmanuel Levinas, "La Trace de L'Autre", p. 351.
[506] *The Mill on the Floss*, p. 529.
[507] ibid., p. 534.

"unnamed" as Maggie and is freed from her name yet her memory still embodies that sign/signifier. In this regard, Maggie's *bildung* is completed and she is herself, no longer merely a *mimesis* of nature, but one who has been transfigured and thereby represented (*bildung*) with and alongside the Other.

In the Conclusion, the narrator makes the following summation:

> Nature repairs her ravages - repairs them with her sunshine and with human labour. The desolation wrought by the flood had left little visible trace on the face of the earth five years after... And every man and women mentioned in this history was still living, except those whose end we know. Nature repairs her ravages - but not all. The up-torn trees are not rooted again; the parted hills are left scarred; if there is a new growth, the trees are not the same as the old, and the hills underneath their green vesture bear the marks of the past rending. To the eyes that have dwelt on the past, there is no thorough repair.[508]

As previously mentioned, Derrida has stated in a recent interview that "what [ultimately] interests me ... is not strictly called either literature or philosophy, but something for which 'autobiography' is perhaps the least adequate name".[509] In *The Mill on the Floss*, Eliots' poetics are indeed something that 'is not strictly called either literature or philosophy but resides in a place between. As a fiction that is more "autobiographical" than any other piece of her fictional work, it is closer to that which is called "Gospel" in its way of telling its timeless story through the particular life of one whose story mirrors that of the author yet is profoundly unique. As a protagonist whose transfiguration provokes both beginnings and endings simultaneously (the town is rebuilt as her death is remembered), Eliot has figured a poetics of Jesus in Maggie Tulliver as a *coincidentia oppositorum*, which is at the very centre of the Christian epic. As noted in the Introduction, Thomas Altizer states that the true Christian story is

> a calling forth and voyage into an apocalyptic totality, and [the

---

[508] ibid., p. 535.

[509] Jacques Derrida, "This Strange Institution Called Literature", p. 34.

> Christian] epic totality is an apocalyptic totality if only because it embodies such a radical and total transformation. Here, this transformation is deepest in envisioning the depths of the Godhead itself, depths that are apocalyptic depths, and hence depths unveiling a new Godhead only by bringing a new Godhead to an end. [510]

Eliot's writing provokes such apocalyptic depths in subjectivity and figuring of the sacred. As in *Scenes of Clerical Life*, these apocalyptic depths are seen in the dissolving of stable society where those who represent Christianity (clerics, the pious) collapse once the mariginalised and rejected (Milly Barton, Janet Dempster) are no longer present. As in *Adam Bede*, this envisioning the depths of the Godhead itself is provoked in Eliot's recasting of word-image relationships and putting them into play to allow recovered meaning to arise and "the possible" not only to be read, but "seen". In *The Mill on the Floss*, Eliot has called forth a voyage into an apocalyptic totality where the timeless and fully present "floods" that which is systemic and seemingly progressive, leaving behind an absence that is ironically more present than the perceived presence had been (Maggie Tulliver) prior to the apocalyptic finality. These elements show a poetics that recovers, remembers, and refigures that which Eliot saw as being "the beautiful story". As I will note in the Conclusion, this one who is recovered, remembered, and refigured within her poetics acts as a "mapping of meaning" for the reader, what I am calling a *poetic cartography of grace*, which is the heart of "true fiction".

---

510 Thomas J.J. Altizer, *The Contemporary Jesus* (New York: State University of New York Press, 1997) pp. xiv, xv, xxiii.

# Conclusion

# A Poetic Cartography of Grace

The search for the basic *shape* of the central doctrine of the Christian faith – Jesus the Christ – goes back to the very foundations of the Church itself. Given the literary basis of Christianity, this shaping activity is manifested in much writing as a *poetics* – "a declaration of principle with regard to the ideas about literature [and writing] that have been embodied in the events [of a given] text [or work]".[511] With Jesus representing the ultimate nexus of subject and sacred in place and temporality, such a declaration of principle regarding how literature functions in relation to *and* as the incarnation of this coming together, as well as what this embodiment within literary space ultimately concerns, is what I have termed *a poetics of Jesus*. As discussed in the Introduction, the question of form has been central to Christianity and its attempt to give voice to the nature of the subject, the figuring of the sacred, and incarnation as nexus of subject and sacred in Christ. From the New Testament to writings of the church such as the Creeds and works of St. Augustine, this favouring of structure to the point of delimiting the "possible" is evident. Yet prior to the Council of Nicaea of 325 CE and the forming of the Symbol of Chalcedon in 451 CE, language used to figure Jesus, as noted by John Hick, "seems generally to have been devotional, or ecstatic, or liturgical (or all three), rather than an exercise in precise theological formulation. *It was analogous to the language of love*, in which all manner of extravagances and exaggerations are entirely appropriate…"[512] What I have sought throughout this study is to assert that this "language of love" – that which comes *before* theological form – is what George Eliot and writers of her spirit sought to recover, remember, and refigure in their poetics. For George Eliot, that which has become the concern of most quests for Jesus is not the "ultimate concern" for the very figure that has been searched for. As

[511] Mieke Bal, *Narratology. 2nd edition* (Toronto: University of Toronto Press, 1997) p. 59.

[512] John Hick, *The Metaphor of God Incarnate* (London: SCM Press, 1993) p. 101.

ones who stood on the top of Pisgah[513] – Baur, Feuerbach, and Strauss – saw in their different ways where the promise was in stepping free from the forms they had inherited and announcing the challenge to move beyond them. Yet they remained tied to the very structures they perceived as deathly. George Eliot became one of the key inheritors of this perception.

Gotthold Müller, reflecting on those theologians who espoused an a/theological approach such as David Friedrich Strauss' attempt in *Das Leben Jesu*, made the following insight:

> In them, the dubiety is not so much about marginal doctrine as about the essence of faith itself: the existence of God. What makes this new phenomenon especially interesting is that these professional theologians do not leave the Christian community or give up theology. They are still preoccupied with the significance of Jesus Christ for human life, and they read and comment on the work of other more orthodox theologians. Nevertheless, they are deeply estranged from the faith and their work reflects this estrangement. They are "unhappy lovers" of Christian theology.[514]

As we have seen, George Eliot exemplifies one who would certainly be counted among those "unhappy lovers". As one whose creative journey as both critic and writer of fiction shows the imprint of the key minds of nineteenth century Anglo-German thought, hers was an "unhappy love" with the systematic renderings of many thinkers of the age such as Kant, Baur, Feuerbach, and Strauss while finding the questions raised by such thinkers nonetheless compelling. Yet unlike these writers, she did not remain at the top of Pisgah. In a unique way,

---

513 Reference to the Pisgah view of Deuteronomy 3: 27, 28 where Moses is allowed to view the Promised Land but not allowed to cross the River Jordan, being told by God that his descendants will eventually enter the land: "Go to the top of Pisgah and look west and north and south and east. Look at the land with your own eyes, since you are not going to cross this Jordan. But commission Joshua, and encourage and strengthen him, for he will lead his people across and will cause them to inherit the land you see".

514 Gotthold Müller, *Identitat und Immanenz: Zur Genese der Theologie von David Friedrich Strauss* (Zurich: EVZ-Verlag, 1968) pp. 252-259. Trans. and cited by Peter C. Hodgson, "Editor's Introduction to Strauss' Theological Development from 1825 to 1840" in *The Life of Jesus Critically Examined* (Ramsey: Sigler Press, 1994) p. xv.

George Eliot entered into the land that was seen but untouched by Kant, Baur, Feuerbach, and Strauss. Hers was a poetics that not only mapped the history of these writers' search and the Christ they sought for, but was a mapping as the very figure of Jesus as the Christ. In particular, as one sees her developing poetics in her early works such as *Scenes of Clerical Life*, *Adam Bede*, and *The Mill on the Floss*, it is notable the degree to which the question of christology – how we "figure" the person of Christ and the ramifications of this person upon the lives of others – continued to manifest itself in both veiled and overt ways. In *Scenes of Clerical Life*, Eliot disturbs the context of seemingly stable society by provoking "gaps" of apocalyptic depths in her poetics that unveil a new figuring of Jesus by bringing present figurings to an end – from Milly Barton, whose death made possible the liberation of her preacher husband to "be" the Gospel he weekly proclaimed and, subsequently, liberate an entire village, to Janet Dempster who upon finding that "Infinite Love was caring for her"[515] realises the limitless depths of true repentance and forgiveness. In *Adam Bede*, Eliot overturns the traditional images of the Incarnation of this 'Infinite Love' held by her culture through visual artists such as Rembrandt and Da Vinci. With her utilisation of a rich iconographic poetics that recalls the visual density of compositional structures, figures such as Dinah Morris and Hetty Sorrel move continually between the word-image opposition and provoke a double, differential reading, which juxtaposes the evoked image against the narrated story, in order to let them (both image and word) interact. The tensions between the stories then produce a recovery of Jesus as a poetics that is, recalling Thomas Altizer, "an apocalyptic totality if only because it embodies such a radical and total transformation" in both evoked image and the 'simple story'. In *The Mill on the Floss*, George Eliot's developing poetics move from looking at the context for the coming together of the self and sacred (*Scenes of Clerical Life*) and the figuring of the incarnation of the sacred (*Adam Bede*), to the ultimate release of the subject into and throughout the sacred as figured in the autobiographical character of Maggie Tulliver. As Maggie grows and develops alongside the Floss (a figuring of the sacred), her encounter with the flooding waters of the Floss where "more and more strongly the energies seemed to come and put themselves forth as if her life were a stored-up force that had been

[515] George Eliot, *Scenes of Clerical Life*, 1857 ed. Jennifer Gribble (London: Penguin Books, 1998) p. 337.

spent in this hour, unneeded for any future" becomes her release.

Where many writers of her time were employing the *evolutionary* poetics of Darwin which are Hegelian in its philosophy, Eliot rests upon the *transfigurational* poetics of Thomas à Kempis as a source for what humanity is truly seeking for. Ultimately, as one looks to the characters framed through her poetics – differing though they are – there are embodied within the lives of these female characters similar questions of meaning that show different expressions of a common face that troubled Eliot from the beginning of her fictional output. This "face" that had troubled her and gave form to her resulting fiction, was found to be central to what she termed "the beautiful story" – the face and person of Jesus. It was this face that she kept before her whilst translating *Das Leben Jesu* and it was "only the sight of her Christ-image and picture [a cast of Thorwaldsen's figure of the risen Christ] that made her endure it".[516] It was "seeing" a re-figuring of Thorwaldsen's figure of Christ – the copy of an artist's work based on the figure of Christ – which provided Eliot with the focus to endure the mistakes of Strauss. As a writer, she did not attempt to render an idealised Christ that was beyond the reach of common humanity, nor did she seek to entrap the figure of Christ within a systematic poetics that, as Matthew Arnold noted regarding Strauss, was an "imperturbable resolution of a … professor in making all the facts suit a theory which he had adopted".[517] As one who was an "unhappy lover" of the Christianity of her era, Eliot saw the reality of Christ as that particular manifestation of the sacred which is constantly appearing and disappearing at the same time, a veiled character whose very absence makes evident a sense of presence desired for, longed for, and always sought for. It was those "German System Mongers" who sought to fashion a system to frame a static and dead Christ that sickened Eliot for their lack of understanding of what they presumed to show forth in their projects.[518]

---

516 Cited by Rosemary Ashton from a 1846 letter to Sara Hennell in *George Eliot: A Life*, p. 52.

517 Matthew Arnold, "God and the Bible" in *Complete Prose Works of Matthew Arnold.* Cited by Rosemary Ashton *The German Idea: Four English Writers and the Reception of German Thought 1800-1860*. (London: Libris, 1980, 1994) p. 150.

518 This loss of the extravagant exaggeration of a language of love and the

In this regard, I argue that Eliot as an "unhappy lover" of the theology of her time due to the unacceptable *systems* that cloud the face of Christ from view, still found a compelling drive to re-tell through her poetics something more akin to Gospel as showing forth Jesus and telling this simple story in both content and form of her fiction. As she stated in *The Leader* prior to her move into writing fiction, she saw the priority of "System" as the "spinning of elaborate cocoons" by those she termed "German system-mongers".[519] As Valerie Dodd notes in *George Eliot: An Intellectual Life*, Eliot affirmed deep and meaningful belief as "an integral part of character, a prerequisite of [a person's] vitality" and was therefore unwilling to "up root tares where we must inevitably gather all wheat with them".[520] In short, Eliot desired that which lived outside the cocoon of systems to be seen through her poetics – that which was alive and which animated life.

In her act of writing throughout *Scenes of Clerical Life*, *Adam Bede*, and *The Mill on the Floss*, George Eliot's search to tell the simple story was a radical departure from the forms of Baur, Feuerbach, and Strauss. Yet her writing remains profoundly centred on questions germane and foundational to much of what these writers sought for: the nature of the subject, the figuring of the sacred, and the point of nexus between the two. As noted by Felicia Bonaparte in her introduction to *Middlemarch*, Eliot was a writer who saw all too well the demise of delimited poetics employed by Theologians of her age:

> [For Eliot] Theology… causes us to ignore the needs of human beings here on earth; diverting our attention too much to *the formalities of the creed*, it causes us to forget its spirit. For a period of time, religion had made its home in theology. But that had been a historical accident, not a necessary connection. Theology in the modern world must be discarded as a dead creed.[521]

---

reinforcement of a employment of mere systems of belief is noted by Martin Heidegger to Engelbert Krebs, the priest who married Heidegger and performed the baptism of his first child. He wrote that his reason for leaving the Catholic Church was due to "epistemological insights, extending as far as the theory of historical knowledge, that have made the *system* of Catholicism problematic and unacceptable to me – but not Christianity and metaphysics". Cited by John Caputo, "Heidegger and Theology" in *The Cambridge Companion to Heidegger* ed. Charles Guignon (Cambridge: Cambridge University Press, 1993) p. 272.

519 Cited by Rosemary Ashton, *The German Idea*, pp. 150-151.

520 Valerie Dodd, *George Eliot: An Intellectual Life* (New York: Macmillian Press, 1990) p. 98.

Writing for Eliot was a means and exercise in framing a *figura* of the subject and the sacred which "assures the unity of the kerygmatic and the eventlike by giving the figure another kind of depth".[522] With regard to framing, I refer back to Jonathan Culler's understanding of "framing" as "determining, setting off the object or event" in such a way that alludes the positivism of "context". As seen in the earlier chapters and exemplified in *Scenes of Clerical Life*, context for Eliot will not sustain subjectivity nor provide an adequate foundation for figuring the sacred. Rather, Eliot utilises the poetic space to show how the subject and sacred are framed rather than grounded, showing "discursive practices, institutional arrangements, systems of value, semiotic mechanisms"[523] that we as readers employ in the figuring of the subject and sacred. In the framing of her poetics, the reader is encouraged to see who approaches and what is offered in this approach. In this way, her poetics resembles the Christ which is figured in the Gospel of St. John in the post-Easter encounter of Thomas and the risen Christ:

> A week later his disciples were again in the house, and Thomas was with them. Although the doors were shut, Jesus came and stood among them and said, "Peace be with you". Then he said to Thomas, "Put your finger here and see my hands. Reach out your hand and put it in my side. Do not doubt but believe". Thomas answered him, "My Lord and My God!"[524]

Her poetics in *Scenes of Clerical Life*, *Adam Bede*, and *The Mill on the Floss*, visually dense and yet thoroughly unsutured in its woundedness, asks the reader to enter into the narrative wounds re-imagined and refigured through reading in the character and context of her female characters – Milly Barton, Janet Dempster, Hetty Sorrel, Dinah Morris, and Maggie

---

[521] Felicia Bonaparte, "Introduction to *Middlemarch*" in *Middlemarch* (Oxford: Oxford World Classics, 1988,1998) p. xiii.

[522] Paul Ricoeur in "The Bible and Genre", *Figuring the Sacred: Religion, Narrative, and Imagination* (Minneapolis: Fortress Press, 1995) p. 189.

[523] Jonathan Culler, *Framing the Sign: Criticism and its Institutions*, p. ix.

[524] John 20: 26-28 NRSV.

Tulliver. The reader is encouraged ultimately to allow this "body" figured in the poetics to come forward and is encouraged "not to doubt but believe". This act is the essence of fiction that in turn is the truest essence of Gospel as true fiction.

When reflecting upon the culminating theme of his life's work, Heidegger reflected that his project was "an *on-the-way* in the field of paths for the changing questioning of the manifold question of Being".[525] This metaphor of "the field of paths" is an apt one. As seen in his idea of *die Lichtung des Seins* or *the clearing of Being* mentioned in "The End of Philosophy and the Task of Thinking",[526] Heidegger draws from colloquial German, *eine Lichtung*, which is the sense of a forest "clearing" made manifest to allow "light" to shine upon Being (*Sein*). Paths to these clearings exist yet are not charted on any maps. Yet, when one undertakes the task of walking through the woods, these woodpaths are evident – there is a way through although not defined or mapped.

This study, in conclusion, has sought to see George Eliot's poetics in her early fiction as an "on-the-way in the field of paths" of the formation of subjectivity and the figuring of the sacred. As Heidegger saw that only by walking amidst the woods would a woodpath be made evident, so it is that writers such as George Eliot see form arise only after being *on-the-way* of writing. In this way, the "paths" formed in her journey toward a poetics exhibit a "poetic cartography of grace" where one can orient oneself and be invited to

---

525 Heidegger's last reflections on his lifework from the unfinished notes to preface *Frühe Schriften* as a review of his collected writings (*Gesamtausgabe letzter Hand*). Cited by Dorothea Frede in "The Question of being: Heidegger's project" from *The Cambridge Companion to Heidegger*, ibid, p. 42.

526 Martin Heidegger, "The End of Philosophy and the Task of Thinking – 1964" in *Basic Writings of Martin Heidegger* ed. David Farrell Krell (London: Routledge, 1996): "We call this openness that grants a possible letting appear show 'clearing'. .. The forest clearing (*lichtung*) is experienced in contrast to dense forest, called *Dicktung* in our older language. The substantive *Lichtung* goes back to the verb *lichten*. The adjective *licht* is the same word as 'light'. To lighten something means to make it light, free and open, e.g. to make the forest free of trees in one place. The free space thus originating the clearing. What is light is the sense of being free and open has nothing in common with the adjective 'light' which means 'bright', neither linguistically nor materially. This is to be observed for the difference between clearing and light... Light can stream into the clearing, into its openness, and let brightness play with darkness in it. But light never first creates clearing. Rather, light presupposes it... *The clearing is the open region for everything that becomes present and absent*" pp. 441, 442.

search for the nexus of the subject and the sacred – to touch the wounds and truly to believe. Where the traditional understanding of cartography is that of mapping space on a two-dimensional field of north/east/west/south, a "poetic cartography of grace", I argue, is the "mapping" not merely of space *within* poetics, but the very fullness of space and time itself – in short, *a mapping of meaning*. In the poetic cartography of George Eliot, the poetics are embodied *and* embody both in the poetics and the reader – you are in Christ as Christ is in you. This "mapping" has no boundary or edge that would announce the end of the world or a limit to the universe that creates a sense of beginning and end, but is fully enclosed and three-dimensional, moving *itself* in the fullest breath, depth, and height of time and space[527] as one who comes unannounced and bearing Gospel - good news.

Derrida states in "This Strange Institution Called Literature" that the power within the space of literature is a "*fictive institution* which in principle allows one to say everything" that is seen in its ability to "break out of prohibitions in every field where law can lay down the law. The law of literature tends, in principle, to defy or lift the law... It [literature] is an institution which tends to overflow the institution".[528] What I have argued is that a poetics of Jesus is an act which "overflows the institution" of writing so that *how* the story is told is as important as the story itself. George Eliot's concern was not only to tell "the simple story", but also a desire for a poetics that finds its very form exhibiting the qualities of a re-imagined incarnation of the Christ whose figuring "made her endure". While most of the so-called Historical Quest for Jesus concerned itself with the content and facts concerning this one who "comes to us as one unknown", it was the form of Jesus and what this person represents that intrigued and gave noticeable shape to the arising poetics of Eliot's fiction and gives a face to this one unknown. As Paul writes in the second letter to the Corinthians, it is deep within the Christian story to figure this face where

---

527 I am seeing this notion of "poetic cartography" as akin to the attempts put forward by women mystics such as Theresa of Avila. See E. Ann Matter "Internal Maps of an Eternal External" and Laurie Finke "Mystical Bodies and the Dialogics of Vision" in *Maps of Flesh and Light* ed. Ulrike Wiethaus (New York: Syracuse University Press, 1993) pp. 28ff.

528 Jacques Derrida, "This Strange Institution Called Literature", p. 36.

> we all, with unveiled face, beholding the glory of the Lord, are being transformed into his likeness from one degree of glory to another... For it is the God who said, "Light will shine out of the darkness", who has shown in our hearts to the light of the knowledge of the glory of God in the face of Christ.[529]

Günther Bornkamm's statement that "no one is any longer in the position to write a life of Jesus"[530] remains before many scholars as we come into the new millenium. While the writing of various "lives of Jesus" such as D.F. Strauss' *Das Leben Jesu* may be seen as a dead end, *writing* which recalls a poetics of Jesus continues to bring new forms and new life to the person of Jesus. This is a poetics that takes its form through a retrieval of Jesus' words at the institution of the Eucharist:

> And when the hour came, he sat at table, and the apostles with him. And he said to them, "I have earnestly desired to eat this passover with you before I suffer; for I tell you I shall not eat it until it is fulfilled in the kingdom of God." And he took a cup, and when he had given thanks he said, "Take this, and divide it among yourselves; for I tell you that from now on I shall not drink of the fruit of the vine until the kingdom of God comes." And he took bread, and when he had given thanks he broke it and gave it to them, saying, "This is my body which is given for you. Do this in remembrance of me."[531]

As evidenced by George Eliot, there is an authenticity that comes in and through the poetic act that is truly a *re*-membrance of Jesus. The directive of Jesus for this remembrance is a creative act as seen in verse 19 where the "do this" (τουτο ποιειτε) of remembrance recalls *poiesis,* which is the root of "poetics". Such was the act of remembrance that George Eliot found in writing. That which was sought for by writers of the nineteenth century – this one who comes as one unknown - does indeed arise in the act of remembrance Eliot celebrated through a poetics of Jesus. As she mused in *Middlemarch* – "Who shall tell what may be the effect of writing?" In the same way, as readers of such poetics we are invited to come, as St. Paul wrote, "with

---

529 2 Corinthians 3:18, 4:6 NRSV. David Ford, in his recent book *Self and Salvation* (Cambridge: Cambridge University Press, 1999), has an extended reflection on this notion of "facing" in relation to the figuring of Christ.

530 Günther Bornkamm, *Jesus of Nazareth*, p. 13.

531 Luke 22: 14-19. NRSV.

unveiled face, beholding the glory of the Lord, are being transformed into his likeness from one degree of glory to another". Such is the invitation to "do this" – *poiesis* – in remembrance of him.

# Bibliography


Abrams, M. H. (1953), *The Mirror and the Lamp*, Oxford, Oxford University Press.

Altizer, Thomas J.J. (1997), *The Contemporary Jesus,* New York, State University of New York Press.

Armstrong, Isobel (1982), *Language as Living Form in Nineteenth Century Poetry*, Sussex, Harvester Press.

Arnold, Matthew (1961), *Poetry and Criticism of Matthew Arnold.* ed. A. Dwight Culler, Boston, Houghton Mifflin Company.

Ashton, Rosemary (1996), *George Eliot: A Life*, London, Penguin.

(1980, 1994), *The German Idea: Four English Writers and the Reception of German Thought 1800-1860*, London, Libris.

St. Augustine of Hippo (1953), *Augustine: Early Writings.* trans. John H.S. Burleigh, London, SCM Press.

(1993), *City of God*, trans. by Marcus Dods, New York, The Modern Library.

(1998), *Confessions,* trans. Henry Chadwick, Oxford, Oxford University Press.

Bal, Mieke (1991), *Reading "Rembrandt": Beyond the Word-Image Opposition*, Cambridge, Cambridge University Press.

(1997), *Narratology 2nd edition*, Toronto, University of Toronto Press.

Barth, Karl (1947, 1969), *Die protestantische Theologie im 19. Jahrhundert*, Zurich, Evangelischer Verlag.

(1947), *Church Dogmatics*, IV, Edinburgh, T & T Clark.

Baur, F.C. (1963-1975), *Ausgewählte Werke in Einzelausgaben*, ed. and trans. Klaus Scholder, 5 volumes, Stuttgart, Friedrich Frommann.

Benecke, Heinrich (1883), *William Vatke in seinem Leben und seinen Schriften* , Bonn, E. Strauss.

Bodenheimer, Rosemarie (1996), *The Real Life of Mary Ann Evans: George Eliot Her Letters and Fiction,* Ithaca, Cornell University Press.

Roder-Bolton, Gerlinde (1998), *Studies in Comparative Literature - Vol. 13: George Eliot and Goethe: An Elective Affinity*, Amsterdam, Rodopi.

Borg, Marcus (1997), *The God We Never Knew*, San Francisco, Harper Collins.

Bornkamm, Günther (1956), *Jesus of Nazareth,* trans. I. McLuskey, F. McLuskey, and J.M. Robinson, New York, Harper and Row.

Buber, Martin (1959), *I and Thou,* trans. by Ronald Gregor Smith, Edinburgh, T. & T. Clark.

Bubner, Rüdiger (1997), *German Idealist Philosophy*, London, Penguin Books.

Butler, Lance St. John (1990), *Victorian Doubt: Literary and Cultural Discourses*, London, Simon and Schuster.

Campbell, Joesph (1973), *The Hero With A Thousand Faces* 3rd ed., Princeton, Princeton University Press.

Carlyle, Thomas (1840), *Chartism,* London, Fraser.

Carroll, David (1992), *George Eliot and the Conflict of Interpretations,* Cambridge, Cambridge University Press.

Cassirer, Ernst (1945), *Rousseau Kant Goethe,* Princeton, Princeton University Press.

Cochrane, Charles N. (1957), *Christianity and Classical Culture*, New York, Oxford University Press.

Culler, Jonathan (1988), *Framing the Sign: Criticism and Its Institutions*, Oxford, Blackwell.

Darwin, Charles (1859), *On the Origin of Species by Means of Natural Selection, or The Preservation of Favoured Races in the Struggle for Life,* ed. John Burrow, London, Murray.

Dawes, Gregory W. ed. (1999), *The Historical Jesus Quest: A Foundational Anthology,* Leiden, Deo Publishing.

Derrida, Jacques (1976), *Of Grammatology*, trans. G.C. Spivak, Baltimore, Johns Hopkins University Press.

(1992), *Acts of Literature/Jacques Derrida*, ed. Derek Attridge, trans. Geoffrey Bennington and Rachel Bowlby, New York, Routledge.

(1978), *Writing and Difference,* London, Routledge Press.

Descartes, Rene (1970), *Philosophical Letters,* trans. by Anthony Kenny, Oxford, Oxford University Press.

(1955), *The Philosophical Works of Descartes*, trans. E.S. Haldane and G.R.T. Ross, Cambridge: Dover.

Detweiler, Robert and Jasper, David ed. (2000), *Religion and Literature,* Louisville: Westminster John Knox.

Dodd, Valerie (1990), *George Eliot: An Intellectual Life*, New York, Macmillian Press.

Dowden, Edward (1892), "The Scientific Movement and Literature," *Studies in Literature: 1789-1877, 6th ed.*, London, Kegan Paul.

Eagleton, Mary and Pierce, David (1979), *Attitudes to Class in the English Novel* , London, Thames and Hudson.

Eliade, Mircea (1959), *The Sacred and the Divine :The Nature of Religion*, trans. Willard R. Trask, New York, Harcourt Brace, 1959.

Eliot, George (1996) *Middlemarch: A Study in Provincial Life*, Oxford, Oxford University Press.

(1996), *Adam Bede* – 1859, Oxford, Oxford Classics.

(1992), *Selected Critical Writings*, ed. by Rosemary Ashton, Oxford: Oxford University Press.

(1990), *Selected Essays, Poems, and Other Writings.* ed. A.S. Byatt, London, Penguin.

(1855), "The Morality of Wilhelm Meister" in *The Leader*, 21st July.

(1860), *The Mill on the Floss*, London, Penguin.

(1963), *Essays of George Eliot*, ed. Thomas Pinney, London, Routledge.

(1856), 'The Natural History of German Life', *Westminster Review*, July.

(1995), *The Impressions of Theophratus Such* – 1879, London, Everyman Press.

(1998), *Scenes of Clerical Life* – 1857, ed. Jennifer Gribble, London, Penguin Books.

(1954-1955), *The George Eliot Letters*, ed. Gordon S. Haight, London, Oxford University Press.

Feuerbach, Ludwig (1957), *The Essence of Christianity*, trans. George Eliot, New York, Harper.

(1966), *Principles of the Philosophy of the Future*, trans. Manfred Vogel, Indianapolis, Bobbs-Merrill.

Fichte, J. G. (1849), *The Way Toward the Blessed Life, or, The Doctrine of Religion – 1806*, trans. W. Smith, London, Chapman.

Ford, David F. (1999), *Self and Salvation*, Cambridge, Cambridge University Press.

Frei, Hans (1974), *The Eclipse of Biblical Narrative*, New Haven, Yale University Press.

Froude, J.A. (1849), *The Nemesis of Faith*, London, George Woodfall and Son.

(1894), *Short Stories on Great Subjects*, London, Longmans, Green & Co.

Gadamer, Hans-Georg (1998), *Truth and Method* 2nd ed., New York, Continuum Press.

Gilson, Etienne (1961), *The Christian Philosophy of Saint Augustine*, London, Golancz Press.

von Goethe, Johann Wolfgang (1988), *Scientific Studies, Vol. 12 : Goethe – The Collected Works*, Princeton, Princeton University Press.

(1988), *The Sorrows of Young Werther* from *Goethe: The Collected Works Volume 11,* ed. David E. Wellbury, Princeton, Princeton University Press.

(1858), *Wilhelm Meister's Apprenticeship* Vol.1, trans. Thomas Carlyle, London, Chapman and Hall.

(1858), *Wilhelm Meister's Apprenticeship and Travels* Vol. 2 trans. Thomas Carlyle, London, Chapman and Hall.

(1949), *Faust: Part One* – 1808, trans. Philip Wayne, London, Penguin Classics.

Goodman, Nelson (1976), *Languages of Art: An Approach to a Theory of Symbols*, Indianapolis, Hackett.

Guignon, Charles ed. (1993), *The Cambridge Companion to Heidegger,* Cambridge, Cambridge University Press.

Haight, Gordon S. (1968), *George Eliot: A Biography,* Oxford, Oxford University Press.

Hamilton, William (1993), *A Quest for the Post-Historical Jesus,* London, SCM Press.

Harris, Horton (1973), *David Friedrich Strauss and his Theology,* London, Cambridge University Press.

Harrisville, Roy A. and Sundberg, Walter (1995), *The Bible in Modern Culture: Theology and Historical-Critical Method from Spinoza to Käsemann*, Grand Rapids, Eerdmans.

Hegel, G.W.F. (1968), *Lectures on the Philosophy of Religion*, vol. 3, trans. E.S. Haldane, New York, Humanities Press.

(1969), *Science of Logic*, trans. A.V. Miller, New York, Humanities Press.

Heidegger, Martin (1996), *Being and Time*, trans. Joan Stambaugh, New York, State University of New York.

(1968), *What is Called Thinking?* trans. J. Glenn Gray – 1958, New York, Harper and Row.

(1998), *Basic Writings of Martin Heidegger*, ed. David Farrell Krell, London, Routledge.

Hemmings, F.W.J. ed. (1974), *The Age of Realism,* London, Pelican Books.

Hick, John (1993), *The Metaphor of God Incarnate,* London, SCM Press.

Hodgson, Peter C. (2001), *Theology in the Fiction of George Eliot*, London, SCM Press.

Hölderlin, Friedrich (1998), "Empedokles" in *Selected Poems and Fragments*, trans. Michael Hamburger, London, Penguin.

Jasper, David (1999), *The Sacred and Secular Canon in Romanticism,* London, Macmillian Press.

(1989), ed. (with T.R. Wright) *The Critical Spirit and The Will to Believe,* London, Macmillian Press.

(2000), "Can We Speak of a Christian Poetics?" *Literature and Religion – The Korean Society of Literature and Religion*, Vol. 5, No. 1 Summer.

Jeanrond, Werner (1994), *Theological Hermeneutics: Development and Significance*, London, SCM Press.

Jolowicz, H. F. (1972), *Historical Introduction to the Study of Roman Law* 3rd ed., London, Cambridge University Press.

Kant, Immanuel (1973), *Kritik der Urteilskraft (Critique of Judgement)* trans. J.C. Meredith, New York, Oxford University Press.

(1965), *On History*, trans. L.W. Beck, New York, Bobbs-Merill.

Kerr, Hugh T. ed. (1993), *Readings in Christian Thought 2nd Edition*, Nashville, Abington Press.

á Kempis, Thomas (1952), *The Imitation of Christ*, trans. and introd. Leo Sherley-Price, London, Penguin Books.

Knoepflmacher, U. C. (1965), *Religious Humanism and the Victorian Novel: George Eliot, Walter Pater, and Samuel Butler*, Princeton: Princeton University Press.

Krueger, Christine L. (1992), *The Reader's Repentance: Women Preachers, Women Writers, and Nineteenth-Century Social Discourse*, Chicago, University of Chicago Press.

Landow, George P. (1971), *The Aesthetic and Critical Theories of John Ruskin,* Princeton, Princeton University Press.

Lessing, Gotthold Ephraim (1956), *Lessing's Theological Writings*, trans. Henry Chadwick, London, Adam & Charles Black.

Lewes, G.H. (1855), *The Life and Works of Goethe* Vol. 2, London, T. Richards, 37, Great Queen Street.

(1874), *Problems of Life and Mind. First Series: The Foundations of a Creed, 2 vols.*, London.

(1876), "Spiritualism and Materialism," *The Fortnightly Review*, Vol. 19.

Linton, Eliza Lynn (1872), *The True History of Joshua Davidson, Communist*, London.

Lovesay, Oliver (1991), *The Clerical Character in George Eliot's Fiction,* Victoria, ELS Monograph Series.

Luxemburg, Rosa (1905), *Socialism and the Churches,* London.

Macksey, Richard and Donato, Eugenio eds. (1972), *The Structuralist Controversy: The Languages of Criticism and the Sciences of Man*, Baltimore, Johns Hopkins University Press.

Macquarrie, John (1989), *20th Century Religious Thought*, 4th ed, London, SCM Press.

Mallock, W.H. (1892), "Amateur Christianity" *The Fortnightly Review*, LVII.

Marsh, James (1822), "Ancient and Modern Poetry", *North American Review* XV, Vol. VI.

McIntyre, John (1966), *The Shape of Christology*, London, SCM Press.

Miller, J. Hillis (1968), *The Form of Victorian Fiction*, London, University of Notre Dame Press.

Moore, Stephen D. (1992), *Mark and Luke in Postructuralist Perspectives*, New Haven, Yale University Press.

Morrissey, Lee (1999), "Derrida, Algeria, and "Structure, Sign, and Play" *Postmodern Culture* Volume 9, Issue 2.

Mueller-Vollmer, Kurt ed. (1997), *The Hermeneutics Reader,* New York, Continuum.

Newman, John Henry (1977), *Apologia Pro Vita Sua* – 1864, London, Fount Press.

(1974), *An Essay on the Development of Christian Doctrine* – 1845,

London, Pelican.
Ong, Walter J. S.J. (1967), *The Presence of the Word,* New Haven, Yale University Press.
Paris, B. J. (1965), *Experiments in Life: George Eliot's Quest for Values,* Detroit, Wayne State University Press.
Pater, Walter (1985), *Marius the Epicurean* – 1885, London, Penguin Classics.
(1973), *Essays on Literature and Art,* ed. Jennifer Uglow, London, Everyman's Library.
Pelikan, Jarosalov (1985), *Jesus Through the Centuries,* New York, Harper and Row.
(1993), *Christianity and Classical Culture,* New Haven, Yale University Press.
Plato (1961), *The Collected Dialogues of Plato,* ed. Edith Hamilton, Princeton, Princeton University Press.
Redfield, Marc (1996), *Phantom Formations: Aesthetic Ideology and the Bildungsroman,* Ithaca: Cornell University Press.
Reimarus, Hermann Samuel (1970), *Reimarus: Fragments,* ed. Charles H. Talbert, Minneapolis, Fortress Press.
Renan, Ernest (1991), *The Life of Jesus* – 1863, Amherst, Prometheus Books.
Ricoeur, Paul (1988), *Time and Narrative,* Vol. 1- 3, Chicago, University of Chicago Press.
(1995), *Figuring the Sacred: Religion, Narrative, and Imagination,* Minneapolis, Fortress Press.
(1981), *Hermeneutics and the Human Sciences: Essays on Language, Action and Interpretation* ed., trans. and intro. J.B. Thompson, Cambridge, Cambridge University Press.
Riffaterre, Michael (1990), *Fictional Truth,* London, John Hopkins University Press.
Rushdie, Salman (1990), "Is Nothing Sacred?" *Granta* 31, Spring.
Ruskin, John (1903), *The Works of John Ruskin,* ed. E.T. Cook and Alexander Wedderburn, London.
(1991), *John Ruskin: Selected Writings,* ed. Kenneth Clark, London, Penguin.
Sandberger, Jorg (1972), *David Friedrich Strauss als theologischer Hegelianer,* Gottingen, Vandenhoeck und Ruprecht.
Sarte, Jean-Paul (1958), *Being and Nothingness: An Essay on Phenomenlogical Ontology,* trans. Hazel E. Barnes, London, Methuen.
de Saussure, Ferdinand (1986), *Course in General Linguistics,* trans. Roy

Harris, La Salle, Open Court Press.
Schäfer, Martin (1999), "The Sacred: A Figureless Figure: On Heidegger", Paper presented at the Conference on Theology and Criticism at Johns Hopkins University, March 4 - 7.
Schama, Simon (1999), *Rembrandt's Eyes*, New York, Alfred A. Knopf.
Scharlemann, Robert (1981), *The Being of God: Theology and the Experience of Truth,* New York, Seabury Press.
Schelling, Friedrich W. J. (1966), "On the Study of Theology", in *On University Studies*, trans. E.S. Morgan, Athens, Ohio University Press.
Schleiermacher, Friedrich (1928), *The Christian Faith.* trans. H.R. Mackintosh and J.S. Stewart, Edinburgh, T and T Clark.
Schwietzer, Albert (1906, 1954), *The Quest for the Historical Jesus: A Critical Study of its Progress from Reimarus to Wrede,* London: A & C Black.
Shuttleworth, Sally (1984), *George Eliot and Nineteenth-Century Science*, Cambridge, Cambridge University Press.
Simons, John D. (1981), *Friedrich Schiller,* Boston, G.K. Hall and Co.
Sloyan, Gerard S. (1988), *Jesus in Focus: A Life in its Setting* 4th Printing, Mystic, Conn, Twenty-Third Publications.
de Spinoza, Benedict (1955), *On the Improvement of Understanding*, trans. R.H. M. Elwes, London, Dover Press.
(1955), *The Ethics.* trans. R.H.M. Elwes, London, Dover Press.
(1989), *Tractatus Theologico-Politicus,* trans. Samuel Shirley, Leiden, E.J. Brill.
Sterling, John (1851), *Twelve Letters by John Sterling*, ed. William Coningham, London.
(1897), *A Correspondence between John Sterling and Ralph Waldo Emerson* ed. E.W. Emerson, Boston, Mass.
Stiver, Dan V. (1996), *The Philosophy of Religious Language: Sign, Symbol, and Story*, London, Blackwell Publishers.
Stockton, Kathryn Bond (1994), *God Between Their Lips: Desire Between Women in Irigaray, Brontë, and Eliot,* Stanford, Stanford University Press.
Stevick, Philip ed. (1967), *The Theory of the Novel,* London, Collins-Macmillian.
Strauss, David Friedrich (1848, 1898), *The Life of Jesus, Critically*

*Examined. 4th Edition*. trans. George Eliot, New York, Swan Sonnenschein and Co.

(1930), *Streitschriften zur Vertheidigung meiner Schrift über das Leben Jesu und zur Charakteristik der gegenwärtigen Theologie,* New York, G. Olms.

Taylor, Charles (1979), *Hegel and Modern Society*, Cambridge, Cambridge University Press.

(1989), *Sources of the Self*, Cambridge, Harvard University Press.

Taylor, Mark C. ed. (1986), *Deconstruction in Context: Literature and Philosophy*, Chicago, University of Chicago Press.

(1984), *Erring: A Postmodern A/Theology*, Chicago, University of Chicago Press.

Templeton, Douglas A. (1999), *The New Testament as True Fiction,* Sheffield: Sheffield Academic Press.

Theissen, Gerd (1987), *The Shadow of the Galilean*, Philadelphia, Fortress Press.

Tillich, Paul (1959), *Theology of Culture,* Oxford, Oxford University Press.

Trollope, Anthony (1974), *The Clergyman of the Church of England,* Leicester, Leicester University Press.

Tyndall, John (n.d.), "Scientific Use of Imagination" in *Fragments of Science,* 6th ed., 2 vols, New York, Burt.

Valdes, Mario J. ed. (1991), *Reflection and Imagination: A Ricoeur Reader,* Toronto: University of Toronto Press.

Ward, Mrs. Humphrey (1888), *Robert Elsmere* 9th ed, London, Smith, Elder, & Co.

Wasserman, Earl (1968), *The Subler Language,* Baltimore, Johns Hopkins University Press.

Watt, Ian (1971), *The Victorian Novel: Modern Essays in Criticism*, London, Oxford University Press.

(1987), *The Rise of the Novel*, London, Hogarth Press.

Welleck, René (1963), *Concepts of Criticism*, New Haven, Yale University Press.

Wheeler, Kathleen ed. (1984), *German Aesthetic and Literary Criticism: The Romantic Ironists and Goethe*, Cambridge, Cambridge University Press.

Whitemeyer, Hugh (1979), *George Eliot and the Visual Arts,* New Haven, Yale University Press.

Wiethaus, Ulrike ed. (1993), *Maps of Flesh and Light*, New York, Syracuse University Press.

Willey, Basil (1949), *Nineteenth Century Studies: Coleridge to Matthew Arnold,*

London, Chatto and Windus.

Wolff, Robert Lee (1977), *Gains and Losses: Novels of Faith and Doubt in Victorian England*, London, Garland Publications.

Wordsworth, William (1979), *The Prelude* – 1805/1850 *Norton Critical Edition* ed. John Wordsworth, London, W.W. Norton.
(1995), *The Prelude – The Four Texts 1798, 1799,1805,1850* ed. John Wordsworth, London, Penguin Classics.

Wright, NT and Borg, Marcus (1999), *The Meaning of Jesus – Two Visions,* London, SPCK.

Wright, T.R. (1981), "George Eliot and Positivism: A Reassessment" in *Modern Language Review*, LXXVI, Spring.
(1986), *The Religion of Humanity,* Cambridge, Cambridge University Press.

# Index of Names